AGREST AND GANDELSONAS

WORKS

WITH AN INTRODUCTION BY ANTHONY VIDLER

PRINCETON ARCHITECTURAL PRESS

Published by
Princeton Architectural Press
37 East 7th Street
New York, New York 10003
212.995.9620

call 1.800.458.1131 for a free catalog of books

Design: J. Abbott Miller and Hall Smyth, Design Writing Research

Cover Photograph: Paul Warchol; Back Cover Photograph: Roberto Shezen

Research: Jasmit Singh Rangr, Dina Radeka

Special thanks to: Seonaidh Davenport, Caroline Green, Clare Jacobson, Bill Monaghan,
Allison Saltzman, and Ann C. Urban of Princeton Architectural Press—Kevin C. Lippert, publisher

Library of Congress Cataloging-in-Publication Data
Agrest, Diana.
          Agrest and Gandelsonas, works.
               p.   cm.
          Includes biographical references
          ISBN 0-910413-28-2 (cloth). — 1-878271-90-3 (pbk)
          1. Agrest and Gandelsonas—Catalogs. 2. Agrest, Diana—Catalogs.
     3. Gandelsonas, Mario, 1938– —Catalogs. 4. Architecture, Modern—
     20th century—Catalogs. 5. Architectural practice, International—
     Catalogs. I. Gandelsonas, Mario, 1938– . II. Title.
     NA737.A34A4 1995
     720'.92'2—dc20   94-30361
                                                                  CIP

FOR JULIA

CONTENTS

REFIGURING THE PLACE OF ARCHITECTURE

Anthony Vidler

> *Architecture is not called "frozen music" in vain ("gefrorene Musik"—*
> *Goethe). At the basis of the composition of its ensemble, at the basis of the*
> *harmony of its conglomerating masses, in the establishment of the melody*
> *of the future overflow of its forms, and in the execution of its rhythmic parts,*
> *giving harmony to the relief of its ensemble, lies that same "dance" that is*
> *also at the basis of the creation of music, painting, and cinematic montage.*
> —Sergey Eisenstein, "Piranesi, or the Flux of Form."[1]

DUOGRAPHY

The genre of an architect's "collected works" has undergone significant transformations since the Renaissance. At first a combination of rule-book, archeological source, and collection of exemplary designs in the publications of Andrea Palladio, Sebastiano Serlio, and their followers, the monograph was reinvested with utopian associations by the Enlightenment in the didactic models and idealized types elaborately illustrated by Étienne-Louis Boullée and Claude-Nicolas Ledoux, and systematized by Jean-Nicolas-Louis Durand. An increasing sense of historicity turned the classified, rationalist collection of the eighteenth century into a chronological narrative of the development of an architect's genius or the birth of a national style in the engravings of Karl Friedrich Schinkel or the polemical works of Augustus Pugin. Modernism, inheriting all these roles, added an avant-garde belief in imminent cultural and social revolution; the *oeuvres complètes* became a complement to the avant-garde manifesto, the manifestation of avant-garde promise, the demonstration that the future might be built in the present, whether in Le Corbusier's Contemporary City or Frank Lloyd Wright's Broadacre City.

Denied the certainty of these authorizing narratives, whether didactic or historicist, the poststructuralist monograph has searched for different grounds on which to base the publication of a genre that, in the late twentieth century, still retains its central place in professional hagiography. The influence of thirty years of critical reflection on reading has allowed for self-reflection, irony, and authorial distance, while the theorization of representation in all its guises permits a textual and visual construction that refuses the linearity of history or the categorizations of positivistic theory. Thus although many recent "collected works" seem to adhere to the known modes of chronological or thematic organization, they nevertheless demand a different interpretative stance on the part of the reader/viewer. More importantly, they implicitly or explicitly propose a new and complex relationship between theory and practice, book and building, in such a way as to implicate the "monograph" in the process of design itself. No longer is the collected work to be seen as the final and objective representation of a lifetime of building; rather, the very way in which the work offers itself up for reading and representation is a part of the design practice, as a whole, that announces itself, so to speak, as "to be continued" at every moment.

The present book, a collection of the projects and buildings of Diana Agrest and Mario Gandelsonas, is, in these terms, a complex example of the genre. Ostensibly a chronological account, and without elaborate theoretical apparatus, it pretends to a calm objectivity, if not laconic distance. This, at first, might be surprising: both Agrest and Gandelsonas have, since the beginning of their careers, been noted for their intense involvement in theoretical and critical debates; both have published widely from the early seventies on; both have been marked by their attachment to structuralist and poststructuralist theory, from their explorations of politics, cybernetics, structural anthropology, and semiotics to their investigations of post-structuralism, feminism, and psychoanalysis. The apparent absence of theory in this monograph, then, might seem inexplicable, requiring the reader to have at hand a companion volume of text, or at least a collection of the architects' previous writings.

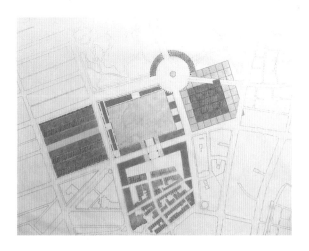

TYPOLOGICAL MORPHING Park Square, Boston, Massachusetts

Interpretation is further complicated by the double origin of the collection, stemming not, as in many cases, from a single architect (perhaps with a second if not secondary partner—Pierre Jeanneret to Le Corbusier), nor from a monolithic firm of supposedly co-equal partners. Here the work is clearly a product of the collaboration of two distinct and equally powerful intellects, each with its own formation, field of discursive reference, and, let it be said, despite enormous commonality, different if complementary architectural tastes. It requires no essentialist or biograph-ical determinism to identify, among many other traits, a preference, on the part of Agrest, for the urban realm as a field of physical and social codes and signifiers both "architectural" and "non-architectural"; for the physical elements of architecture as related in a play of forms that shift and recom-pose according to context; for the typological, considered as a mode of non-reductive analysis; and, finally, for the filmic, as experience and form. On the part of Gandelsonas, we might detect a delight in abstraction, in complex geometrical constructions, and in all systems of thought that somehow undermine and destroy any utopian purity in such organizations; for Gandelsonas, we might hazard, it would be the musical analogy that, in its very nonphysical aspects, informs architectural composition. For Agrest's Alfred Hitchcock we might pose Gandelsonas's John Cage. No less important, theoretically as well as professionally, would be the distinction of gender and its relation to the "body" of architecture. In these terms the book would not be a "monograph" but a "duograph": "duograph: *n.* in photoengraving, a picture in two shades of the same color, made from two half-tone plates produced by setting the screen at different angles." (Webster)

Such an evident theoretical foundation should perhaps alert us to the fact that its "absence" from the text of the present work might be deliberate; that we are being asked to read the works in a different, if not theoretical, way. Or, rather, that we should see the works themselves as standing in for, or taking the place of, discursive theory; that the designs do not illustrate theory but enact it. Further we should certainly not mistake the chronological ordering of the projects as implying any form of development or progress, much less as recounting an architectural *bildungsroman* or biographical story. If there is a story, it is one told by and with the architecture, as if, in some way, the buildings have gained an animate status. We might imagine using this monograph like a flicker-book, where one image imperceptibly transforms itself into the next, so as to compose a world of images in motion, all making up the "city" that is an important locus of Agrest and Gandelsonas's concerns.

Thus from the first project in the book to the last, we may detect an overlapping of themes that, in formal terms, are represented at different and continuously changing scales. The central space of a villa becomes, at another scale, the public square of a town, which, at the scale of the city, is transformed into a huge modern agora. In reverse, the forms and elements that define large-scale urban places are, at a smaller scale, evoked in groups of buildings, houses, and domestic interiors. Cafes and restaurants are so many internal public domains. At the smallest scale of all, furniture and fittings become so many small buildings, assembled into miniature cities in rooms. It is as if the architects have joined Leone Battista Alberti's celebrated maxim — the house as a small city, the city as a small house — to his concept of a building as a horse, putting both in motion, like some Eadweard Muybridge sequence taken literally for architecture.

ARCHITECTURE AS MISE-EN-SEQUENCE
La Villette, Paris, France

Clearly architecture presents itself to Agrest and Gandelsonas as a willing victim for analytical decomposition; its elements and types, repeated and transformed over time, its different combinatorial strategies, themselves subject to historical change, and its modes of representation, from the Renaissance to the present, have all been re-envisioned as so much material for new compositions. This process has called for at least two primary levels of analysis: the identification of generalizable elements and types, and the formulation of new modes of transformation. It has as a precondition that architecture is at root both an open semiotic system and a text, visual and non-visual, that might be decomposed and rewritten. We are reminded of Ferdinand de Saussure's celebrated architectural example serving to distinguish the two relations of the sign, syntagmatic and associative, where the former relies on linearity, on sequence, and gains meaning by way of opposition, and the latter depends on meaning formed external to discourse, within a "potential mnemonic series."

> *From the associative and syntagmatic viewpoint a linguistic unit is like a fixed point of a building, e.g., a column. On the one hand, the column has a certain relation to the architrave that it supports; the arrangement of the two units in space suggests the syntagmatic relation. On the other hand, if the column is Doric, it suggests a mental comparison of this style with others (Ionic, Corinthian, etc.) although none of these elements is present in space: the relation is associative.*[2]

Such distinctions have informed the work of Agrest and Gandelsonas from the outset, and a cursory examination of every project illustrated reinforces the effectiveness of the structural analogy.

In their work, however, the commonplaces of an applied semiology have been replaced by an extended discussion of the nature of the architectural signifier, and of architecture and urbanism as complex systems of signs. Here, architecture has been seen not as a "language" but rather "as an area of production where the subject works in a transgressive way with the notion of rules as a limit,"[3] that is, as a form of "writing." This mixed status allows for the interpretation of the architectural element as something between a "letter" and a "hieroglyph," and thence "de-ciphered," as if it were a form of visual figure of speech, a trope in space, or rebus. This notion of tropical space informs not only the questioning of the building, but, more importantly, inserts the building as a complex of signifiers into a field constituted by the urban context. This field, in turn, is subjected to analysis, as if it were a rhetorical text in its own right — one produced by texts (discursive and visual) and communicating through its own textual orders.

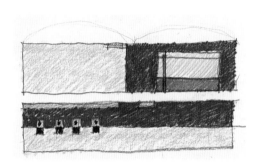

150 WOOSTER STREET A Restaurant in Soho, New York City

But while structuralist analysis in architecture and urbanism, as manifested in theory during the seventies, tended to substitute one static analytical system (the linguistic, the anthropological) for another (the architectural) with a too easy confusion of the notion of "structure," Agrest and Gandelsonas's work has been consistently suspicious of reified analogies, finding in poststructuralism, rather, a mode of setting architecture in motion, of unseating its rigid formalities and empirical stabilities. For Agrest, sociocultural codes are not "a classification and abstraction of an inventory that finds fixed sets of regularities and rules," but rather are forces produced by dynamic processes; "the problem," writes Agrest, "is how to reveal these forces without reducing them to a system, to a closed construction."[4] Instead, she developed the notion of a reading that sees these codes as "enchained" and "dispersed," allowing for an open interpretation and, of course, an active strategy of intervention:

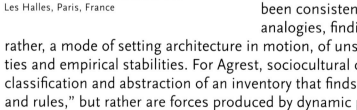

A CRITICAL READING OF THE URBAN TEXT
Les Halles, Paris, France

The complexity, the heterogeneity that accepts contradiction as a constitutive part, must be retained in opposition to the unifying reductionism that eliminates them. Rather than closing the system—characteristic of architecture—this principle opens it, permitting thus the articulation of many readings, signifying chains. The reading is conceived as a process of chaining, which constitutes a structuring force. The multiplication of sense produced by the readings, by the infinite chains of signifiers, by this explosion of sense, makes us enter a new dynamic space similar to the work of the dream, that of the production of sense.[5]

CINEMATOGRAPHY

Here the notion of buildings in animation and the search for analytical models have come together in the common analogy with film. For if there is a theory of reading that will guide us through this book and the architecture it represents, it is one derived from film theory developed in Agrest's critical writings.[6] Making sense of the film, of course, has been a primary task of modernism since the end of the nineteenth century, but more recently a revived interest in the cinema has appeared, adopting the interrelated notions of framing, montage, movement, and narrative displacement in order to inform both architectural representation and composition (we think of the filmic strips of Bernard Tschumi's *Manhattan Transcripts*, or the literal unrolling of the thematic parks in La Villette). On another, less obvious, level, the transformational sequences of Peter Eisenman's "House" permutations, or the perspective distortions of Frank Gehry's assemblages, rely on techniques already well tried in the cinema. Such examples of the formal methods of the movies transposed into architecture have been paralleled, if not criticized, by inquiries into the theoretical conditions of visuality, the psychoanalytical position of the viewing subject, and the role of the frame and the screen in the gender and power positions of this subject, as in the experimental installations of Elizabeth Diller and Ricardo Scofidio.

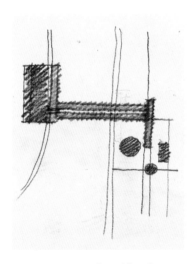

OBJECT AS FABRIC Porta Vittoria, Milan, Italy

Predating all these examples, the notion of the filmic for Agrest and Gandelsonas is not adduced with any of the overtones of space-time collapse or Bergsonian memory psychology that characterized its avant-garde years, film nevertheless allows for a dynamic reading of the static in a way that is essentially non-linear. The obvious reference is to Sergey Eisenstein's theory of the shot, and its de-composition and re-composition through montage, where architecture in some way anticipates the sequential framings of montage, requiring only the "explosive" vision of the filmmaker to set it in motion.

In his article "Montage and Architecture," written in the late thirties as a part of the uncompleted work on montage, Eisenstein contrasted two "paths" of the spatial eye: the cinematic, where a spectator follows an imaginary line among a series of objects, through the sight as well as in the mind—"diverse positions passing in front of an immobile spectator"—and the architectural, where "the spectator moved through a series of carefully disposed phenomena which he observed in order with his visual sense."[7] In this transition from real to imaginary movement, architecture was, in Eisenstein's view, film's predecessor. Where painting "remained incapable of fixing the total representation of an object in its full multidimensionality," and "only the film camera has solved the problem of doing this on a flat surface," "its undoubted ancestor in this capability is...architecture."[8]

But where, for Eisenstein, architecture gives way to the film—having, so to speak, prepared the way—for Agrest and Gandelsonas the film anticipates architecture, in the sense of viewing architecture with a filmic eye, for its own, not film's, sake. In this context, architecture is treated as film, and its procedures assumed to be identical on at least two levels. The first is that procedure of juxtaposition that Roland Barthes, following Roman Jakobsen, identified as metonymic:

> metonymy is the prototype of signs which signify through a contiguous relation, through contagion one might say...and we'd be tempted to say that in films, all montage, i.e., all signifying contiguity, is a metonymy, and since the cinema is montage, to say further that the cinema is a metonymic art (at least at present).[9]

In architecture, too, one might say that its fundamental elements and types signify "by contagion" and through juxtaposition, and certainly a reading of these collected works as constructed through montage would not lead us astray.

TYPO-GRAPHY

But there is, of course, another level of signification presented by architecture that refuses both elemental decomposition and meaningful juxtaposition, that level that relates an entire composition or ensemble to culture in general, its "allusiveness" or ability to evoke a disseminated field of reference far beyond framed intentionality or local specificity. This would be the realm of metaphor, which, in architecture, is as difficult to fix and bind as it is in film. On this level, one architectural element might be substituted for another, through similarity; an entire architectural system might stand for another—as in the attempt of Le Corbusier to reformulate the classic villa in the guise of its modernist substitute. We might be presented with an entirely functional element that through a metaphoric procedure is endowed with bodily or physiognomic characteristics, and so on.

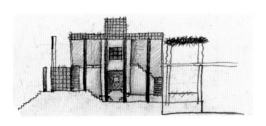

DOORS Summer House for Two Lawyers, Punta del Este, Uruguay

On this metaphoric level, too, these collected works may be read as so many ways that architecture might "stand in" for culture, and substitute itself for former architectures, classical or modernist. Hovering behind the buildings and urban projects of Agrest and Gandelsonas are their shadowy prototypes, so many pre-images of works from Palladio to Le Corbusier—works selected themselves for the way in which they condense former architectures with synthetic, metaphoric intensity.

At neither the level of analysis nor that of synthesis, however, are we confronted with any simplistic stylistic or formalistic reference; there are no

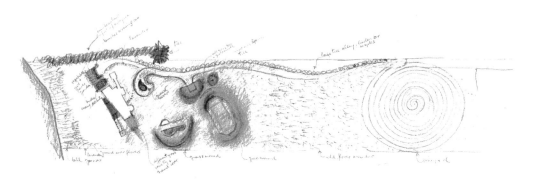

HOUSE ON SAG POND Southampton, New York

Palladian "Serliana" or Corbusian nautical motifs, no pediments, capitals, fragments of classical archeology, or any of the proliferation of historical references favored by postmodernism. Rather, the play with historical precedent is internal and abstract, buried in the geometries, the compositions, the formal correspondences beneath the surface. The Palladian villa is certainly the basis for the centralized plan and geometrical organization of Doors (1977), but its presence is more that of a diagram constructed by Rudolf Wittkower to demonstrate the rhythmic grid, than that of overt quotation.

It is this abstraction of reference that paradoxically enough allows works derived from a "rationalist" canon and framed within a tradition defined more by Aldo Rossi than by Robert Venturi to take on a contextual character. Extending beyond the simple "resonance" of individual building types to their cultural milieu, and refusing to camouflage urban interventions in the styles of the past, Agrest and Gandelsonas have developed a number of strategies by which to embed their designs in specific contexts. On a fundamental level, these begin at the scale of the element. Where, for Rossi and many of the neo-Rationalists, the building type remains the indivisible unit of architecture, for Agrest and Gandelsonas, the unit is smaller. A tower, for example, is separated (as in Agrest's own analysis of the skyscraper as "anagram") into its constituent parts, including tops, shafts, and bases, and these, far from being confined in their roles to skyscrapers, are easily displaced into other "tower-types" and their elements, to the extent that there remains a direct affiliation of form and meaning between such apparently distant buildings as the small skyscraper Manhattan Addition 2, New York City (1979–1980) and the House on Sag Pond, Southampton, New York (1989–1990). At the same time, this distance allows for each set of elements to take on precisely calculated affective values—that of the "church" in the case of the New York City project, and those of a combination of "lighthouse" and "silo" in the rural context of Southampton. Thus buildings may be built up out of elements that recall former buildings, with a deliberate play on the migration of forms that occurs.

PANOROGRAPHY [10]

A second contextualizing device, one that also follows the filmic analogy, is that of movement, now considered not as suggested between building and building, but as residing in the composition itself, either as implied between elements, or in the empirical realm, the movement of the subject through space.

Here we may return to Eisenstein's analysis of architectural montage. In his essay, the film director, a former architect and an admitted "great adherent of the architectural aesthetics of Le Corbusier," used an example of the architectural "path" that precisely paralleled that studied by Le Corbusier himself in *Vers une Architecture* to exemplify the "promenade architecturale": the successive perspective views of the movement of an imaginary spectator on the Acropolis constructed by Auguste Choisy to demonstrate the "successive tableaux" and "picturesque" composition of the site.[11] Eisenstein cites Choisy's analysis at length with little commentary, asking his reader simply "to look at it with the eye of a film-maker."

> *It is hard to imagine a montage sequence for an architectural ensemble more subtly composed, shot by shot, than the one which our legs create by walking among the buildings of the Acropolis.*[12]

For Eisenstein the Acropolis was the veritable answer to Victor Hugo's assertion of the cathedral of a book in stone: "the perfect example of one of the most ancient films."[13] Eisenstein finds in the carefully sequenced perspectives presented by Choisy the combination of a "film shot effect," producing an obvious new impression from each new, emerging shot, and a "montage effect," where the effect is gained from the sequential juxtaposition of the shots. The film-maker speculates on the desirable temporal duration of each picture, finding the possibility that there was a distinct relationship between the pace of the spectator's movement and the rhythm of the buildings themselves, a temporal solemnity being provoked by the distance between each building.

Le Corbusier, who was apparently less faithful in his reproduction of Choisy's sequence, concentrates on the second perspective, shown together with the plan of the visual axis of entry from the Propylea to the former statue of Athena.[14] For the architect, this demonstrates the flexibility of Greek "axial" planning, as opposed to the rigidity of the academic Beaux-Arts: "False right angles have furnished rich views and a subtle effect; the asymmetrical masses of the buildings create an intense rhythm. The spectacle is massive, elastic, nervous, overwhelming in its sharpness, dominating."[15] The plan of the mobile and changing ground levels of the Acropolis is only apparently "disordered." There is an inner equilibrium when the entire site is viewed from afar.

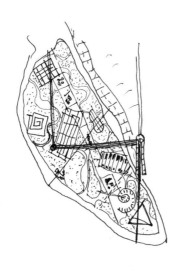

URBAN READY-MADES 1 AND 2
Goose Island, Chicago, Illinois

In this common reliance on Choisy we might be tempted to see the final conjunction of architectural and filmic modernism; the rhythmic dance of Le Corbusier's spectator (modeled, no doubt, on the movements of Émile Jaques-Dalcroze) anticipating the movement of Eisenstein's shots and montages. For both analysts, the apparently inert site and its strangely placed buildings are almost literally exploded into life, at once physical and mental. For both, the rereading of a canonical monument has provided the key to a "true" and natural modernist aesthetic.

And yet, as both ceaselessly reiterated, such correspondences were, when taking themselves too literally, false to the internal laws of the two media—architecture and film. If Le Corbusier agreed that "everything is Architecture," he also called for film to concentrate on its own laws; Eisenstein, similarly, abandoned a career as an architect and stage designer precisely because film offered a new and different stage of representational technique for modernity. For Eisenstein architecture remained only a *potential* film, a necessary stage in aesthetic evolution, but already surpassed; for Le Corbusier architecture was a setting for the athletic and physical life of the new man; its objects and settings the activators of mental and spiritual activity through vision.

Agrest and Gandelsonas take this composite tradition of the picturesque promenade further, eliding the boundaries drawn up by Eisenstein and Le Corbusier between film and architecture, in order to instill in their projects a sense of the one in the other, to be read through the same interpretative lens that characterizes their monograph as a whole. Here building and representation, intention and interpretation, merge into a generalized "third sense" that we have characterized as the filmic imaginary. This is achieved precisely through the medium of architecture, and without losing any of the specificity called for by Le Corbusier. In the House on Sag Pond, for example, the intersection of two axial compositions, both stable in themselves, not only provokes implicit movement in the plan, but creates a complex landscape by means of the grid of six towers cutting through the central barrel-vaulted volume. In turn, the actual walkways, internal and external, that link the towers to each other and to the ground, and that themselves intersect with the movement patterns within the central volume, construct an architectural promenade that defies beginnings and endings, in the ritual sense developed by Choisy and Le Corbusier, and refuses montage symmetries, such as those set up by Eisenstein out of Choisy's perspectives. An architecture of the random, of the planned chance, has replaced that of the framed spectacle or the goal-oriented path; all the ambiguities detected by Paul De Man in William Butler Yeats's meditation on the relations of dancer to dance are here transferred to architecture—the promenade is, so to speak, experienced by the architectural elements themselves.

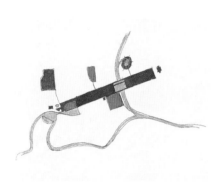

VISION PLAN Des Moines, Iowa

CARTOGRAPHY

On an urban scale, of course, such promenades have traditionally taken on the characteristics of *flânerie*, the slow, meditative, quasi-random strolling of the dandy and the poet, which, in the view of Walter Benjamin, constituted one of the principle ways in which modernity was able to comprehend the modern city, the metropolis. To turn the city into a landscape—a favorite theme of urban writers from Sébastien Mercier to Georg Simmel—was at once a means of rendering the unnatural natural and of aestheticizing, through the lens of the picturesque, what on the surface had no aesthetic qualities. The representation of *flânerie* has equally permeated modernism, whether in the textual "tableaux" of Mercier, the combinatorial genre of the Baudelairean prose poem, the rapid sketches of Constantin Guys, the photographs of Jean Atget, or the filmic montage of Walter Ruttmann or Fritz Lang.

In this context we might see the attempt of Agrest and Gandelsonas to refigure the place of architecture in the city as set in a long tradition of modern "snapshot" theory culminating with the metropolitan film. But once again, we are insistently returned to architecture, and to its own systems of representation; if it was Walter Benjamin's desire "to make a film of the plan of Paris," these architects are more concerned to interrogate the internal nature of city plans themselves.

Thus in the project for Park Square, Boston, Massachusetts (1978), the proposal is presented in ostensibly traditional form: a plan of the site and proposed intervention at the center, with a border of vignettes illustrating aspects of the scheme in perspective. The three-dimensional projection of the central plan, and the surrounding *tableaux*, follow the representational conven-

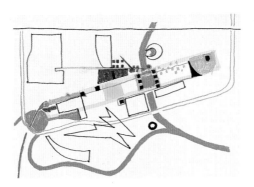

VISION PLAN Des Moines, Iowa

tions of seventeenth- and eighteenth-century city maps, where a city plan, generally in bird's-eye-view perspective, is bordered by topographical scenes of monuments and street life. This cartographic presentation, no doubt the visual antecedent for Mercier's and Charles-Pierre Baudelaire's literary *tableaux*, presented, as Louis Marin has demonstrated, a kind of utopical display of the city. On one level the map presents a totalizing view of the city, but from an entirely imaginary vantage point; on the other the city is revealed as an itinerary, its successive stages marked by squares, monuments, and quarters as depicted in the vignettes. Marin, in his analysis of two Paris maps (Mérian's of 1615, and Jacques Gomboust's of 1647) details these levels as they intersect in order to provide a key, spatially, to the hidden discourses of the city:

1. *The city map represents the production of discourse about the city.*
2. *The deconstruction of this representation uncovers the ideology controlling it.*
3. *The city map is a "utopic" insofar as it reveals a plurality of places whose incongruity lets us examine the critical space of ideology.*[16]

For Marin, these combinatorial maps, mingling narrative and discourse, implying significant routes through the city while neutralizing their status by merging them in the totality of routes, slyly showing aspects of monumental and social signification while hiding others, frame an urban vision that is far from disinterested, or "real." It is significant that this convention largely disappeared with the emergence of functional urbanism coinciding with geometrically accurate surveys at the end of the eighteenth century; the maps of Pierre Patte and Charles de Wailly, both recording the city in plan at the same time as indicating the nature of possible transformations in accompanying vignettes, refuse perspective representation.

Thus the deliberate revival of the older, pre-rationalist, classical convention by Agrest and Gandelsonas carries an implicit critique of modern urbanism and its instrumentalities, while postulating the active play of coded representations enchained, in sequence, turning around an equally active bird's-eye view. Among the former, the subject traces spatially marked trajectories through the site; from the latter, the subject is restored to an apparent position of omnipotence — apparent because put into question at every moment by the contradictory movement of the vignettes. This very decentering of the classical observer further allows for a radical substitution of subjects. For Agrest, the subject is now woman, a "female *flâneuse*" in Janet Wolff's terms, whose special kind of reading of the urban puts formerly static and hierarchical scenes in motion. As Agrest writes, speaking of the problematic relation of woman to the street, *"this subject, woman, writes as she reads where the repression has failed, where the system is fragmented, and where she does not want to be reconstructed by finding in it the reflection of an enclosed homogenous unitary system.... The street is the scene of her writing."*[17]

The presence of this subject as architect in the city radically transforms its reading and its reconstruction; no longer are we presented with a denial of the margins and what Agrest calls "non-architecture." Rather we are inserted into a field rich with semantic potential and, despite the aura of critical negation that has pervaded the vision of metropolitan life from Simmel to Benjamin and Theodor Adorno, this field carries sudden possibilities. If Benjamin called for an interpretation of modernism that might "comprise Le Corbusier and Andre Breton in a single glance," then Agrest and Gandelsonas ask for that late-twentieth-century viewpoint that might activate the sensibility of Nadja herself as a force for producing a theoretical practice that refuses the nihilistic *tabula rasa* of the Moderns: *"Nadja, because in Russian it is the beginning of the word "hope," and because this is only the beginning."*[18]

NOTES

1 Sergey Eisenstein, "Piranesi, or the Flux of Form," *Nonindifferent Nature*, trans. Herbert Marshall (Cambridge, England: Cambridge University Press, 1987), 140.

2 Ferdinand de Saussure, *Course in General Linguistics*, eds. Charles Bally and Albert Sechehaye in collaboration with Albert Riedlinger, translated with an introduction and notes by Wade Baskin (New York: McGraw-Hill, 1966), 123–124.

3 Mario Gandelsonas, "From Structure to Subject: The Formation of an Architectural Language," *Oppositions* 17 (Summer 1979): 28.

4 Diana I. Agrest, "On the Notion of Place," *Architecture from Without: Theoretical Framings for a Critical Practice* (Cambridge: MIT Press, 1991), 24.

5 Diana I. Agrest, "The Misfortunes of Theory," *Architecture from Without: Theoretical Framings for a Critical Practice* (Cambridge: MIT Press, 1991), 76.

6 Diana I. Agrest, "Design versus Non-Design," *Architecture From Without: Theoretical Framings for a Critical Practice* (Cambridge: MIT Press, 1991), 48–65.

7 Sergey Eisenstein, "Montage and Architecture," *Towards a Theory of Montage*, vol. 2 of *Selected Works*, edited by Michael Glenny and Richard Taylor, translated by Michael Glenny (London: BFI Publishing, 1991), 59.

8 Ibid., 60.

9 Roland Barthes, "On Film," *The Grain of the Voice. Interviews 1962–1980*, trans. Linda Coverdale (New York: Hill and Wang, 1985), 15.

10 According to Maximilien-Paul-Émile Littré, the "panorograph" was an instrument invented in 1824 "to obtain immediately, on a flat surface, the development of a perspective view of the objects that surround the horizon." As cited by Jacques Derrida, "Force et signification," *L'ecriture et la différence* (Paris: Editions du Seuil, 1967), 12–13.

11 Auguste Choisy, *Histoire de l'Architecture*, vol. 1 (Paris, 1899), 413.

12 Eisenstein, "Montage and Architecture," 60.

13 Ibid.

14 Le Corbusier, *Vers une Architecture* (Paris, 1923), 31.

15 Ibid.

16 Louis Marin, *Utopics: Spatial Play*, trans. Robert A. Vollrath (Atlantic Highlands, NJ: Humanities Press, 1984), 200.

17 Diana Agrest, "Architecture from Without: Body, Logic, Sex," in *Architecture from Without: Theoretical Framings for a Critical Practice* (Cambridge: MIT Press, 1991), 191.

18 Andre Breton, *Nadja* (Paris: Gallimard, 1984), 75.

DOUBLE INTERVIEW

Mario Gandelsonas interviews
DIANA AGREST

MG: I would like to ask you two sets of questions in relation to the theoretical strategies deployed in your practice of architecture. The first "within" architecture, the second "without" architecture.

Within Architecture
How did you enter the realm of theoretical work and what was your object of criticism?

DA: Theoretical work cannot be separated from practice in my case. I say this because it is from the shortcomings and crisis of architectural practice I encountered after graduating from school that I "entered" the realm of theory or theoretical work, with almost no transition.

I was searching for answers to new questions that I posed for myself and confronting the available models, in particular those proposed for the city and urban architecture (such as the Japanese Metabolists, and the English Team 10 and Archigram.)

This critical/theoretical work led me to the criticism of functionalist ideology and modernist urbanism. As a result of the articulation of theory and practice within this problematic system a reversal of scales of influence took place. Instead of thinking from the building — the small scale — to the city — the larger scale — as is traditionally the case, I started thinking from the city to architecture. Certain notions were instrumental in this operation, in particular the question of *public place*. This notion was not conceived of in a sentimental, picturesque way, but rather within the scope of the question of communication and culture with and

Diana Agrest interviews
MARIO GANDELSONAS

DA: What is the position of critical theory in architectural discourse today?

MG: In order to answer your question I need to start by describing the role of critical theory in our work as a response to the paradoxical social conditions of the contemporary practice of architecture. While our society continued to value architecture (ideologically) throughout the twentieth century, it rendered its craft, its principles, and its values impossible to realize (pragmatically).

This contradiction has been reflected in the work of the architectural avant-garde since the sixties with the acknowledgment of the *impossibility of architecture*, the *loss of its object* through different modes of disappearance of the architectural building, which is repeating now as another form of the same avant-gardism. This contradiction is also reflected through its denial in the work of the other side of the avant-gardist position, the traditionalist position that promotes the absurd notion of a *return to past convention*.

For me, starting from our earliest work, the issue has been to focus on the *conditions for the survival of architecture* through the redefinition of the role of critical theory and its relationship to practice, and the need to confront and deal with past conventions rather than suppress them, that is, to confront architectural ideology and reinstate the urban question. *In this space of confrontation, critical theory finds its place in architecture.*

The importance and relevance of critical theory lies more in its power to transform ideology than in its capacity to "explain." And with that I mean not just the conscious but also and fundamentally the "unconscious" of ideology. The role of critical theory has not changed. Besides, it is still the against the ever-growing development of the non-place of nonmaterial communication, what is more commonly known now as "cyberspace."

MG: From the beginning, your practice took different forms and developed in different spaces. Where and how was this critical practice implemented? What were the critical notions developed in this process? How do they relate to your practice?

DA: I developed my work in three parallel discourses and practices, the pedagogical (teaching), the theoretical (writing), and the practice (design, drawing, building).

In teaching both at Princeton University and the Institute for Architecture and Urban Studies, starting in 1974, I developed an approach in which design started from a *reading of the city*, more specifically, of parts of the city where the relationship between building and public place could be seen.

The city was recreated, redesigned through the *reading* that became the first step in the process of formal production. The split between theory and practice was erased, the boundaries separating these two modes were blurred. An important concept underlying this approach is that of the impossible gap that exists between the omnipotent logocentric, anthropocentric, (male) architectural subject and the social historical conditions within which the practice is developed. In this *reading* a radical critique of the architectural subject is performed, and its position is transformed creating the conditions for a different articulation between subject and history.

Starting from the city as a constant production and transformation of form, as an open text, as a complex intertextual relationship outside the books of architecture, the question of style that encloses the architectural discourse for easy consumption was avoided from the start.

These issues were explored in theory, particularly in the "Design versus Non-Design" essay (1972–75) where the

indispensable mechanism of surveillance of the economic/political/cultural conditions of architecture.

It is actually the "outside" that has provided the most potent tools and strategies, starting with the possibility of a theoretical production given by the displacement towards the semiotic and textual critical work in the late sixties and early seventies—Roland Barthes, Julia Kristeva, Jacques Derrida. These tools have allowed criticism of both an architecture that tends towards formalism and fetishism (because of the suppression of the city) and a conservative architecture nostalgic of the past (because of the suppression of history).

DA: What are the tasks of a critical theory today?

MG: I see two major tasks for a critical theory today. First, it needs to *unmask* an *ideology* structured as an opposition between avant-gardism and traditionalism as two sides of the same coin/Möbius band, an alternation that obscures the fact that they are two faces of the same ideology.

Second, if the question of theory was the issue in the seventies, the battle for the political and social connection is the issue now. Architecture needs to *claim* the *city* and criticize a production of fetishistic objects refusing to confront it.

A critical theoretical practice today should confront an architecture that tends towards formalism, *because of the suppression of politics; towards* fetishism, *because of the suppression of the city; and towards* nostalgia, *because of the suppression of history.*

DA: Is there still room for a critical practice?

MG: I believe that the notion of a critical practice best defines our work. Critical practice is a conception of architecture that opposes the notion of the autonomy of architectural theory, a discourse disconnected from the practice of architecture.

It is an overdetermined notion that persists in our work after all these years as a mechanism that allows the resonance of the discursive theoretical practice in the

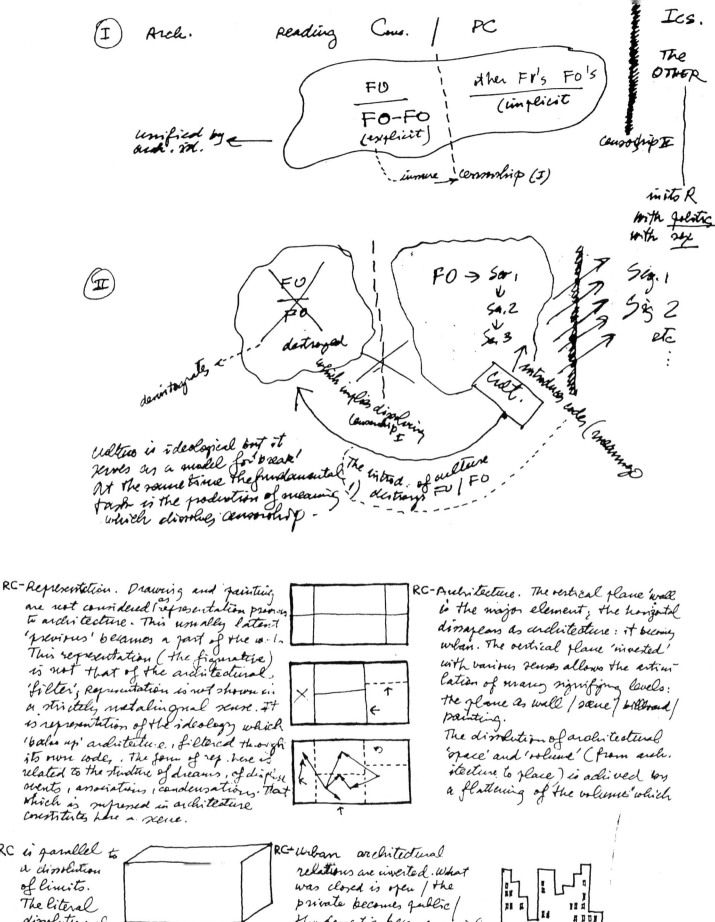

I Arch. reading Cons. / PC   Ics.

THE OTHER

FU | other Fr's FO's
FO-FO (implicit
(explicit)

unified by ←
arch. rd.

censorship II

inner → censorship (I)

into R
with politics
with sex

II

FU/FO destroyed
which implies dissolving
censorship I

FO → Sa.1
↓
Sa.2
↓
Sa.3

Sig.1
Sig.2
etc

Cult.

introducing codes (meaning)

disintegrates ←

culture is ideological but it
serves as a model for 'break'
At the same time the fundamental
task is the production of meaning
which dissolves censorship —

the introd. of culture
1) destroys FU / FO

RC–Representation. Drawing and painting
are not considered representation previous
to architecture. This usually latent
'previous' becomes a part of the work.
This representation (the figurative)
is not that of the architectural
'filter'; Representation is not shown in
a strictly metalingual sense. It
is representation of the ideology which
'backs up' architecture, filtered through
its own code, the form of rep. here is
related to the structure of dreams, of diffuse
events, associations, condensations. That
which is repressed in architecture
constitutes here a scene.

RC–Architecture. The vertical plane 'wall'
is the major element; the horizontal
disappears as architecture: it becomes
urban. The vertical plane 'inverted'
with various senses allows the articulation of many signifying levels:
the plane as wall / scene / billboard /
painting.
The dissolution of architectural
'space' and 'volume' (from architecture to place) is achieved by
a flattening of the 'volume' which

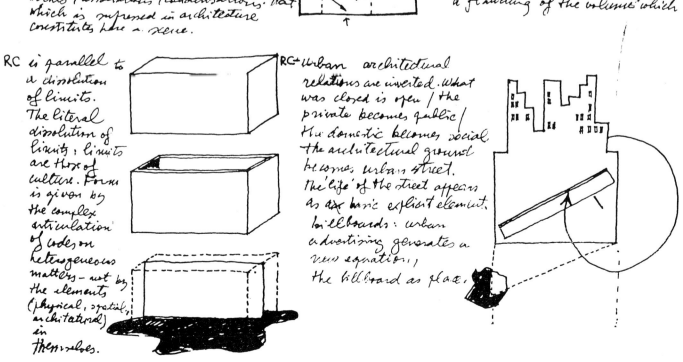

RC is parallel to
a dissolution
of limits.
The literal
dissolution of
limits; limits
are those of
culture. Form
is given by
the complex
articulation
of codes on
heterogeneous
matters – not by
the elements
(physical, spatial,
architectural)
in
themselves.

RC– Urban architectural
relations are inverted. What
was closed is open / the
private becomes public /
the domestic becomes social,
the architectural ground
becomes urban street.
The 'life' of the street appears
as a basic explicit element.
billboards: urban
advertising generates a
new equation;
the billboard as place.

position of architecture in culture and in relation to the city was moved from a privileged position to an equal one, in relation to other cultural systems. In this repositioning, an opening is created and the architect is placed in the position of the *reader*. Another essay important in this context is the "Misfortunes of Theory," where the reciprocal ideological influences of the discourses of urbanism, planning, and architecture were explored as leading architecture to the loss of its own object, which in fact is the problematic concept that led me to theory and criticism.

The mode of articulation of these discourses in relation to practice is not always conscious, as an application, and they do not always relate in a linear before-and-after fashion. In the project for Roosevelt Island, for example, we can see the reading of Manhattan's juxtaposition between high-rise and low-rise structures. But project, the public domain permeates through our entire project, not as a neutral field as in modernist urbanism, but as an articulation of places where the transitions between public and private become essential. This is not done in a nostalgic manner trying to emulate the historical European city but as a way to inspect the specificity of the American city.

The repetition of the towers can be related to issues explored, for instance, in my essay "Architectural Anagrams," where the question of the symbolic performance of the skyscraper is inspected by questioning its symbolic role as a single object in the city, by seeing it in its relationship of "value," a syntagmatic relationship, with other skyscrapers in Manhattan.

In a small-scale project like "Les Echelles," the house is a double object; it may become a public place, a stage for performance independent from the interior private domain, while at the same time there can be a constant interface between the inside and outside.

The architecture here is not only conceptually affected by the urban but is also articulated with other cultural systems.

production of design, and its articulation to a particular historical conjuncture. In other terms, it is a mechanism that provides both internal and external surveillance of the logic of development of a project as well as the political and ideological implications within and without architecture.

DA: Do the political-historical events in the recent past and the present state of changing economic forces in the world have an impact on architectural discourse and practice?

MG: The recent transformations of the global map, where political frontiers have been radically transformed, are redefining the role of cities and states. The fragmentation of the socialist world, and the resurgence of the nation-states in Eastern Europe, parallels the erasure of the economic boundaries in western Europe. Some walls have fallen (Berlin), while new conservative walls are being built menacing the fragmentation of the nation-states.

The other side of the instability of boundaries is the resurgence of the city in different and contradictory directions: a conservative regression to medieval city-states reviving their role as war machines (Sarajevo); a progressive movement towards a network of city nodes where the flow of informational and economic global processes intersect. The cities still have the role of economic dynamos. However, the dynamos have radically changed.

A new global city that functions both in cyberspace and as a physical city, and therefore a new object for architecture and urbanism, has emerged. Finally, the present economic restructuring will certainly have an impact in the practice of architecture, which will also be restructured.

DA: A number of years ago, we started developing theoretical critical work related to the need for criticism of inherited ideologies as they related to the overall structure of society; a major figure in our work was Louis Althusser. Has this need disappeared? Has it changed, has it transformed?

MG: How does the wide range of practices (from interiors to large-scale projects) affect the making of architecture?

DA: Intervention at many different scales is in the tradition of architecture, clearly in modern architecture in the work of Frank Lloyd Wright, Le Corbusier, and Mies van der Rohe.

I consider them different "scenes" in the architectural drama. Following the question of the city, I would say that this even affects the interiors, which are, for the most part, "urban." This happens in two ways: on the one hand, urban notions such as transition, sequence, and place are present in the interiors; on the other hand, these interiors can be seen as an interface between the city and the private realm. They occur behind the mask of the building's facade. One could say that this is the architectural reality of the city, a fabric and a world behind it. This is very clear in the Central Park West apartment interior where there is a sequence from park front to interior of a typical Upper West Side Manhattan block. This is reordered in the series of openings from the open park views to the fragmented, more fabric-like views through interior openings.

The organization of the interior is also affected by the notion of sequence and framing that comes from my work on the city and film, among other things. In relation to these questions, the nature of interior spaces such as that of "room" versus open plan are explored both in plan and section.

The interior also allows for the focusing on materiality and visuality, on the projections of desires and of the body, through the material realization of the place: materials that one can touch or caress, that reflect, mirroring city and subject at once, mechanisms that regulate the screening or exposure of the body. Of course some of these issues appear in the houses and/or the buildings.

The buildings, residential for the most part, are the result of the articulation of city and architecture, a building in the city

MG: The early years of the Institute for Architecture and Urban Studies were the years of the most intense production of critical theory. I proposed "Oppositions" as the name for the magazine to convey the sense that its pages were meant to be a place where the ideological struggle would take place. This gesture was definitely influenced by Althusser's writings.

Our work started at a point in time that was ineradicably marked by Althusser, as Jacques Derrida said "by what he searched for, experimented with, and risked at the highest price." This is crucial for critical work because "in thought…one must run risks, otherwise there is no responsibility." What became most relevant for our work was the notion that theory could be transformed into a "revolutionary practice"—the practice of the avant-garde—within architecture and urbanism. In addition the notion of "critique," which is the core of our critical practice, is not only an essential motif in Althusser's discourse and project, but also an indispensable notion for our practice today. The ongoing interest and the continuing vitality of the intellectual tradition associated with his writings on both sides of the Atlantic reminds us of the relevance and pertinence of his work for our time.

DA: Is there a real avant-garde? What would an avant-garde be now?

MG: We need to differentiate avant-garde from the avant-gardism I mentioned above. We also need to criticize the notion of an official architectural avant-garde.

A history of painting—where Marcel Duchamp and the surrealists represent a separate nonlinear development from the Paul Cézanne/Pablo Picasso lineage that moves from impressionism to abstraction via cubism—is being rewritten. This other development has always been the remainder of the official history of the avant-garde. The problem for historians now is to show that there are not two histories—the official line and a remainder—that half the facts cannot be suppressed for the sake of the internal consistency of the historical narrative.

is more than itself and also less than itself. This is exemplified in Buildings 1, 2, 3 and 4 designed as "two buildings" or "three buildings" or "one building in front of the other." In Manhattan Additions 1 and 2, buildings are made of urban fragments addressing different aspects of the city and of a building in the city. In these, some of the notions explored in "Architectural Anagrams," such as the tripartite organization of the skyscraper, reappear. Each of these scales of intervention affect each other. The architecture is not seen as a subjective, "expressive," freestanding fetishistic object, but as the place of intersection of all the forces that traverse architecture and the creative subject.

MG: Why is your practice of urbanism (and your large-scale projects) focused on the American city?

DA: Although we have designed a number of urban projects for European cities, the referent, if not the focus, of our urban work is the American city.

The American city *is* the modern city in its origins and in its development towards the negation or restructuring of an urban order. The American city is in fact the product of the Cartesian order claimed by Le Corbusier in his urban projects. Most American cities were developed by layering abstract grids of circulation on virgin land, on a "neutral green." And if not originally founded that way, their subsequent developments take the form of the grid, e.g., Manhattan's development according to the 1811 gridiron. From a building point of view, the type *par excellence* of the modern city — the skyscraper — is also American. One could say that the morphology and typology of the modern city are fundamentally American while the vocabulary of modernist urbanism developed in Europe. The transformation of the city with the changes in capitalism can also be best seen in the American city, in its conflict between the urban, the suburban, and the exurban.

While the official line in painting (pre- and post-cubist) reverberates in architecture through modernism (promoted by Sigfried Giedion and Colin Rowe), there are also architectures that develop beside the modernist lineage—Adolf Loos, Louis Kahn, Robert Venturi—and since the seventies, what we designate as a radical critical practice *on architecture*, where we include our work.

DA: How is Duchamp important in the development of critical work in theory and/or in practice?

MG: First, in our theoretical work, Duchamp's position has been helpful for a reflection on the question of the avant-garde today inasmuch as it clarifies the question of avant-gardism as the other side of the conservative movements of architecture in the twentieth century, and opens up the possibility of another avant-garde.

Second, in our practice not only Duchamp's notion of *tabula rasa* and its connection to the notion of *ready-made*, but also his break from the exclusive *optical* conception of painting and the reintroduction of the questions of *language, text*, the *body* and *desire*, are crucial for our conception of an urban architecture, and for the implications that they bring into the practice of architecture.

In our work the critique on the notion of *tabula rasa* is performed through the notion of *writing* as a form of *reading*, which brings up the question of the previous *text*. This notion, which is present in every one of our projects, acquires particular relevance in the urban projects.

The *ready-made* appears in different forms, from objects, such as the pantry door in the Central Park West interior, to urban projects, such as the Goose Island, Chicago, Illinois master plan.

The break from a purely optical conception of architecture is also very important in our work since it is developed through several texts, in which the written text acquires particular importance not only in themselves but in their reverberations with the optical and in their mutual dependency.

MG: How do you see the relationship between style and architecture?

DA: Style is the way in which a critical practice, by its reduction to fetishism, gets absorbed into pure consumption.

Each project represents a certain exploration in which forms are developed in a consistent way. While there is a certain continuity or familiarity in the formal development of projects, we cannot call it a "style"; actually it is a plus when a project cannot be easily classified stylistically. I would even leave out the term "postmodern," since this covers just about everything and reduction to stylistic naming seems quite banal. We could say that postmodernism starts after WWII, more specifically in the fifties, with cultural and technological changes, the development of communications and cybernetics infiltrating every level of life as mass culture and mass media within which any juxtaposition, no matter how odd, is possible.

When starting from a reading of the city as a generator in the process of production of architecture, the question of style is avoided. The city generates formal configurations of its own that do not belong in the books of architecture. We could speak of a textual architecture, rather than one of books, that is open, not necessarily consistent or unified. This is what architecture as *reading* and *rewriting* the city is about. The city itself (particularly the American city) as an apparent reality has no unity, closure, consistency, and is beyond style. An architecture that is generated by an urban reading should transcend the limitation of stylistic boundaries. This is not the same as eclecticism, which, again, is not of text but of books; it is within style and not beyond it.

Without Architecture
MG: How have the notions developed in your theoretical critical practice reshaped the fields of architecture and urbanism and their relationship in your practice? How do these notions affect the understanding of the ideology of modernist urbanism?

DA: Is the role of the city now equivalent to that of architecture in the past? Or, what is the place of urban discourse in relation to an architectural discourse? What is the role of architectural discourse in relation to an urban discourse?

MG: The city has been the object of architectural desire from the moment architectural discourse was established. As such, it has always eluded the architect; it has always been unreachable. In its pursuit of the city, architecture can only approach the city, "it never gets there." It is too slow or too fast; it rebuilds the past or projects the future, but it can never set itself in the present.

The city as the object of architectural desire is supposed to fulfill a fundamental lack in architecture, always focused on the building as object. As you said, "From the position of architecture as a critical practice, the city looks at architecture from without. It is beside, beyond its field of vision, something that, in looking back at architecture, constantly redefines it, again and again through history: in the baroque, in the enlightenment, at the beginning of the twentieth century with modernism, and now again with the radical restructuring brought by the global and informational city. The movement of the choreography of desire flows back and forth from architecture to the city, from the architectural to the non-architectural, and then back from the city to architecture."

It is important to note that to view architecture from without is not necessary to "stay" *outside*, but *beside*—to find the strategies that will allow discourse to confront and break apart from the conservative historical forces expressed in the compulsive repetition or in the violent denial of history.

DA: How do you see the American city? Is it mutating? In which way?

MG: From the beginning, the American city was founded with a specific formal structure. Since the independence of the United States, the American city, as the physical support of democratic and capitalist

DA: The question of urbanism and its relationship to architecture transcends the specificity of the city as locus. We live in an urban culture and therefore everything we do is filtered through it, whether consciously or unconsciously. The city, however, has certain configurational characteristics that make various possible settings for architecture. In this respect the question of *fabric* and *object* is a major one in defining different historical and ideological modes of addressing the formal relationship between architecture and the city and between architecture and urbanism.

These two conditions — fabric and object — have been seen since the turn of the century as opposites, until now. The city was seen either as a continuous fabric with public places and monuments, such as the historical city, or as a collection of objects — freestanding buildings — with no public places, as in the modernist city.

Our understanding of this relationship has been at the core of the urban projects we present in this book — fabric and object acting upon each other, not as opposites. Rather than repeating an ideological opposition, we propose condensations and displacements, producing new and more powerful notions to deal with the new conditions of the contemporary city. In working with these notions we have replaced the *or* by *as*. We say *object as fabric* — this can be seen in the projects for Roosevelt Island, Minneapolis, Park Square, etc. — or *fabric as object* — in the Goose Island "urban ready-mades," and in the Des Moines residential neighborhood of Hillside.

This is also a way to bring the question of nature back into the urban discourse, which has been absent from it for the past forty years, and establish a more dialectical critical relationship between the principles (and projects) of modernist urbanism. It was at this time that the city entered the realm of architecture as part of its discourse.

The question of the relationship between the ideologies of architecture,

systems, has developed with a unique formal/symbolic character. A mapping strategy based on the colossal scale of the Jeffersonian one-mile grid covers the territory west of the Appalachians, creating the conditions for a "continental city."

This city includes not only the nineteenth-century and early twentieth-century dense and continuous city-of-fabric but also other species of cities, such as the pre- and post-Second World War suburban cities, the late twentieth-century city-of-objects, and now the exurban edge cities. Maybe all of these apparently new forms are perceived as new because they are not yet consolidated as cities, but rather appear as very young urban formations of which the more mature forms are yet unknown.

We are at a point where some crucial decisions need to be taken in relation to the urban geography created since the second half of the twentieth century. Besides the political and economic problems inherent to democracy and capitalism that, without any doubt, affect our cities, there are issues concerning how/what we produce, exchange, and consume, how/where we live, move, and use our free time, etc.

The American city is one of the most vibrant laboratories that propose and answer these questions.

DA: How do you see the relationship between image and style in the development of a critical practice?

MG: I would define that relationship with two questions: first, the question of the image in terms of the reduction of architecture to an exclusive imaginary dimension; second, the question of style in terms of the figural and discursive coding of architecture that makes possible its circulation and consumption, which is another form of reduction.

The confinement of architecture to an *imaginary* scene is the inevitable result of the flow and exchange of shapes and images that circulate in the architectural scene. However, there is another scene, structured by unconscious forces and desires and traversed by political and social forces, where the *symbolic* dimension of urbanism, and planning is essential in my view to understand the crisis of architecture that was most obvious about thirty years ago and that led to the development of the postmodern condition in architecture.

MG: How does the city as the unconscious of architecture affect the practice of architecture?

The first time I used the statement "the city is the unconscious of architecture" was in the essay "Design versus Non-Design." In that context I developed the notion of placing the architect in the *position of the reader*.

The architect as a reader is a detective or a psychoanalyst bringing the not readily apparent configurations and symbolic performances that affect us all at a conscious level. This was later developed as a teaching method that I have now been applying for many years. There are myriads of possible formal conditions that the city develops outside architecture with it or without it—an open text for us to read. The architect reads and rewrites this text. The focus of this reading in my theoretical approach and in the projects has, for the most part, been the *public place*, the field of maximum cultural identity and intersections, the places that make a city urban, and not just a collection of objects. The subject reading and rewriting engages and articulates him/ herself with history.

architecture is played. One of the paradigmatic places that constitutes this scene is the city, the *other* of architecture.

The emergence and appearance of the symbolic scene in the imaginary scene tends to confuse, slow down, or even block the successful flow, exchange, and consumption of images required by the practice of architecture.

The notion of style represents another form of reduction that obliterates the textual dimension of architecture to coded, recognizable configurations, to stereotyped representations. Style facilitates the circulation of images, their instantaneous, uncritical visual consumption. A critical practice presupposes a form of visual resistance (to instant consumption) that initiates a process of reading and writing the architectural text. The notion of style does not have a place in our practice. Our buildings are neither modernist nor classical; they resist stylistic categorizations.

DA: What do you see as a formal strategy that would be anchored on a relationship between theory and practice?

MG: The most important formal strategy in our work is *reading as a form of writing*.

The tactics that implement this strategy are based on the deployment of a multiplicity of displacements:

The displacement of the *reading apparatus*—as in the filmic reading proposed in your article "Design versus Non-Design," with the implications of the establishment of sequences and the reintroduction of the text—and the displacement of critical theory within the practice as a surveillance mechanism that resists stereotype and styling.

The displacement of the *object of reading*, when reading the American city as architecture, where the city acts as a formal generator, as both a lexical and syntactic reservoir of architectural configurations and forms.

The displacement of the *writing apparatus*, in our latest experiments with computer/video.

The displacement of the *object of writing*, in the simultaneous work contrasting scales from that of furniture to the colossal scale of the metropolis.

PROJECTS

LES ECHELLES

House for a Musician, Mallorca, Spain, 1975

Diana Agrest

The site is a hillside overlooking the Mediterranean Sea. The program required a living room, a bedroom, a studio or guest room, a garage, a kitchen, and a bathroom. The house is conceived not just as an interior private space, but also as a building that has an outside life of its own—two buildings that may be experienced independently or together.

The house is also conceived as a public object, as a cultural event utilizing the public potential of its exterior surface. The client, who is a composer, pianist, and conductor, could create musical and theatrical events there. Groups of musicians and actors could be set on the various terraces as well as along the staircase; the house would then become a stage. Thus, the house does not remain just an enclosed private space, but can acquire social meaning. The staircase, illuminated from inside at night like a light cascade, further emphasizes these qualities.

This house accentuates and incorporates the dimension of pleasure in architecture. It tries to make the body a part of architecture—the movements up, down, and through space, the effort, the vertigo, the surprise, the pleasure of culture and the pleasure of the body in action come together in this house.

Certain aspects of the building relate to the immediate context, such as the very simple mode of construction and some forms and openings; others were taken from the more formal context of Spanish-Islamic tradition, such as the use of outside spaces and of different modes of transition between them. The whole house becomes a sequence of gardens or fragments of gardens, ranging from natural elements to an abstract cultural grid, organized along various modes of transition—staircase, bridges, doors, or passageways.

The glass-block staircase provides the traditional access to the house as well as an approach to the terraces. It is possible to ascend it entirely without entering the house, or to use it to go directly to the bedroom or the swimming pool levels. The staircase establishes a dynamic connection with the hillside to create a dialectical relationship with the static cubic volumes. The top of the staircase, a space for only one person, becomes a significant place for the house. From here one may watch the sunset, reflect, or play music. The staircase and the terraces form a relationship between inside and outside on the front of the house. There are similar relationships on the back side of the house: a direct access to a vegetable garden from the living-room level, a bridge toward the hill from the bedroom level, and the staircase to the "air."

The interior is treated as a neutral space where the only articulated elements are those that refer to the outside of the house. This allows the space to be organized freely. The construction system has deliberately been kept very simple in order to make use of the local technology. The structure is concrete and the walls are concrete blocks with cerulean blue stucco finish. The staircase is a glass-block and steel structure incorporating an interior lighting system. The intention is to make a simple house that would open itself up to rich cultural readings, to the plurality of sense.

right: Conceptual model with glass-block stairwell, lit at night

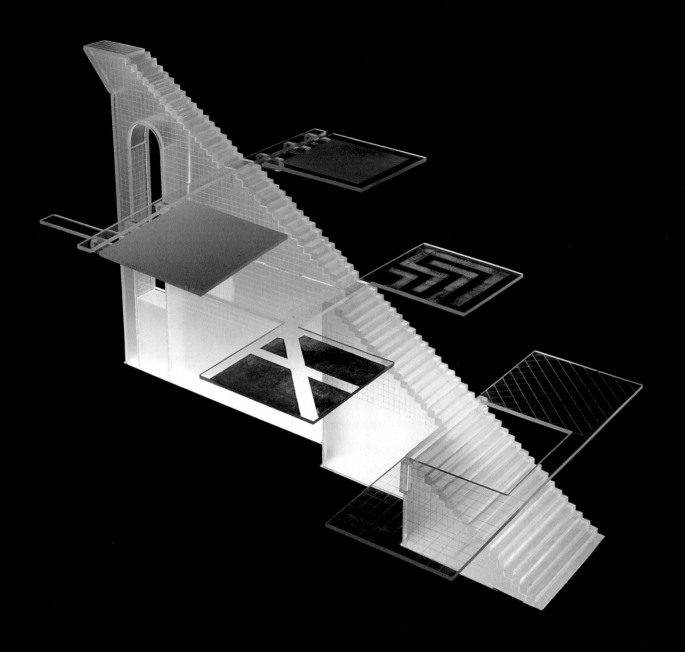

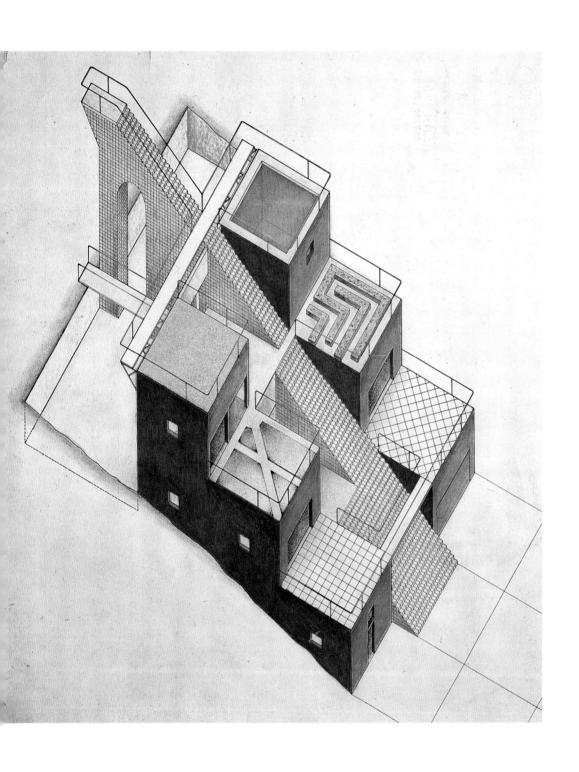

above: Back garden side carved into the hill
left: Hillside facing the sea

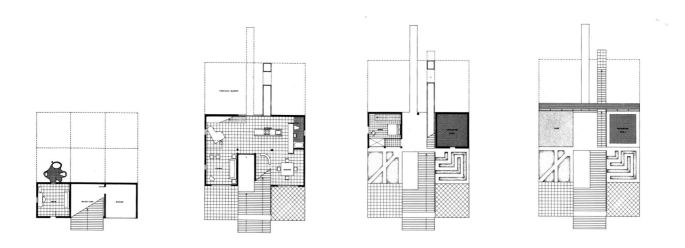

above, left to right: First floor plan; Second floor plan; Third floor plan; Roof plan with garden terraces

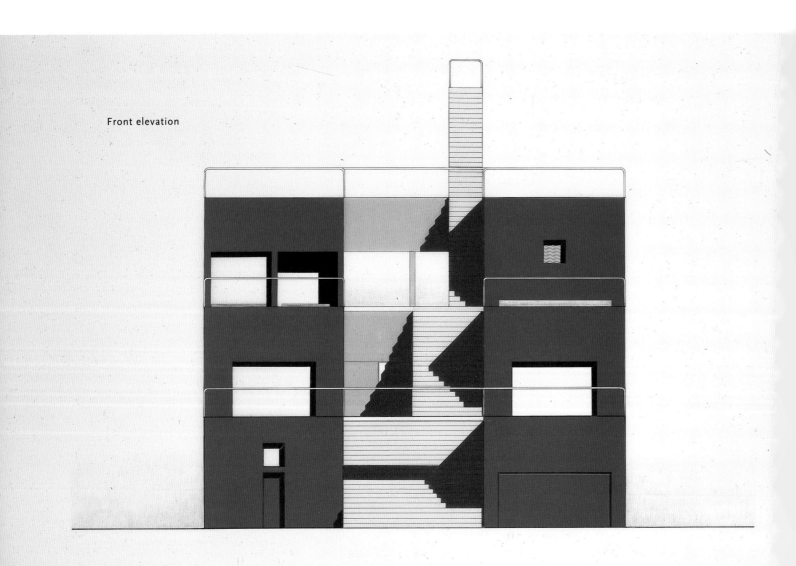

Front elevation

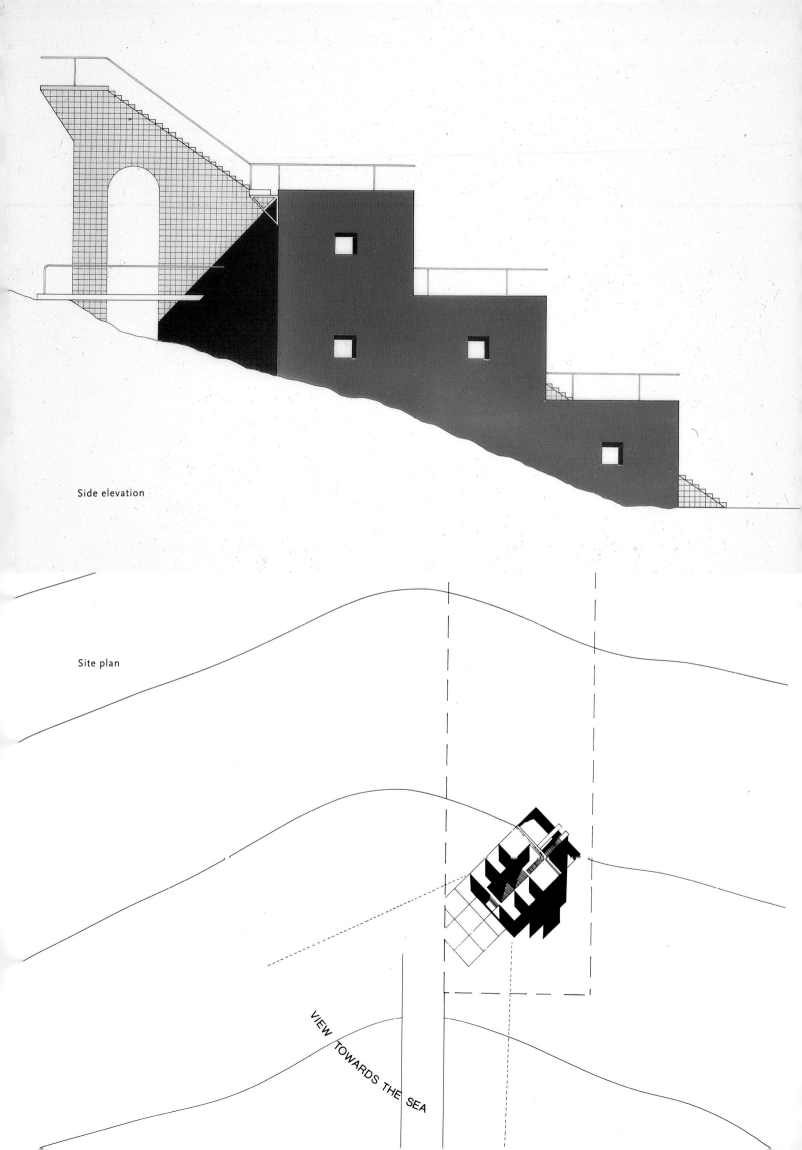

Side elevation

Site plan

VIEW TOWARDS THE SEA

BUILDING AS CLASSIFIER 1967–1975

Mario Gandelsonas

An articulation between building and body is the condition for the development of this project. The architecture is explored for its possibilities to produce and organize a series of physical sensations such as compression, expansion, acceleration, and delay, and psychological sensations such as tension, relaxation, vertigo, and claustrophobia. This new role of the building affects both the vocabulary and the alternative formal developments that generate the project.

These sketches develop a series of ideas for the design of a building as a classifying device. Classification of functions has always been one of the roles of building, but in this case the building acts as a human classifier. The entrance, marked with a black, square floor, leads to corridors of different lengths that classify bodies according to weight, height, sex, and age by means of architectural devices that reveal these differences (the design of these devices are not shown in the sketches).The last flight of the staircase, which vertically links the different corridors, articulates the physical and psychological classifiers of bodies. When people arrive at the top, there exist three alternatives for descent, each possessing a different physical and psychological nature. The first is a "monumental" staircase with a slope of forty-five degrees and steps five feet high with intermediate steps of two and one-half feet high. The second is a spiral sliding ramp, which arrives at an underground level where its axis intersects the forty-five degree axis of the staircase. The third is a double sliding ramp, which hangs from points where the two vertical planes parallel to the building meet. It arrives at the red circle, the point at which the exits from the monumental staircase and spiraling ramp converge.

"I come now to speak of monuments erected for preserving the memory of great events; Our Ancestors when having overcome their enemies, they were endeavoring with all their power to enlarge the confines of the Empire, used to set up Statues and terms to marvel the course of their victories, and to distinguish the limits of their conquests. This was the origin of Pyramids, Obelisks and the like Monuments for the distinction of limits." (Leone Battista Alberti, *Ten Books on Architecture,* book 7, chapter 16)

"This distinction between simultaneous or successive comprehension which is based upon the degree of openness or closeness of surfaces defining individual spaces coincides in the main with the difference between ecclesiastical and secular architecture.

"To understand a secular building we must get to know it as a whole, by walking through it from end to end, from cellar to roof, through all its outstretching wings. The entrance, the vestibule or passage leading to courtyard or stair, the connection between the several courtyards, the stairs themselves and the corridors leading away from them at each level like veins of our bodies—these are the pulsating arteries of a building." (Paul Frankl, *Principles of Architectural History,* chapter 1)

this page: Section-elevation
following pages: Plan; Axonometric

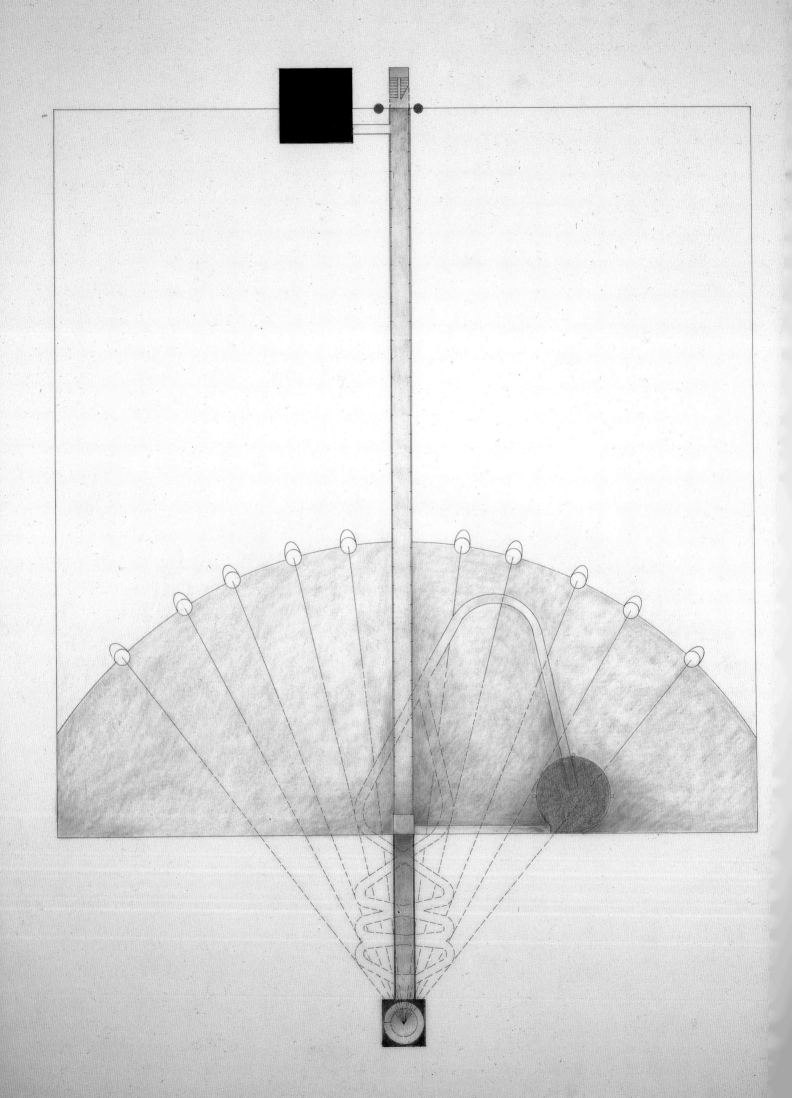

"Preliminary sketches for a building that classifies human bodies according to physical and psychological characteristics and stands as a monument to the progressive nature of western secular architecture"   D.V. 1975

DESIGN AS READING

Roosevelt Island, New York City, 1975

Given the particular conditions of the Roosevelt Island Housing Design Competition—historical (economic/political/ideological), contextual (New York, principal city of the nation), and concurrent (the present period in architectural history)—we decided that the program requirements could not be answered by improving an existing reality (ideology) in the area of housing, or by a cultural (regressive) or technological (progressive) program— the traditional alternatives of architectural Utopias.

We decided instead that the competition ought to be treated as material for considering a series of questions concerning the housing problem. In this regard, our project should be understood as part of the more general work of reflection on architectural ideology, that is, on the problem of the production of sense in building design and construction.

THE CITY

Architectural ideology needs to be displaced toward a new definition in which notions of design and reading, as operations of production and transformation of the meaning of the constructed world, play a fundamental role. In our proposal the displacement is effected by the introduction of formal repositories and operations derived from the architectural urban configurations— that is to say, the architecture of a production not completely controlled by architectural codes but rather subject to extra-architectural determinants, to "other" logic systems governing production of meaning in design. In design as well as in reading, meaning is derived from a chain of fragments rather than from a content adhering to a form.

THE OPERATIONS OF DESIGN

In design, the operations are closer to transcription, juxtaposition, and transformation than to invention.

Transcription deals with existing typologies. Examples of this operation are apparent in the variation of facades on Main Street (which transcribe the variation of facades in the city), the town houses, the waterfront, the towers, the setback, etc. Examples are also evident in the transcription of architectonic fragments such as Mies van der Rohe's curtain wall or Le Corbusier's *fenetre en longueur*.

Juxtaposition appears out of a logic in which fragments act as neutral elements in contraposition to the articulations that come to play a principal role. In this sense, and in terms of the articulation between fragments, public places occupy a fundamental role. Public places weave through and are continually blended with the dwellings, as in the stoops of town houses, streets, belvederes, etc.

Transformation allows for the creation of elements that transform the original meaning. Examples of this process are apparent in the transformation of towers, such as those found on Sixth Avenue, into colonnades, of the high rise into a wall, and of the typical brownstone or town house into another

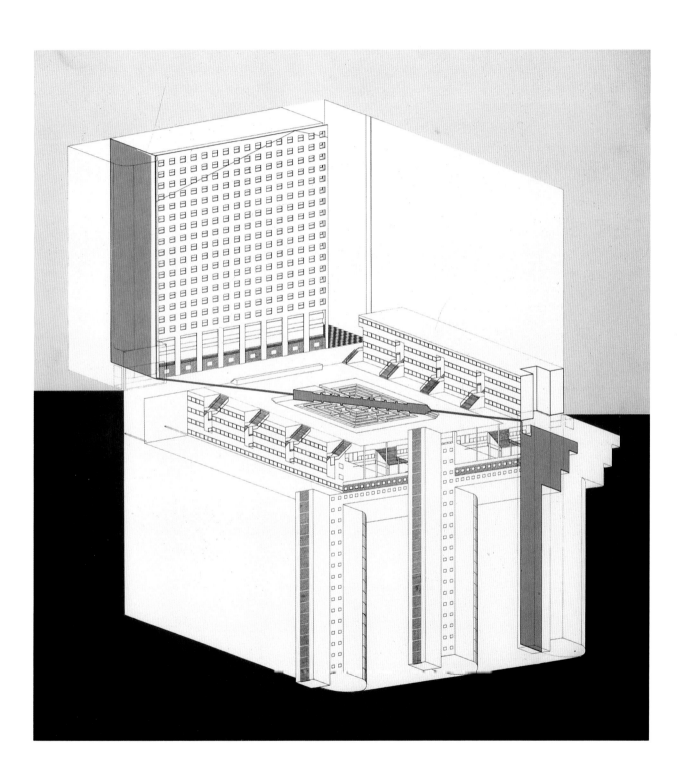

Unfolded block

type of low-rise housing, which is simultaneously transformed into terraced dwellings. These last, in conjunction with the towers in colonnade formation, produce the typical setback configuration of New York skyscrapers. We attempt here to pose the problem of the dissemination of meaning—of the production of meaning—as open signifying chainings. Our project attempts to organize a dispersion as a dialectic between the ideological tendency to reduce meaning (to enclose it completely in metaphors) and the possibility to eventually escape from this reduction. A dialectic is thus created between monument and city, architecture and housing, where housing in its urban logic may still be read as a mega-monument, recovering in another dimension the architecture it has denied.

The urban configuration of the project is based on Manhattan's structure, taking what is in fact a typical configuration of the Manhattan block: high rise on the avenue, low rise on the side street. The area is thus organized in a series of streets, perpendicular to the Main Street and East River edge promenade. One of the most important streets in this context, Seventy-second Street, is emphasized in our project as a link, a mark between the wall and the colonnade. Between the streets, in the core of the block, there are open spaces like piazzas, which are articulated with Main Street. Dominating Main Street is the twenty-one-story-high "wall"; parallel to the river is the colonnade, a series of towers that mark the repetitive rhythm of this type of high-rise building. Between these two are town houses.

THE WALL

The wall appears as a homogeneous screen oriented towards the city, separated from the volume of the building and thus allowing for the provision of terraces in the intermediate space. Its continuity is interrupted only by urban scale doors, which relate the wall to towers and the streets to town houses in a play of solids and voids. Toward Main Street the facade is articulated by openings reflecting the interior space, with its different apartment types. Thus one side of the wall functions at a monumental public scale in relation to Manhattan, while the other refers to the variety of scales found inside the island.

TOWERS

The glass towers refer to the repetitive rhythm of towers in the city, like those on Sixth Avenue, while, in their relationship to the wall and the doors, they appear as a monumental colonnade. The towers, in connection with the low-rise buildings, create a setback in profile, transforming both elements. While they function symbolically at the scale of the city toward the interior of the project, i.e., the courtyards and streets, these two types—towers and stepped housing—are a more complex and fragmented phenomenon. As seen from the wall, the towers relate to the urban landscape of the Manhattan skyline as accents between the ample vistas of the city. This effect is accentuated by the towers' long, lit, glass shafts with small perforated windows, which play with the glittering lights of Manhattan across the river.

right: View from the East River

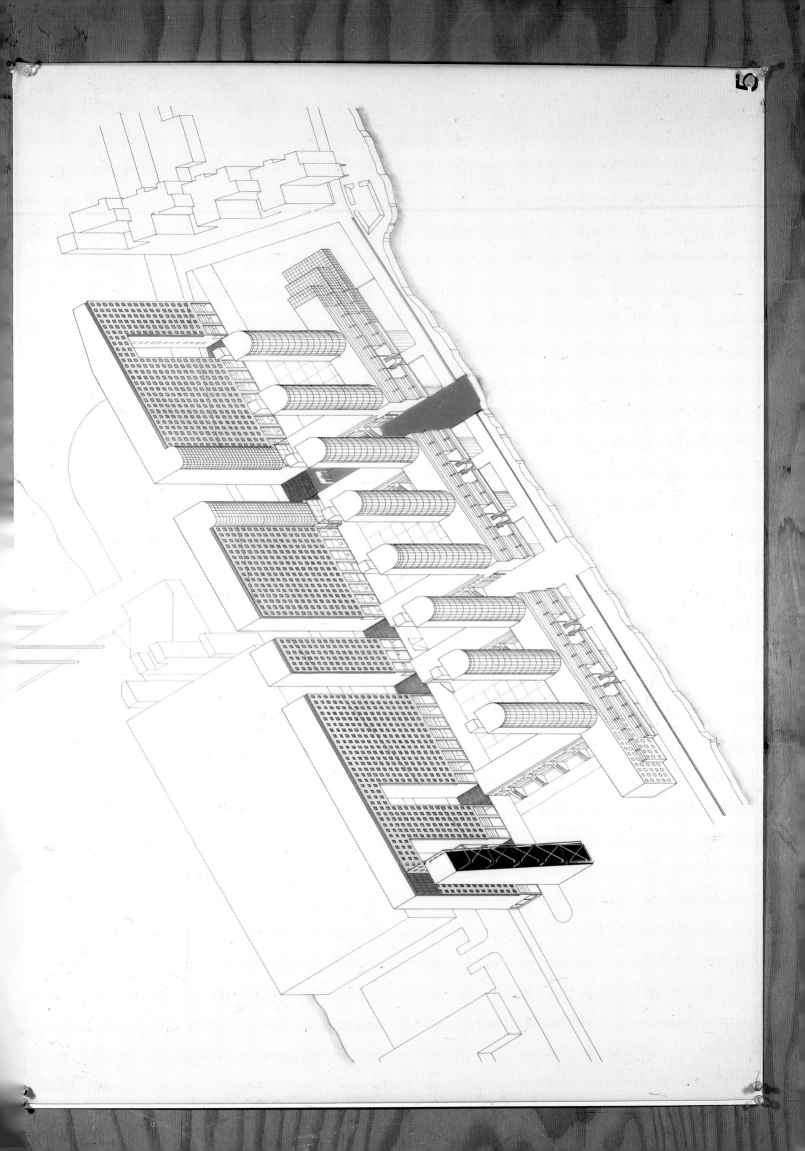

TOWN HOUSES

The typical town house has been transformed. The stoop has become a public element that articulates public spaces through the building, connects streets with squares. The facades towards the streets or piazzas are treated in different manners, addressing the particular character of the space.

STREETS

The wall emphasizes the direction of Main Street and, at the same time, generates a parallel street. Between these two, in the depth of the wall, there are commercial and community facilities. The access to stores is on the side facing the low-rise buildings. Perpendicular to these, there are streets following the Manhattan grid.

SQUARES

These replace the private backyard of the town houses. They are not only physically connected with the streets but also visually connected with Manhattan through urban "windows" that perforate the stepped housing and act as belvederes framing the waterfront landscape. Thus from all parts of the project there are vistas towards the river. The scale of the project allows for a range of different types of gathering places. The plaza is only one place in a sequence of public and semipublic places. From Main Street, one passes through the doors of the wall, along the promenade to the court-yards that are connected by the stoops *qua* bridges, to the streets, to the secondary promenade connecting the towers and providing access to the belvederes, then down to the boardwalk, passing over the water pools.

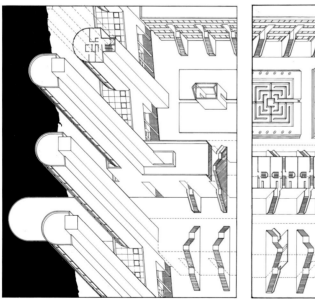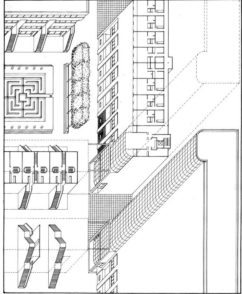

above: Articulation of types and relationship between public place and private space

right: Elevations

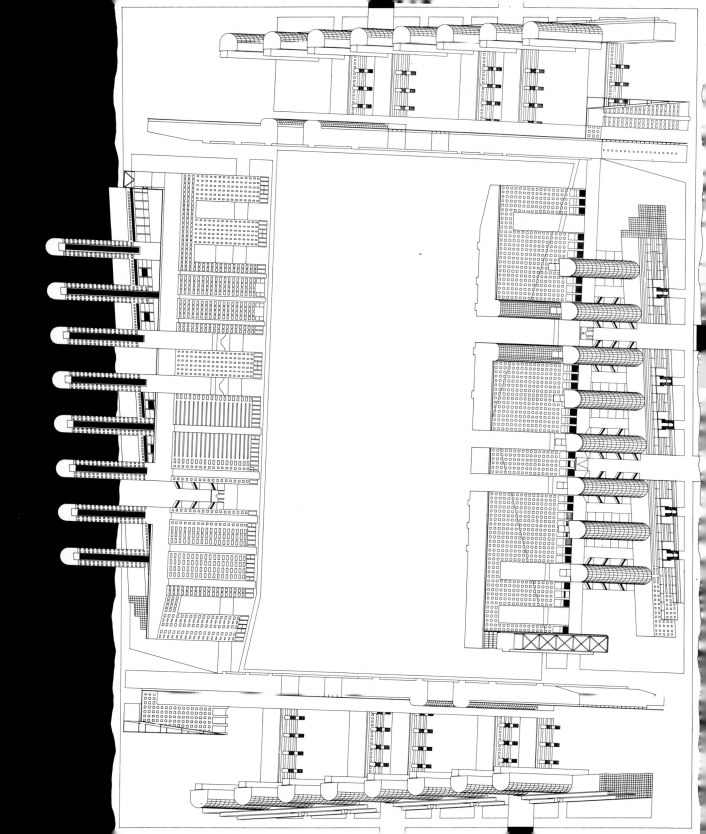

Site plan

Floor plan, ground level

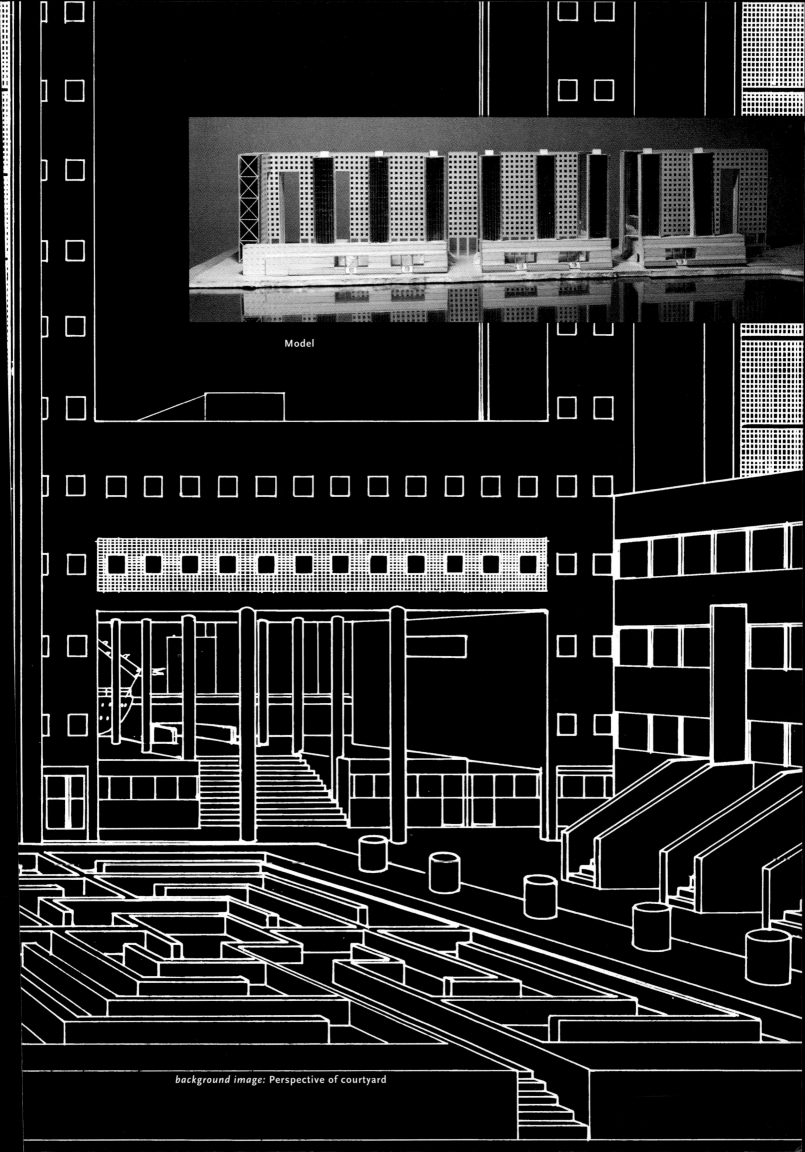

Model

background image: Perspective of courtyard

HOUSING IN PARIS

Programme Architecture Nouvelle, 1975

This project approaches the question of housing on the basis of a critical reevaluation of some key notions that have been elaborated from the 1920s to the present about housing and its architecture. This can be illustrated by the two extreme and antithetic positions that define the spectrum of design strategies of this century in terms of control versus participation. On the one hand is the canonical proposition of the Modern Movement, expressed by the Congrés Internationaux d'Architecture Moderne postulates, which implies total intervention and control of the environment by the architect. On the other hand is the populist "theory," an inversion of these principles as a reaction to the "failures" of modernism. It proposes the users' participation as the determinant force in the configuration of the environment.

This project intends to displace the focus from the architect/user opposition to the question of *reading* and *writing* the architectural text itself. By posing the question in terms of reading and writing it recognizes the existence of a specific architectural knowledge that deals with form giving and it restates the question of the user in terms of reading. Design as reading presupposes the selection, combination, and transformation of forms and meanings, which have a cultural tradition, rather than the direct participation of a user in the design process.

This displacement is accomplished through the notion of type as a mediator between architecture and urbanism. Building types developed through centuries in urban agglomerations are significant cultural elements. The persistence of their "functional" and symbolic codification is a proof of their institutionalized nature. They are recognized, understood, and accepted by their users as the norm. The urban context supplies the material from which types can be inferred and transformed generating a range of possible combinations and articulations.

The relationship between architecture and the city is accomplished by a mechanism of *mise-en-sequence* applied to different specific urban situations. In this process operations of transformation and articulation of types are performed.

This approach represents the contradictions between the forces of culture and the economic forces of the development of the city. It bypasses historicist and stylistic issues.

Our approach recognizes that building types represent only one element of the urban fabric, and that the articulations between public, semipublic, and private spaces are the elements that are essentially urban.

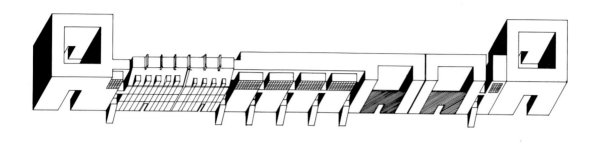

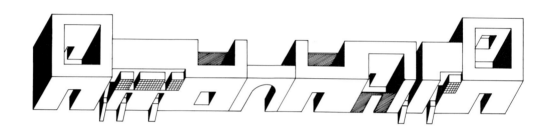

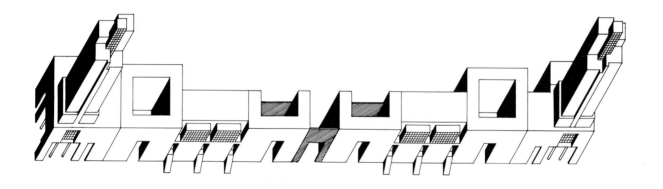

Three sequences

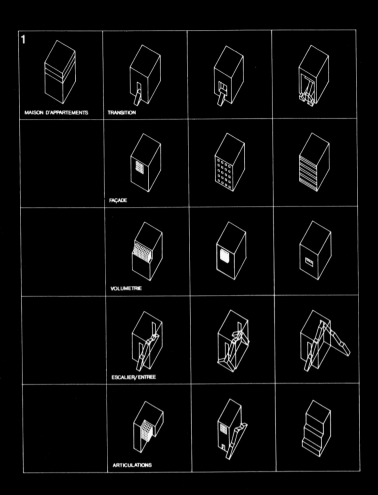

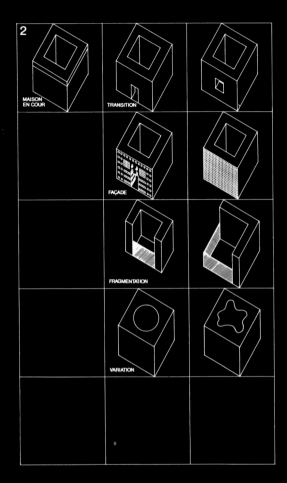

Architectural types

Dialectic between urban configuration and architectural type

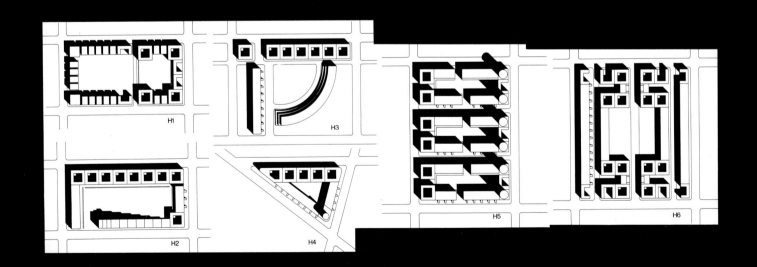

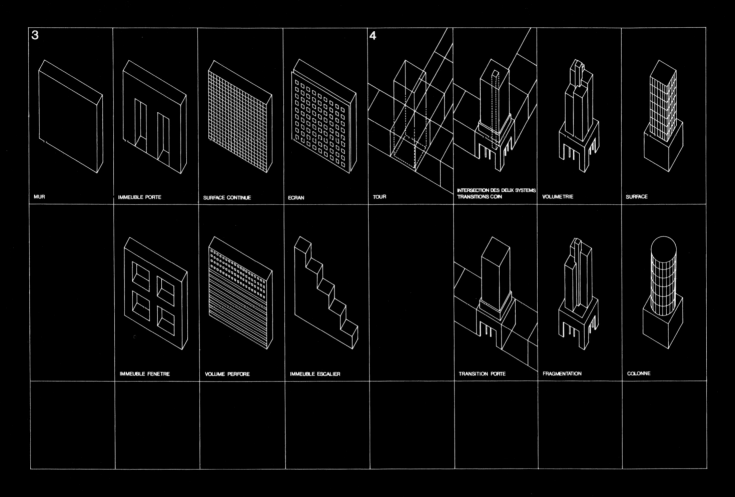

3 MUR · IMMEUBLE PORTE · SURFACE CONTINUE · ECRAN · **4** TOUR · INTERSECTION DES DEUX SYSTEMS TRANSITIONS COIN · VOLUMETRIE · SURFACE

IMMEUBLE FENETRE · VOLUME PERFORE · IMMEUBLE ESCALIER · TRANSITION PORTE · FRAGMENTATION · COLONNE

Architectural types

Plans

Thus, parallel to the housing types, we also propose a typology of connections or articulations developed almost independently of the housing, resulting in the enrichment of the chosen housing types through their connections. As a result of this operation, the traditional elements of entries, staircases, galleries, etc. allow for multiple readings. Thus the entry to one type—the apartment house—is at once a door, a staircase, a transition between city and house and between sidewalk and square, and a communal area for the units grouped in the building.

By combining, articulating, and transforming a given context of urban configurations, the *mise-en-sequence* models itself after the process by which the city develops.

Block interior elevations

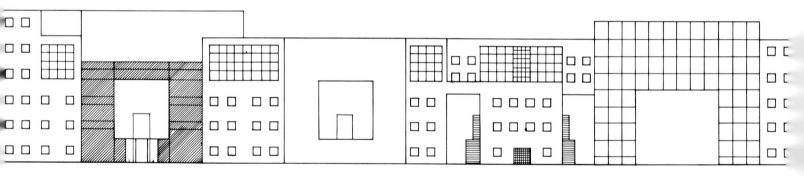

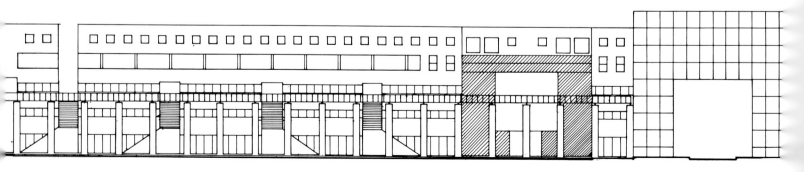

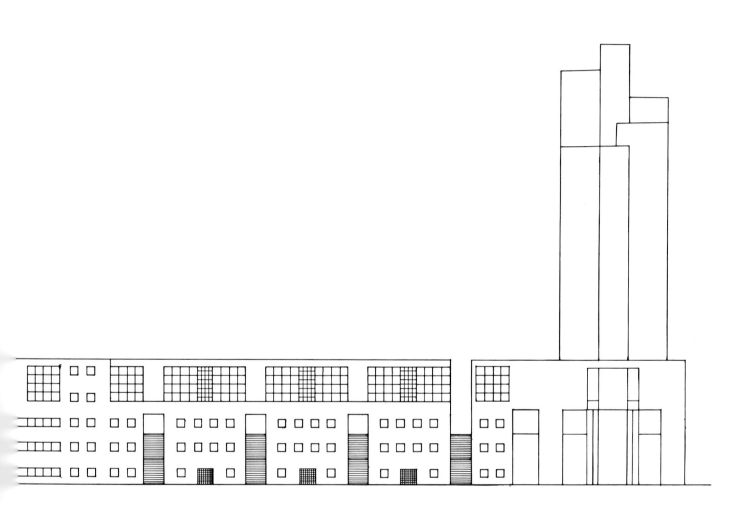

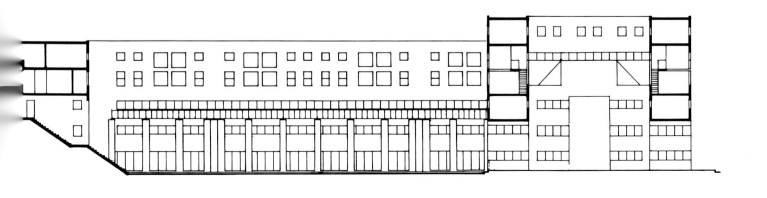

ARCHITECTURE AS MISE-EN-SEQUENCE

La Villette, Paris, France 1976

This project confronts the issues of history and historicism in relation to the design of urban form; it is thus a critical response to the urban design principles of the Modern Movement. Historicism is the mechanistic, arbitrary use of history, the paraphrase without transformation, the quotation out of context, the realistic replica and the picturesque kitsch.

We attempt neither to return to an idealized past nor to use all the historical examples of architecture we happen to like. We want to establish with the past a dialectical relationship in which the modern period is considered a part of history; we want to look at both the classical and the modern with the same critical eye.

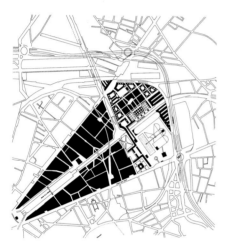

above: Massing
right: Sequential arrangement of public places

Our project at La Villette is a critical reading of the relationship between urban structure and architecture. This reading implies the articulation between history and the subject (the creative subject, the subject of the unconscious). Reading the city—its public places, its built forms producing not only an architectural reading but also other cultural readings—allows our project to articulate with the cultural context of the city of Paris, with its history and the history of architecture, with conscious images and unconscious representations.

This reading of the cultural and historical determinations in the city, denied by the economicist and anti-historical approaches to urbanism, implies an understanding not only of the types of spaces and buildings but also of the symbolic performances of such types. In the process of *reading* and *rewriting*, a transformation takes place, generating new configurations. It is precisely through transformation that the necessary relationship between the old and the new, between history and subject, can be established.

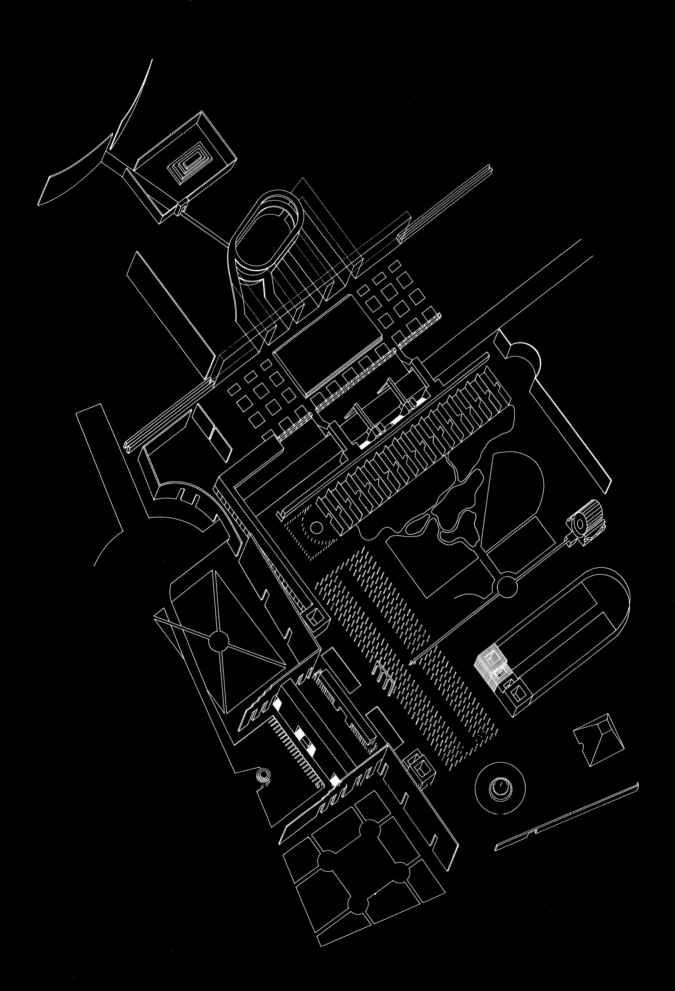

THIS NOTION OF READING IS DEVELOPED IN TWO WAYS

First, public spaces are treated formally as positive spaces and not as leftover space between monumental buildings. Instead of considering the project as a set of buildings on a neutral plane, the project develops as a multiple sequence of public places, of transitions and articulations between open and closed, public and private spaces. Streets, squares, courtyards, parks, and doors designed at an urban scale traverse the built volume and link it to the surrounding neighborhoods and to the rest of the city. In this traversing, edges and elements of transition (such as doors, loggias, stairs, arcades) become very important in allowing for sequential articulation.

Second, through typological articulation and transformation, types transform into each other and thus generate new spatial and typological conditions. This makes an architecture of sequence and juxtaposition rather than an architecture of geometry.

FORMAL CONFIGURATION

This project creates a variety of zones rather than treating the built volume as a homogeneous totality. The project incorporates counterpoints, nuances, and rich modulations, which are the essence of spatial and symbolic experiences offered by the city through its multiplicity of places and *parcours*.

The project is divided into two parts that oppose and relate to each other—a dense urban fabric and a park. A sequence of public places, penetrating through these parts, interrelates them. The two main elements of the program—the building and the park—are divided by the Canal de L'Ourq, which becomes a symbolic line between architecture and nature. The project is organized by a grid perpendicular to the canal; this grid is then modified by the forces of the city.

The built area is developed mostly to the north of the canal through a very dense fabric of streets, perimeter blocks, and squares related to the surrounding neighborhoods. The streets penetrate through the Grande Salle, which has been incorporated into the fabric, its carved center forming an open space. In this space, a shifted axis introduces the city grid and then continues through four doors in the Facade Building, which covers the Grande Salle and frames the square of La Villette on the edge of the canal.

The square of La Villette is enclosed on all sides in different forms addressing various conditions and articulating different possible sequences. On a platform in the center of this square there is a small group of courtyard houses that represent an idealization of their type; the group forms a monument to mass housing that *makes La Villette architecture.*

While nature penetrates the architecture on the urban side, architecture transforms nature on the park side. The Place de La Villette is related to the river edge by means of an arcade connecting towers, by its connection to a market place (which is a nodal point in the relation between north and south), and by the intersection of the two canals and the point at which the transformation of the housing type from fabric to building occurs.

right: Ground level plan

1. Residential
2. Technological school
   and Science Museum
3. School
4. Offices
5. Hotel
6. Ateliers
7. Amphitheater
8. Park
9. Marina

HOUSING

The urban side, on the north, is organized with perimeter block housing. Two types of buildings have been used: the courtyard apartment building and the narrow apartment building. The former is a transformation of the French hotel type. While the front courtyard belongs to the individual building, the back garden, or courtyard, becomes the semipublic center of the block. The sequence from street to garden is preserved and transformed to address the more public nature of these spaces. The apartment building type is a transformation of the seventeenth-century Parisian apartment building. Its major public elements (the lobby and the stair) have been emphasized. They connect the street and the garden in a continuous sequence towards the private apartments.

The grid is modified when it crosses the Canal de L'Ourq. The movement towards the south side starts in an urban block transformed into a marketplace and then into buildings as objects. Residential buildings define the western edge of the project and incorporate both the water and the surrounding neighborhood into a series of plazas and squares.

The buildings are elements of the park—part arcade, part gate, part port—articulated with and through the public places they frame. Thus, although different in scale and character to the housing located on the north side, they are also a transformed type, the modernist slab, which has incorporated the structural aspects of public space. The edge defined by the buildings is a very important element in that it represents the relationship between the two grids, that of the project itself and that of the city, referring respectively to the new and the old.

THE CANAL

The Canal de L'Ourq dividing the north and south is treated as an urban architectural element, the usual role of water in European cities, and particularly in Paris. While the north embankment is framed by a built arcade linking the base of the towers, the south embankment is organized with green sloping grass framing the stairs, with a promenade through topiary trees, and with a continuous pergola. While the architecture of the north has been penetrated by elements of nature, such as the grand square, the nature of the south has been treated as an architectural element.

Mise-en-sequence of public places
facing page, top to bottom:
Northern Square; La Grande Salle;
Place de La Villette; Market Square

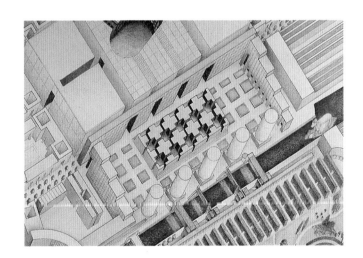

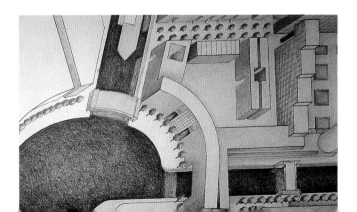

THE PARK

The park is modeled on a reading of the historical French gardens. A three-bay zone, accentuating the east-west axis and framed by a forest-like area, acts as a filter to the industrial area and Peripheric Boulevard. Each of these three bays is different. One is made up of water mirrors and is terminated by an existing neoclassic pavilion, which is replicated as an aviary. The center bay is formed by a fountain and lawn. The third is a formal garden with an axis perpendicular to the Canal de L'Ourq. From this garden springs a romantic garden that ends in a promenade made of topiaries, which connects the arts-and-crafts center to the amphitheater and is parallel to the continuous pergolas along the water. The existent bridges become part of the park. Stairs and sloped green grass connect the pergola level with the embankment below.

The whole project is traversed by green spaces at the scale of buildings or even neighborhoods. The park itself has been conceived to function at the scale of the city. Louis-Pierre Baltard's Grande Halle, incorporated into the park, establishes a transition between the urban zone and the park of the project. At the same time, it shifts the axis of the park and allows the articulation of the various directions involved in this project.

THE MONUMENTS

Some specific points are emphasized by the placement of monuments: projects by Jean-Jacques Lequeu, Claude-Nicolas Ledoux, and Étienne-Louis Boullée. A sculpture of a cow by Lequeu refers to the cows that have been killed in La Villette's turn-of-the-century slaughter houses. It is placed in the Canal L'Ourq and is on axis with Ledoux's Barriere de La Villette in the Place de Stalingrad. The House for the Guardian of the Waters by Ledoux is reinterpreted as a fountain in the garden. Its position emphasizes the axis perpendicular to the Grande Halle. Finally, the Cenotaph to Newton by Boullée is reused as a planetarium in the park. These monuments are critical and political developments of architectural thought and form. Furthermore, they are monuments to all those architects whose projects remain on paper.

Mise-en-sequence of public places
facing page, top to bottom:
La Promenade des Parallèles; Marina;
Parc de La Villette; The Guardian of
the Water, Planetarium

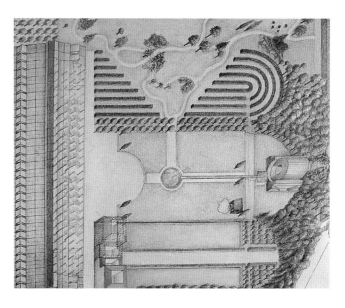

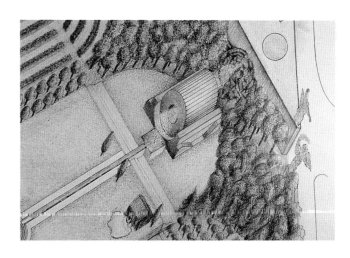

DOORS

Summer House for Two Lawyers, Punta del Este, Uruguay, 1977

The door, a basic element of architecture, is the generating notion for this house in a garden. The door separates nature from culture, open from closed; it is a threshold, a transition, abrupt or articulated, not only between exterior and interior, but also between public and private, between architecture and the city.

This house is generated by the forces of architecture and the city. Public space is incorporated in this most private domain — the house — and articulated with the basic notion of the villa type — the piano nobile. This superimposition generates a series of transformations based on the frontal versus centralized forces in the project.

The building is articulated by three monumental doors: two lateral doors, which permit visual and physical access from the front to the back garden without entering the house, and a central door, which unfolds into a series of doors in the central interior space, which acquires the quality of exterior space.

this page and facing page: On Perspective

In approaching the central door, one must climb a set of steps to a podium, as if ascending to a *piano nobile*. Once through the door, one must descend another flight of steps in order to get into the central space. With this gesture, one is "out" again, so to speak, into a court with doors on all four sides. A set of columns forms a cube within this court. Four perspectival spaces open out from these columns. Each is transformed by the specific articulation of the columns with stairs, walls, and openings. This articulation is the result of the superimposition of frontality and centrality. This collision produces the explosion of the volume and the sequence of transitional elements and places that continually relate outside and inside, garden and house. Frontality is marked by a freestanding screen with three doors cut into it, by wings penetrating the central space, by a loggia in the garden, and by a triangular pond in the back. Centrality is marked by two interior and two exterior "rooms" that extend the central space in a biaxial scheme.

The door becomes a frame where architecture and nature confront one another; rather than represent one another, they meet. The door plays the role of mirror where one side is the image of the other by inversion. It is the locus of the transformation of the oppositions it implies. This set of oppositions is constantly inverted; it generates the resolution of this project as a series of transitions between various "outsides." The transitions emphasize the aspects of permanence and change, through static and dynamic spaces, and are essential to making place.

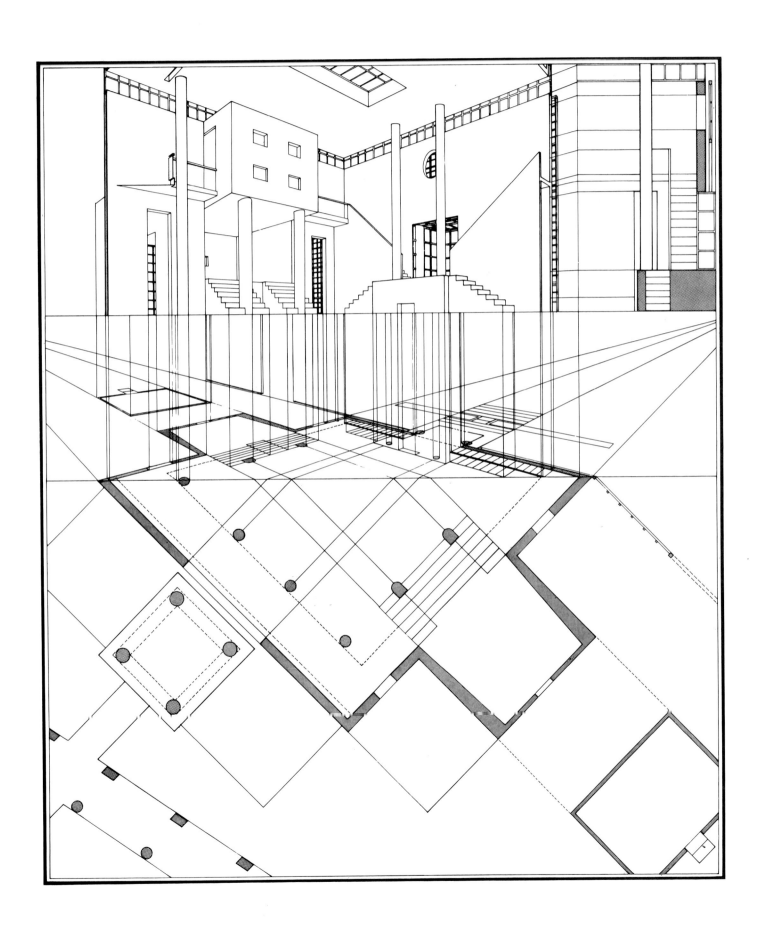

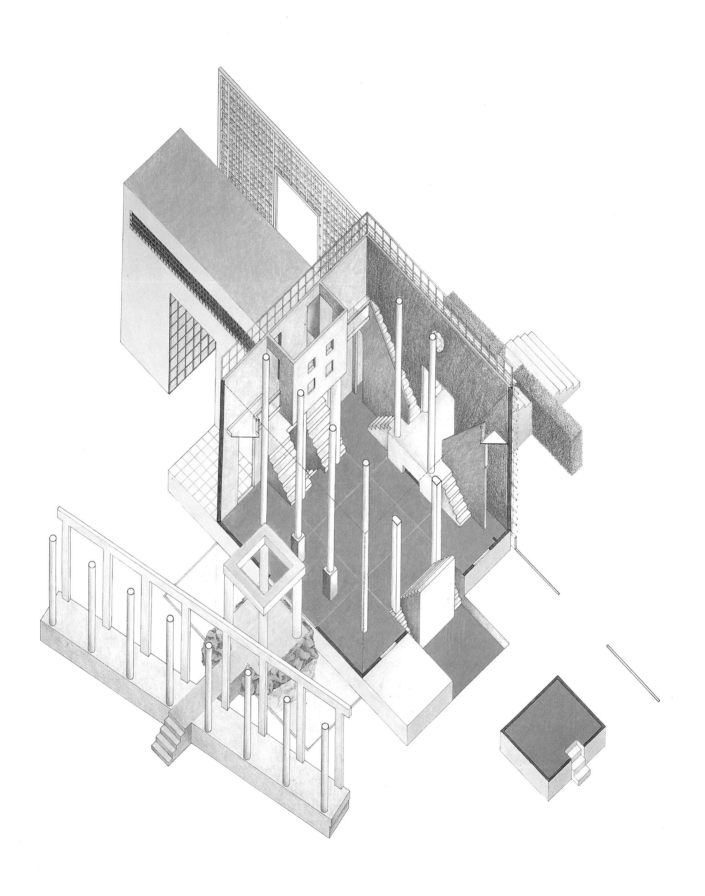

this page: Indoor/outdoor from front to back
facing page: Indoor/outdoor from back to front

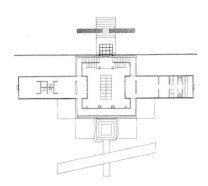

this page, top to bottom: Third level plan;
Second level plan; Ground level plan;

below: Roof plan

facing page, top to bottom: East side view;
Entrance side view; Longitudinal sequential
section

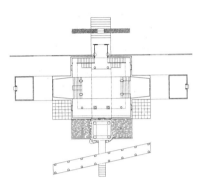

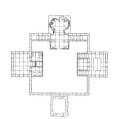

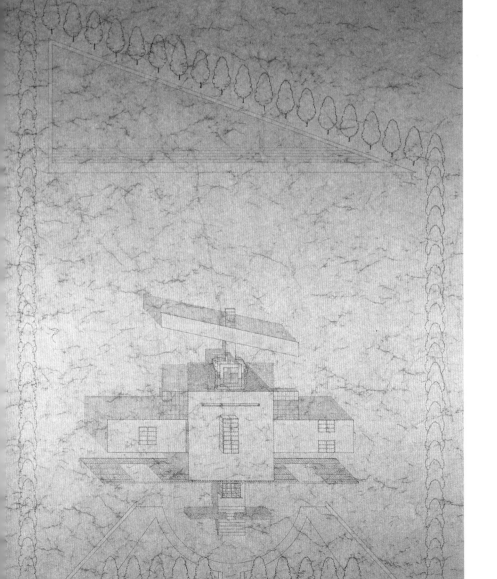

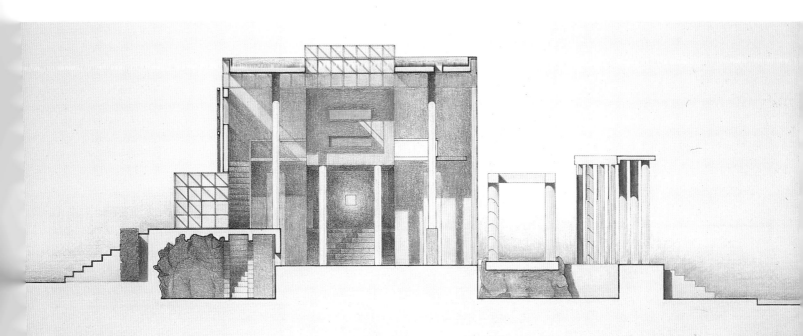

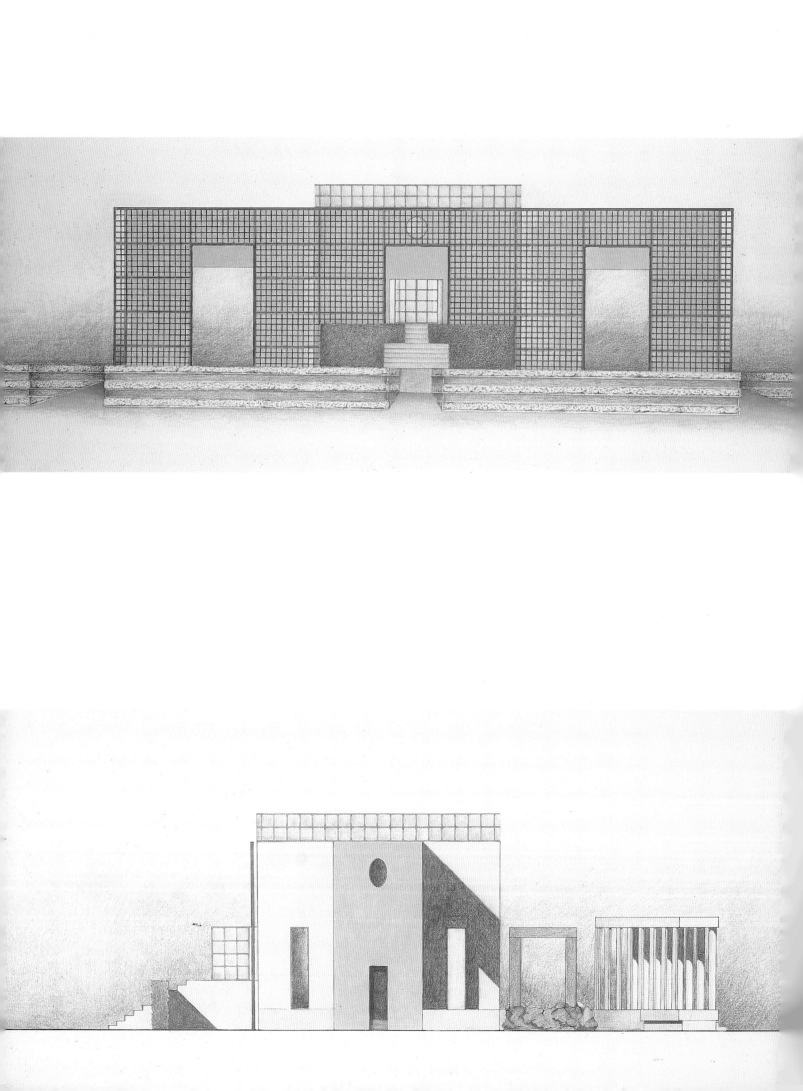

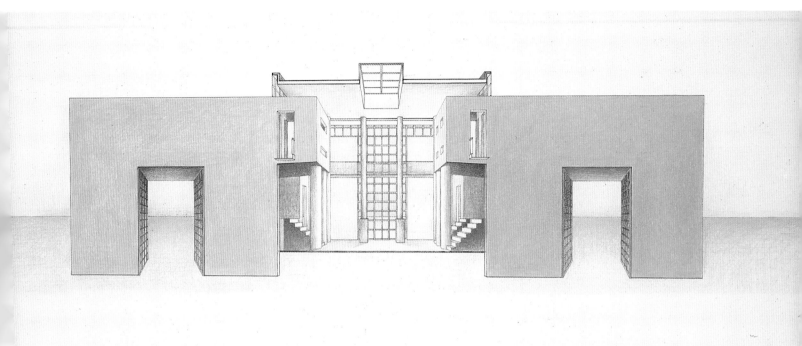

facing page, top to bottom:
East elevation; North elevation

this page, top to bottom: Section;
South elevation

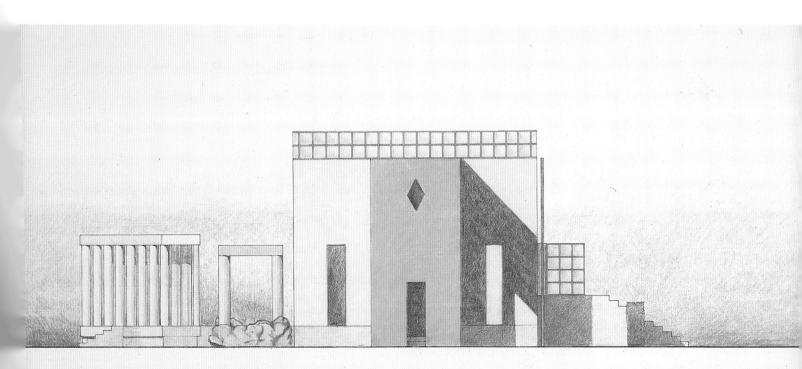

ARCHITECTURE
BETWEEN MEMORY AND AMNESIA

Suburban Center on the Mississippi, Minneapolis, Minnesota, 1976

Design is rewriting architecture. Design is a process of transforming existing configurations, both architectural and urban, both buildings and places. Design implies a dialectic between the new and the old.

But design is also production of meaning—the transformation of the old into the new and the mutation of the known into the unknown. Design is a process of losing memory as a possibility of invention—design is amnesia. This project explores these ideas by examining the relationship between the urban and the suburban realms.

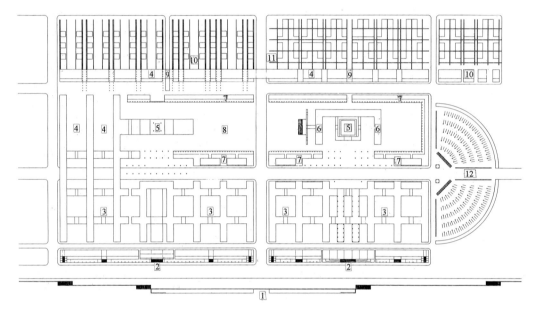

above: Ground level plan: 1. waterfront, 2. waterfront housing, 3. courtyard housing, 4. row housing, 5. high-rise office and apartment towers, 6. shopping mall, 7. arcade, 8. parking, 9. underground parking, 10. single-family houses, 11. courtyard houses, 12. drive-in movies

facing page: Site plan

following four pages: Urban/suburban intersections 1, 2, 3, and 4

First, we consider typologies of buildings and places that characterize the suburban landscape and that are not yet part of history, the memory of architecture. The sparse suburban landscape that characterizes most of the United States is in opposition to the urban density that characterizes most of Europe.

Second, we juxtapose these two opposing situations to create another kind of space. The urban order invades the suburban disorder, but the suburban condition alters the forms and meanings of the urban space. Moreover, the project extracts and develops new potential forms that appear when the urban and the suburban interact and contradict each other in a close and violent way.

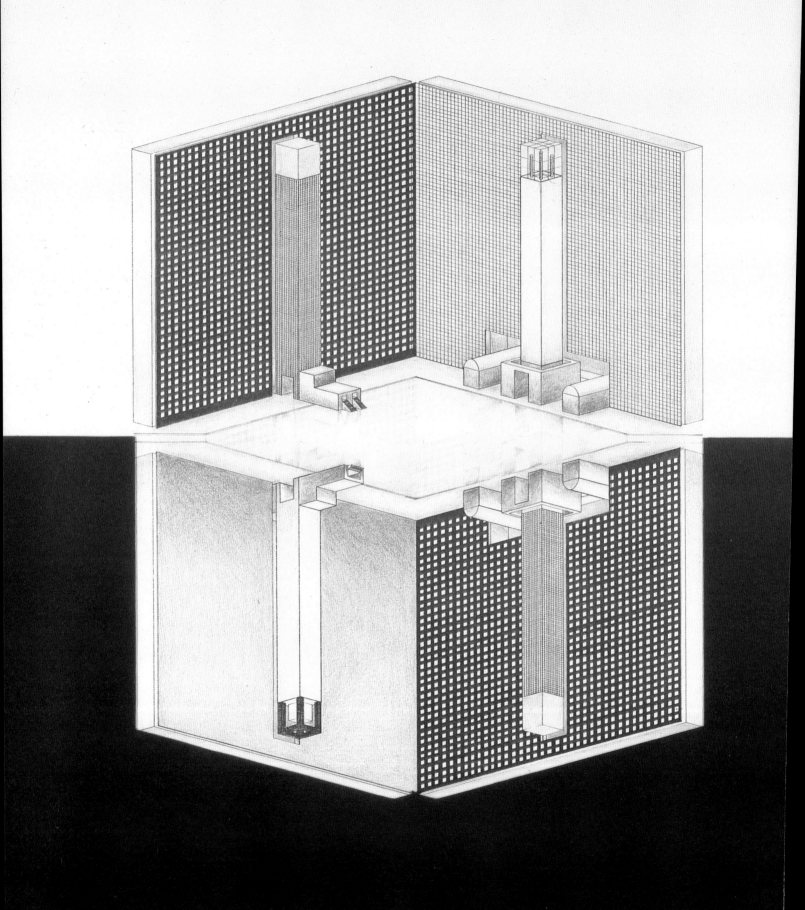

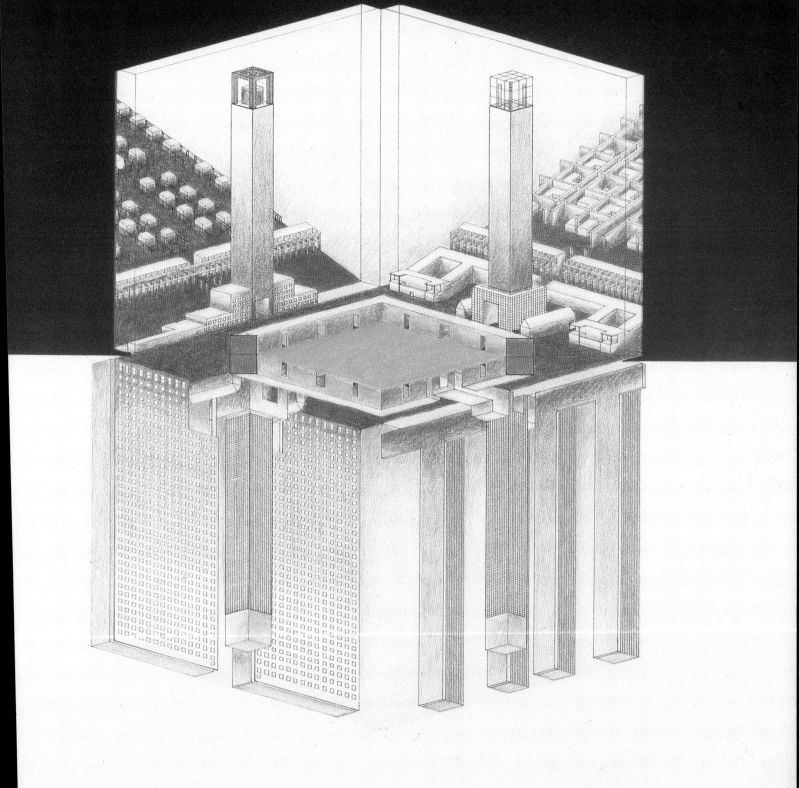

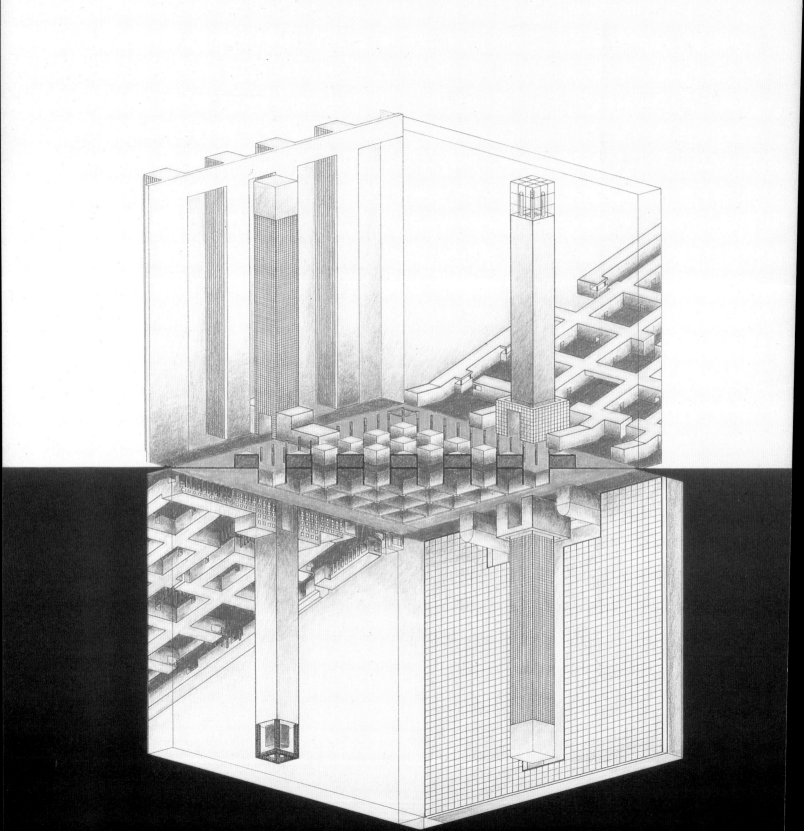

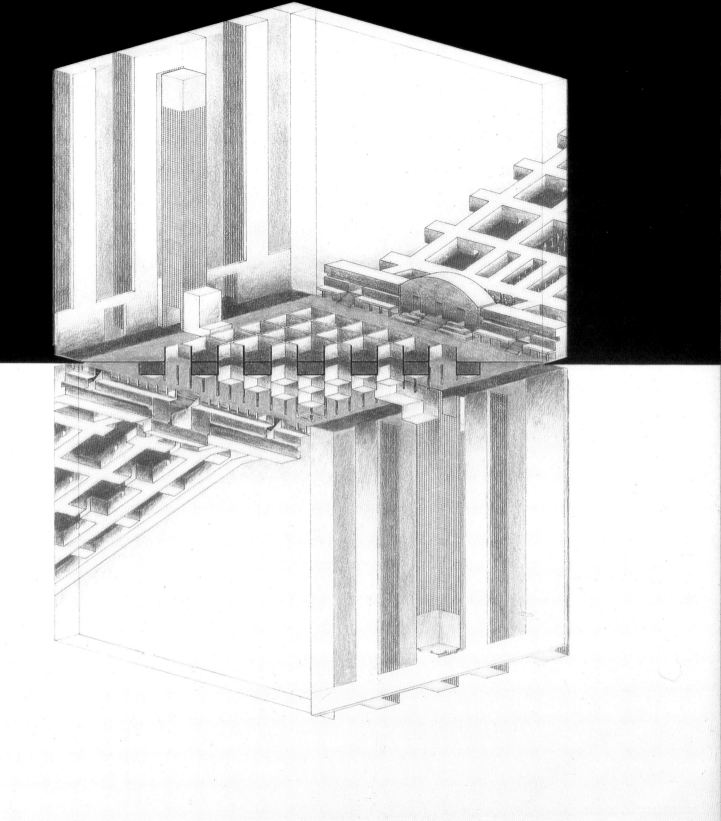

THE NOTION OF GRID

The project is for the city of Minneapolis, on the east bank of the Mississippi River, in front of Nicholet Island. The existing context absorbs the typical suburban sprawl within a grid and negates the river. The grid, which is one of the structuring devices for our project, reflects a basic characteristic of the American city, one that gives no place to the monument and that is planted indifferent to the relationship between the city and the river, or water in general.

Rewriting the American city grid, the project introduces variety through its fragmentation, superimposition, and change of scale. The urban grid transformed into a set of different grids is articulated by a sequence of public places and by two skyscrapers that act as monuments in punctuating the urban landscape. The skyscrapers are like two lighthouses, like two signs of the organizing power that transforms the suburban order. They transform the symbolism of the unique monument—representing the unity of architectural language—into an empty center, a street that does not lead anywhere, in the middle of a dialectic field of grids that cannot be made linear by a single discourse, by a unique interpretation—a text that dissolves architectural language.

PROJECT DESCRIPTION

1. The grids transform alternately into streets, squares, and buildings.
2. The urban grid takes the configuration of a *superblock* (eight city blocks) divided into two smaller superblocks (four blocks each) by a street marking the center. The wall of superblocks faces the river.
3. Each superblock has an axis, perpendicular to the river, that creates a door at the intersection with the waterfront. A center is marked in each superblock.
4. The linking of the two centers produces a street parallel to the river that divides one superblock longitudinally into two blocks: one gridded and the other, a large perimeter block, a plaza that mediates between the urban and the suburban spaces.
5. The two centers, realized as two towers, are displaced and located as centers of the plaza.
6. The *perimeter block* works as a transition between high density and low density and creates three conditions: high density interacting with public places, low density interacting with public space, and low-density suburban houses interacting with private and semipublic spaces.
7. The organized suburban space is developed in two different modalities: the *house as a freestanding volume* on a horizontal plane, and the *courtyard house* defined by a double system—vertical plane and volumetric grid. The first typology is transformed when the volumes are linearly linked and when the front-to-back distinction is introduced; the second is transformed when the semipublic streets produce the fragmentation of the total grid. Both types dissolve towards the existent suburban sprawl.
8. The axis parallel to the river becomes the public axis, linking the housing, the high-rise apartment building, the *shopping mall*, and the high-rise office building and culminating in two *drive-in cinemas*.
9. The buildings relate to the specific urban/suburban conditions of the public spaces they frame.

right: Massing plan and views of possible modes of relationship between architecture and public place

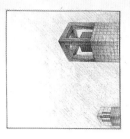

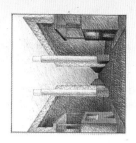

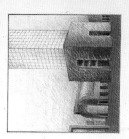

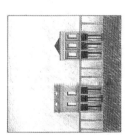

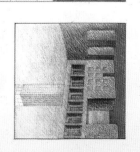

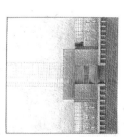

top to bottom:
Mississipi-type single-family house
Drive-in cinema screen gate
Objects as fabric — quadrangle
Half courtyards
Mississippi Plaza

left to right:
Object as fabric
Mall

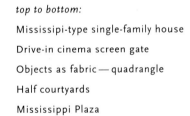

WATERFRONT BUILDINGS: continuous arcades at the level of the promenade, interrupted by gates and doors; upper level marked by atelier-type windows.

QUADRANGLE APARTMENTS: intermediate urban/suburban type with court-yards; permeable to green, air, and light.

SUBURBAN BOULEVARD APARTMENTS: courtyard type sliced; top emphasized to give a particular rhythm and configuration to the boulevard.

SQUARE APARTMENTS: perimeter buildings defining the edge of the square; arcades address the ground floor; double height windows establish a rhythm at the top.

SINGLE-FAMILY HOUSES: prototypical suburban house presented in two transformed versions: detached family house—horizontal southern Mississippi type linked by verandas in various ways; courtyard type—the organization of the solids and voids of the houses and the interplay of small streets and alleys establish the grid.

SKYSCRAPERS: respond to each other and to downtown Minneapolis, establishing their meaning through a syntactic relationship rather than as symbolic objects. The bases of the buildings relate to the square gates and boulevards, and the tops respond to the city of Minneapolis. One of the towers has a hollow base, which houses a public exhibition space surrounded by a shopping mall. Its top is a digital clock within a cubic frame made of glass block lit from inside. The other tower has a solid base with offices in it and a glass cube at the top containing a swimming pool.

left: Skyscraper with mall base and digital clock top

right: Skyscraper with hotel base and swimming pool top

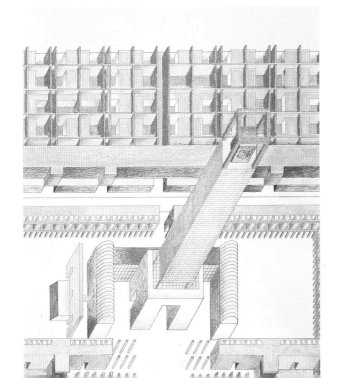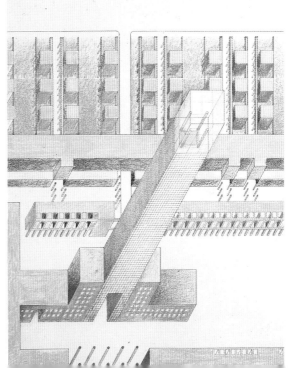

URBAN FRAGMENTS 1977

This project, comprising three buildings located in different areas of the same city, explores the relationship between architecture and the urban context.

It has been a tradition for many years to design individual buildings without considering their particular urban insertion. For us, it is precisely the more general context of the city, not just the immediate physical context, that determines the design of buildings. What makes the context of the city recognizable is its building typology as much as its monuments—a typology that sometimes develops through history as a result of cultural and economic determinations, and other times is generated by building codes.

All three buildings respond to the same type—the urban type *par excellence*, the building between parti walls—with all the constraints and limitations given by the building code. But they represent different aspects in the development and transformations that occur when this type and the building code provide points of departure.

A building in a city is always more and less than itself. It relates to other buildings by juxtaposition, accumulation, and reference. These buildings are fragments of a discourse that is established among buildings in the city. Each building takes one aspect of the type and/or the code and produces a particular transformation. Also, each building is considered as more than one building: one building is set in front of another and connected to it through a courtyard with vertical circulation, another building uses the set-back regulation to generate recessed "buildings," and the third building produces an interpenetration where one building is designed inside another building.

IN BUILDING 1, a punched box is placed in front of a slab structure with a curtain-wall facade, superimposing two types: the box with punched windows with the slab with curtain wall and strip windows.

IN BUILDING 2, three "buildings" are juxtaposed/superimposed in such a way that they allow a formal and symbolic sequence to develop. From a curtain-wall facade, fragments are extracted and become windows of a second facade, which in turn are also fragmented and exploded to create a third facade of punched windows that produce an ambiguous change of scale, a flattening of the typical urban view of juxtapositions.

IN BUILDING 3, two "buildings"—an office building and an apartment building with a central courtyard "broken" in two corners—interpenetrate each other to produce a sequence of three spaces that starts with a strong symbolic door.

right: Superimposition detail

BUILDING I

Buenos Aires, Argentina, 1977

Building I develops the idea of an urban intervention that focuses on the relationship between buildings and between the buildings and the city.

This is achieved by conceiving Building I as more than one building, as two buildings juxtaposed and by taking the building code envelope restrictions as a basis for design.

Building I is a double building, one structure set in front of another, separated by a courtyard and connected by vertical circulation. Their massing avoids the pragmatic configurations determined by the building code envelope by eliminating the setbacks in the first building and adding the volume to the second building within the allowed maximum height, producing two abstract volumes.

above: Second structure from neighbouring street

right: Street view with two structures superimposed

The first lower structure is treated as a solid with perforated windows and an arcade at the base. A portal marks the public face of Building I engaging the first three floors emphasizing the door as the starting point in the formal sequence that articulates the two buildings. The sense of abstraction of the facade is heightened by deep recessed balconies.

The second structure is a taller slab building with strip windows that presents a curtain wall in the top floors facing the street. The strategy of the double building blurs the opposition between front and back as the back of Building I is the front of the second structure.

The two buildings are separated by a courtyard and connected by a sequence of public spaces that transverse the double building from the street to a small garden in the back. The stair splits in two in the lobby and articulates the two buildings at the point of disjunction.

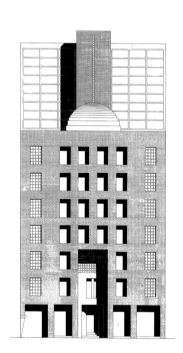 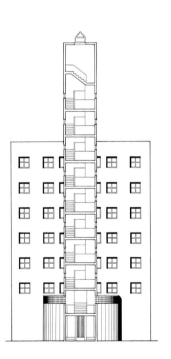 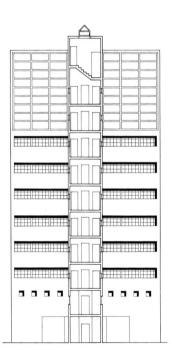 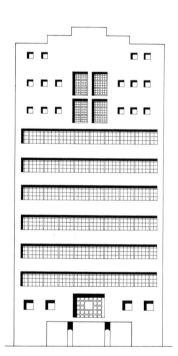

above, left to right: Front 1; Courtyard 1; Courtyard 2; Front 2

right: Frontal view

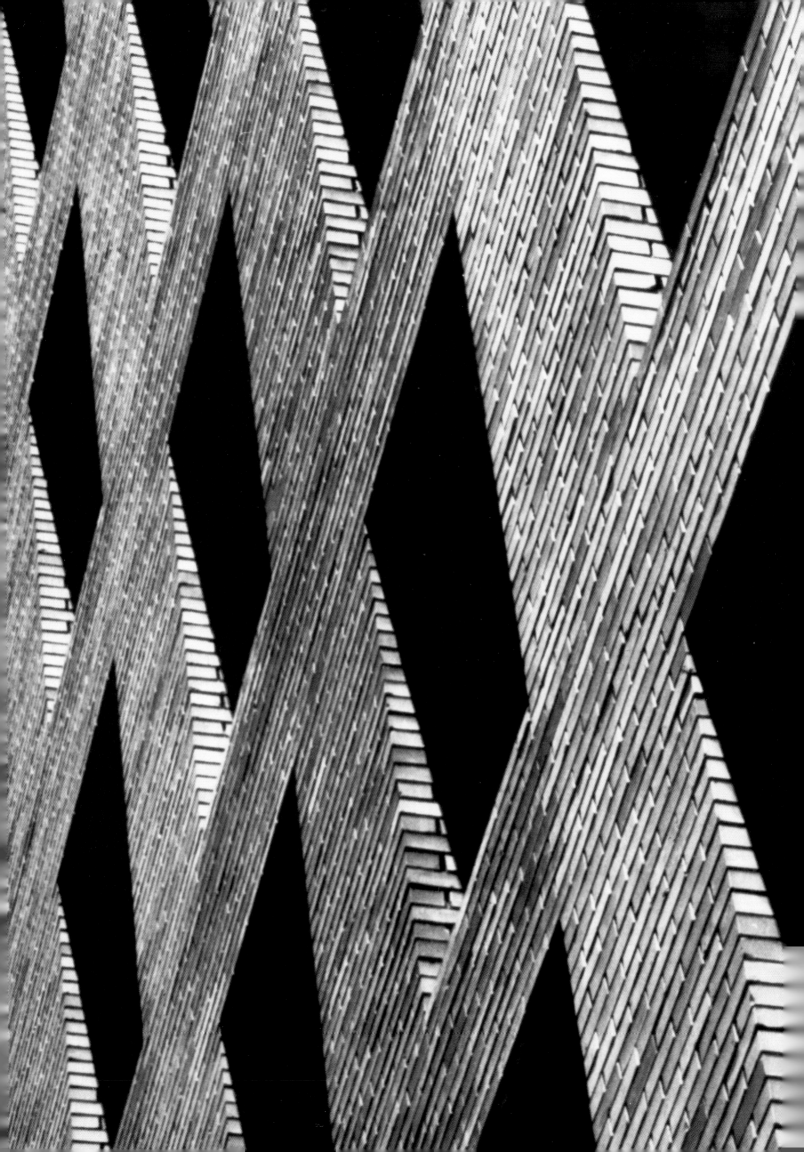

above: Apartment living room

left: Facade 1 detail

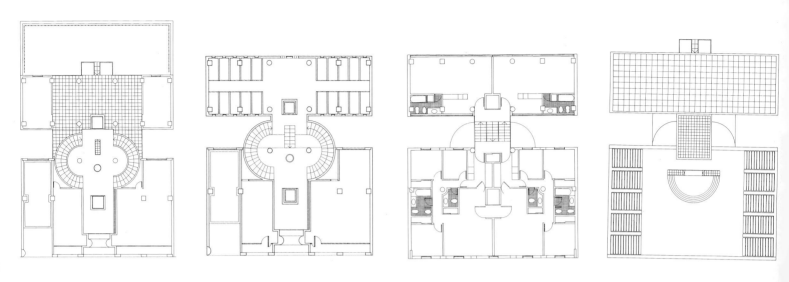

above, left to right: Ground floor plan; Mezzanine plan; Typical floor plan; Roof plan

below: Articulation of two volumes through common spaces

facing page: Entry hall articulation between two volumes

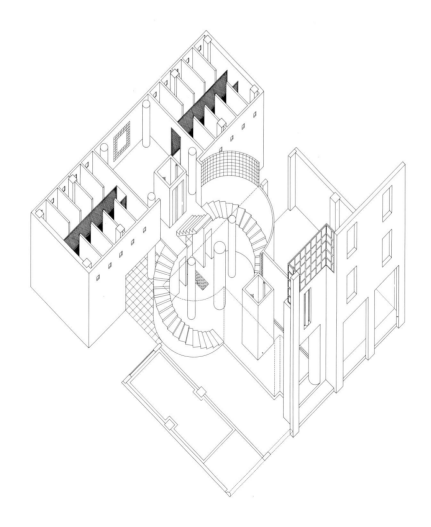

above and above left: Entry hall

right: Entry hall, connection with parking

above left: Roofscape

left: Duplex

facing page: Back courtyard facade

BUILDING 2

Buenos Aires, Argentina, 1977

This building is conceived as three superimposed "buildings" that are syntactically articulated. The project is developed as an interpretation of the building code, which requires that the building be set back horizontally when it reaches a certain height. In this case the building has also been set back vertically, thus creating the effect of three buildings represented by three facades. These facades have been treated as though each one belonged to a different building with its own axis of symmetry. Each one in turn refers to a different surface and scale treatment. The first facade is a glass curtain-wall surface, where the scale of the openings is not obvious. The middle facade has square-shaped windows following the same grid used for the curtain wall, these are the only "real scale" windows. The third facade is a punched wall with windows the size of one of the modules of the curtain wall. This completely distorts the scale, creating nine windows to a room.

above: Garden facade

right: View from street

These superimposed facades with openings decreasing in size emphasize a typical urban perspectival effect. The axis of symmetry of each facade, which is not too obvious because of the superimposition, is marked by different elements such as a column, a window, or a door. The building, however, has an overall asymmetrical configuration, contradicted by a symmetrical entrance at the ground level.

The formal organization of the facade and volume generates the internal organization of the apartments; the articulation of the various axes and the superimposition of the three buildings become the space-organizing elements.

above, left to right: Street side elevation; Ground floor plan; Typical floor plan; Apartment axonometric view

below: Courtyard

facing page: Garden side view

above: Apartment interior with recessed terrace

right: Curtain wall with recessed terraces

BUILDING 3

Buenos Aires, Argentina, 1977

In Building 3, two "buildings," an office building and an apartment building with a central courtyard "broken" in two corners, interpenetrate each other to produce a sequence of three spaces that starts with a strong symbolic door.

The building consists of sales and management for a factory on the first three floors. Floors four through thirteen contain studios and one-, two-, and three-bedroom apartments. The area totals 45,000 square feet.

This building is two things at once: it is a corner building addressing the issues that are implied by that particular condition, and it is a courtyard building. The corner not only relates the building to the street but also articulates the courtyard. The building is broken at the corner; this is emphasized by the vertical rupture. The open space required by code, instead of being partitioned, is used to make one major and one minor courtyard.

Building 3 is two buildings; it is one building within another. Here this doubling is dictated by the program—up to the third floor a multiple-use building, and from there up, apartments. The entrances to the apartments are placed on either street; at the corner, an entrance of a more public nature is placed for the first three levels. The entrance to the administration building is a triple-height space articulating the various levels through a set of stairs that change as they go up, and by two elevators that appear as two columns flanking the entrance.

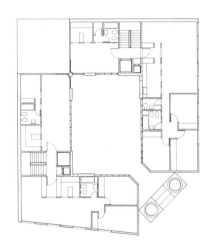

above: Typical floor plan

right: Corner elevation; Street elevation

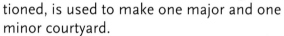

The corner is marked by a break. At the top of the building, the corner is treated as a break relating the building and the city; at the bottom, the corner is treated in a more monumental manner. The main courtyard connects with another courtyard at the opposite corner, creating a sequence from the street to the center of the block. The articulation between these two courtyards is literal at the level of the third floor and virtual through translucent surface treatment at the angles throughout the height of the building. The facade of the residential building sits on the street and frames the facade of the commercial building behind it; this expresses the idea of a building inside another building. There is a contrast between the formal and repetitive treatment of the front facade and the more functional treatment of the facade behind it, which appears as if displayed in a shop window.

The interiors of the apartments are parallel to the edges of the courtyard and are organized with an arcade that separates the services from the main spaces, creating a more rhythmic circulation than the one provided by the standard corridor.

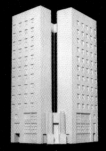

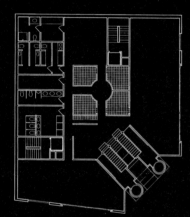

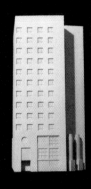

left, top to bottom: Plans: Ground floor plan;
Second floor plan; Third floor plan

right, top to bottom: Model views: Corner;
Two side streets; Back courtyard

facing page: Section through corner entrance

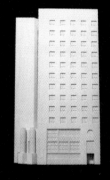

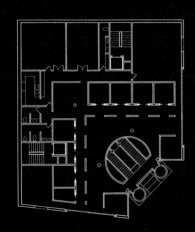

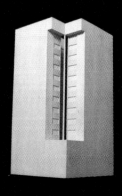

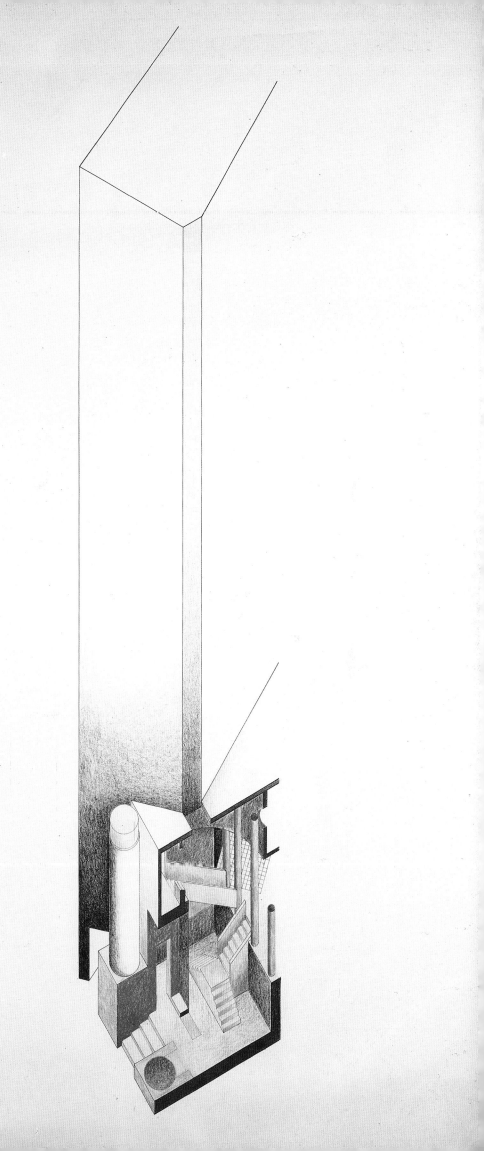

TYPOLOGICAL MORPHING

Park Square, Boston, Massachusetts, 1978

Diana Agrest

The project (which I like to call "A Fiction") for the renewal of the Park Square area in Boston, is not a "real" project, and it is not a Utopian vision of the city. It implies the struggle—in Andre Gide's terms—"between the real, reality itself, and the representation of reality."

This project redefines the area within the historical context of the city and within its own more immediate surroundings. It contends with the layers of history of Boston's development and the various types of buildings involved in the development.

The basic operation of this exploration, of this fiction, involves the inspection of the *tabula rasa* as an urban operation. Here, the *tabula rasa* plays a productive role, rather than the destructive one it has been assigned in the development of cities, and allows for the articulation of the different forces that bear on this historic place—the intersection of the old and the new, of the historical past and the modern past, of the city fabric and the buildings that constitute it, of nature and architecture.

above: Park Square in Boston context

right: Concept axonometric

This project deals with the tradition of the city without mimicry or easy picturesqueness. The operation of *tabula rasa* is used here in order to produce a new reading of the city. The project itself is the result of reading the real city and rewriting it through the eyes of the architect as filmmaker.

At each of its edges, Park Square identifies itself with a different section of the city. At Park Square, the four quadrants generated by the forces that configure the city intersect. This intersection is both literal and symbolic. It is the intersection of two axes, that of history and that of the negation of history: modernity. The relationship and articulation of these various forces is rendered by a repertory of public spaces and places that are essential to the form and culture of the city: streets, squares, and plazas, and transitional elements such as arcades, gates, doors, and stairs.

The north and south quadrants define the traditional north-south axis, and join Bay Village, the Public Gardens, and Beacon Hill. As developed in this project, the axis works with the city fabric. The intersection of nature and the city—the public park—generates the north quadrant. Two elements have been added to define this quadrant: a partition in the center of an existing lake and a row of trees by the sidewalk facing Park Square. The urban fabric governs the south quadrant. In the design, the small-scale area of Bay Village, whose boundaries are already eroded, is framed on three sides by a wall of housing. The wall preserves the identity and quality of this area of small-scale town houses and small streets. The wall is interrupted where it intersects with existing streets.

The west and east quadrants define the east-west axis of modernity that runs from the Prudential Center to the Government Center district, incorporating Back Bay as a modern urban development. This axis offers an example of the completion rather than the destruction of the city. This axis contains buildings or groups of buildings, typical of the post World War II urban ideology, that have been built in the recent past without concern for the urban fabric. Exemplary of this are the new Prudential Center to the west of Park Square, and the new Government Center to its east, an example of object-oriented urban architecture. In contrast to the anti-urbanity of the commercial developments stands Back Bay, one of the most powerful urban developments in the United States. Conceived and realized as a landfilling operation in the nineteenth century, the development combines a grid of streets and alleys of different widths and a building typology of brownstones and brick town houses.

Though the west quadrants are on the axis of modernity, they incorporate its nineteenth-century neighbor, Back Bay. The arcade building type, a remnant of which remains on the site, governs the development of the west quadrant. This type, repeated and combined with the nineteenth-century grid of Back Bay, produces a marketplace of arcades and streets.

The east quadrant is organized by urban architecture, incorporating the modern high-rise building type as an economic necessity for city growth. The towers of the east quadrant sit on a plinth connected to the street by grand stairs. The scale of the plinth establishes a relationship with the street, and this relationship allows the base of the tower to be turned into a public place. The buildings are not designed as finished pieces of architecture but rather as indications in relation to the public spaces they frame.

In the northeast quadrant of the square, a traffic circle displaces the center of the square. A diagonal runs from the statue in the center of the traffic circle to the corners of the square, creating a line that defines the edge of Boston Neck—the old water edge of the city.

right: Massing plan with possible moments relating buildings and public place

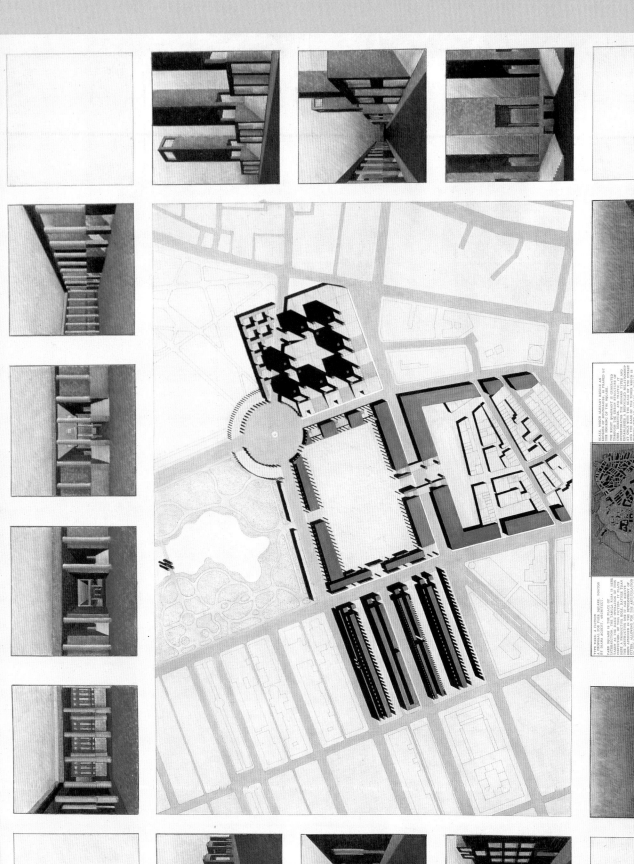

TYTE WARD, A FUTION
A PRODUCER OF PLACE SQUARE, BOSTON
BY DIANA AUDET, ARCHITECT.

PARK SQUARE IS THE PLACE OF
UNCERTAINTY AND DOUBT. PLACE IS HERE
TAKEN AS THE BASIC OPERATION OF THE
URBAN STRUCTURE.

HERE A PRODUCTIVE ROLE, RATHER THAN
BEEN AFFORDED IN THE DEVELOPMENT OF
CITY TO SUPPORT FORCES THAT BEAR ON
THE PART OF THE OPERATION WHICH
OF THE HISTORICAL PART AND THE MORE
SURFACE TO THE WAY WHICH THE URBAN
FABRIC AND THE BUILDING MUST CON-
DITION IT, IS NATURE AND
ARCHITECTURAL.

PARK SQUARE ARTICULATED AS A
SURFACE AS A SPECIFIC SECTION OF THE
QUADRANTS, THE QUADRATION OF THE
GRID STRUCTURE, THE DIFFERENT MODE OF
COMMON FORMED SPACE, THE DIFFERENT MODE OF
COMMON MAY ALWAYS WITH THE
POWDER WHICH PRODUCE IT.

THE LEFT QUADRANT IS GENERATED
FROM A PRODUCTIVE BODY WHICH
NINETEENTH CENTURY COLD OF BACK BAR
FABRIC. THE SPECIFIC PLACE OF
ARCADER AND STREETS.

THE BOTTOM QUADRANT IS GENERATED
THROUGH THE CITY FABRIC. CITY SMALL

SCALE, WHICH REACHES BEHIND AN
INVESTMENT OF THE SQUARE, ENCLOSED BY
THE HOUSING OF THE SQUARE.

THE SPECIFIC PLACE IS GENERATED
THROUGH THE URBAN STRUCTURE OF
PARK SQUARE, WHICH AFFORDS AND
INCORPORATES THE MODERN TYPES AND
AT ONCE WITH THE SCALE OF THE STREET
IN PART WITHIN THE CITY RELATES THE
PLACE INTO AS MACHIC, A PUBLIC
PLACE.

THE TOP QUADRANT IS GENERATED

THE LEFT AND RIGHT QUADRANTS
DEFINE THE PRUDENTIAL CENTER TO THE
HOUSING OF THE SQUARE BY INCOR-
PORATING BACK BAT AS A MODERN URBAN
FABRIC AND STRUCTURE HAS ALMOST
THE AXIS OF TRADITION THE PART.
THE TOP QUADRANT OF THE SQUARE
INCORPORATES THE SQUARE INTO A PUBLIC
HARDMEN AND BEACON HILL.

THE RELATIONSHIP AND ARTICULATION OF
THESE QUADRANTS AS THE PART OF PUBLIC
SPACES AND PLACES AND THAT RELATES TO THE
FORM AND CUSTOM OF THE CITY.

NEW YORK, 1974

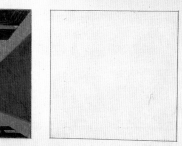

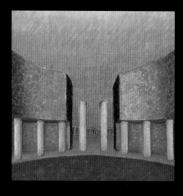

left: Sequence of moments

facing page: Axonometric of site

top left: Residential wall around existing fabric

top right: Arcade district

center: Park Square with residential (south), hotel (north), offices (east), and retail (west)

bottom left: Office towers on urban plinth with theaters

bottom right: Public park with added trees and fountain

URBAN FRAGMENTS

Building 5, Buenos Aires, Argentina, 1978

This small apartment building set between parti walls is treated as more than one building by unfolding the front facade into two superimposed facades to create a space in between them.

The front facade, which follows the geometry of the city, is a "pure" formal facade and openings are simple perforations with no glass, having no real functional requirements. This facade is different from the second facade, which relates to the interior spaces of the building.

above: Courtyard view from neighbouring street

right: Street view

The second facade, which follows the geometry of the building, is recessed from the first one and encompasses the actual apartment windows and openings. It has large gridded openings at the top and bottom. Its door is only a larger version of these gridded openings. The visual continuity of the openings from the ground floor to the top emphasizes the shift between the two facades. The interplay between these two facades, separated by a wedge-shaped space, indicates the relationship between architecture and the city within one building.

The back facade of this building is clad in brick in opposition to the stone stucco of the front. The top of this facade is emphasized recognizing that, while being the back of the building, it becomes a front in the context of the city as seen from neighboring avenues.

The interior of this building has been developed so that each apartment has a space of transition between the very narrow street and the interior. The void between both facades, which runs most of the height of the building, provides for this transition.

facing page, left to right: Typical floor plan;
Eighth floor plan with front and back duplexes;
Street elevation; Back courtyard elevation

below, left to right: Duplex 1; Duplex 2 terrace;
Typical street-side terrace

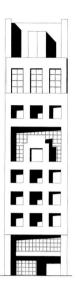
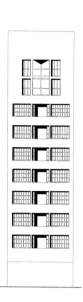

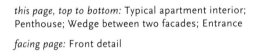

this page, top to bottom: Typical apartment interior; Penthouse; Wedge between two facades; Entrance

facing page: Front detail

HOUSE FOR TWO PSYCHOANALYSTS

Buenos Aires, Argentina, 1978

A sequence of spaces and buildings accommodates working and living quarters for two psychoanalysts and their children in a party-wall lot and defines a transition from the public realm to the private world. This transition is established through a dialectic between the monumental and the domestic.

The house is organized around the contradictions between fragment and whole, individual and family. The house is vertically structured by the contrast between communal family space (living room, dining room, kitchen) along an axis perpendicular to the party walls, and four, autonomous, double-height cells (bedroom-bathroom), one for each member of the family. Individual access to these cells is provided by four enclosed spiral staircases, which are perceived as four corner columns in the living area. These four rooms are whole, independent volumes that are interconnected only by a very light *passerelle*. From the common space below, the rooms are perceived as individual floating volumes. This organization provides the context for a *mise-en-scène* of a way of life and of a mode of architectural writing. The users can be seen as a typical family (father, mother, boy, girl), as a hierarchical, pyramidal structure. However, the formal organization of the architecture suggests the break of this structure and the possibility of a reorganization where four people live as individuals or as part of a family group interrelated through a variety of associations.

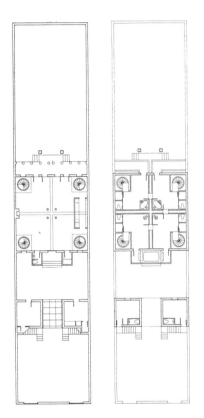

above: Ground level plan: common space with projection of four volumes on second level; Second level plan

facing page: Model, central space view looking up

The model of the house has been built to condense and multiply the representative power of the architectural model and drawing. The traditional architectural drawing fragments the building to produce a knowledge of its parts and relationships while the traditional model verifies the building as an object. In this case the specific qualities of drawing are displaced to the model. This displacement introduces a temporal dimension that fragments the model as object and impregnates it with narrative and sequential qualities.

Since psychoanalysis could be seen as one of the most recent liberal professions to appear in Western culture, this House for Two Psychoanalysts is proposed as a possible late addition to Claude-Nicolas Ledoux's typology of houses for the ideal city.

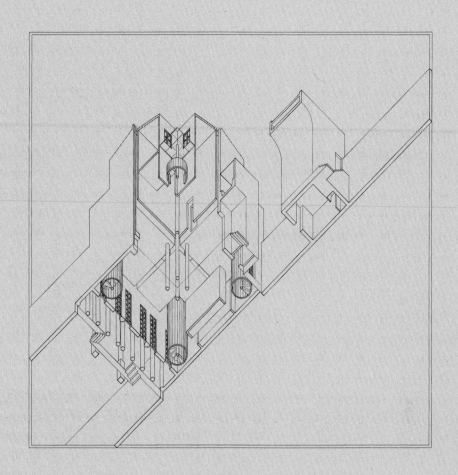

facing page, top to bottom:
Model—Sections and elevations; Plans

this page, top to bottom: Sectional
axonometric looking up; Sectional
axonometric

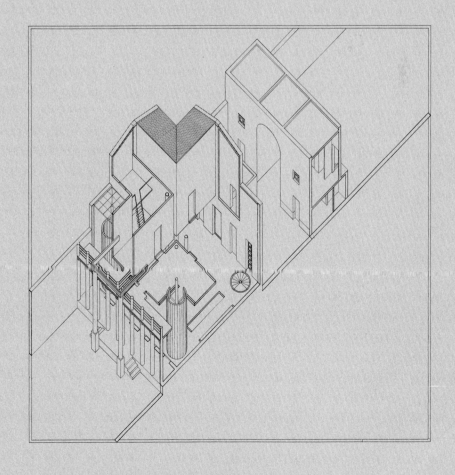

MANHATTAN ADDITION 1

Upper East Side Historic District, New York City, 1979–1980

This project is a multiple-unit building consisting of the renovation of an existing 20,000-square-foot town house and the addition of a new 36,000-square-foot structure.

The project approaches the pragmatic problem of incorporating a new structure into an existing urban context within the boundaries of established zoning (the Upper East Side Historic District [UESHD]) and building codes and against the background of the history and theory of architecture and the city.

New York, like most cities in the world, reflects layers of history in its physical configuration. This physical manifestation of the city as a historical yet changing artifact gives it its cultural richness. This building proposes an articulation between past and present, developing an architecture rooted in an historical tradition, yet modern. The building represents a concern for the city and its history while it responds to specific requirements such as type, scale, and materials.

A building in the city is never seen as an isolated object, but as an integral part of a larger context. It has been designed acknowledging the existent elements of the district, the avenue, the street, and the block in terms of their forms, sizes, scales, and materials. A major characteristic of the UESHD is the presence of low-rise structures in constant juxtaposition with high-rise structures. This mixture provides the particular profile and quality of this area. Both low-rise and high-rise buildings have been part of the development and the history of the district for over fifty years, a history determined by zoning regulations. The building proposes an interaction of characteristics and qualities of 71st Street and Madison Avenue by leaving the low-rise buildings on the avenue and the street intact and by adding a tower that marks the corner and provides an articulation between vertical and horizontal configurations.

The existing building has been transformed into the base of the new building. It has been partially modified to better relate the adjacent corner building as base and the new tower as top.

The east elevation facing the avenue is treated as a clock tower, thus making a civic building out of an apartment tower.

The building establishes a dialogue between the district and the city at two different levels: the untouched base at the level of the street preserves the sense, nature, and scale of the street and the avenue, and the new top interacts with the skyline that has become a symbol of New York City itself. The project is conceived as an architectural reading of the symbolic performance implied in the tower as a building type, such as a tripartite formal organization (base, shaft, and top), as a vertical mark in the townscape.

right: UESHD, axonometric

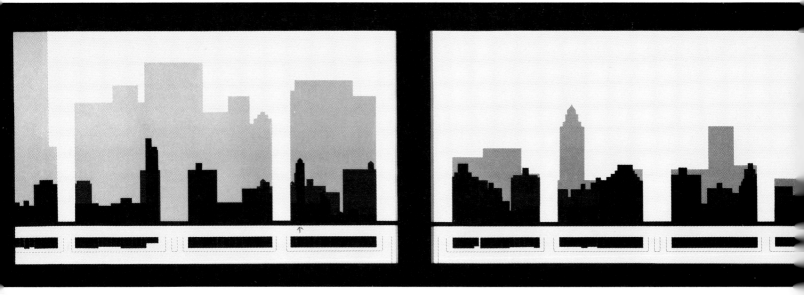

above: Section through East 71st Street, (left) looking downtown and (right) looking uptown

below: UESHD model

facing page: Site plan

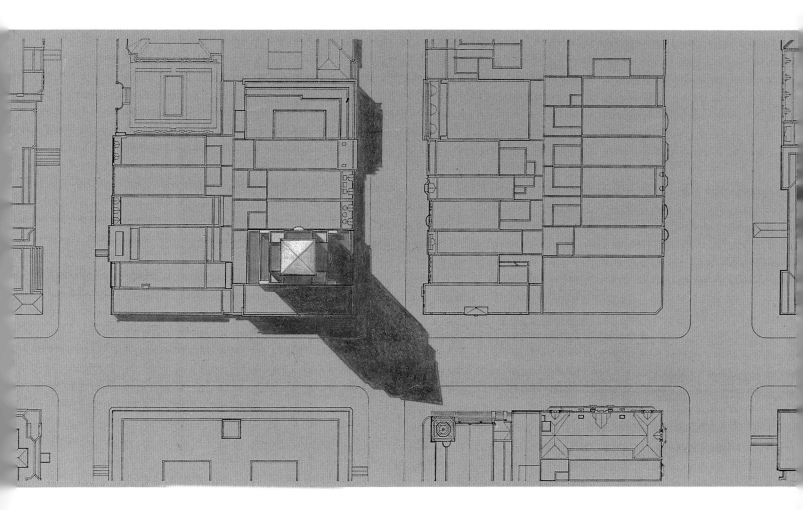

above left: North elevation

above right: West elevation

facing page: East elevation

MANHATTAN ADDITION 2

Upper East Side Historic District, New York City, 1979–1980

This project, a multiple dwelling located in Manhattan's Upper East Side Historic District, addresses its immediate urban context, in which buildings represent both the history of New York and the history of architecture.

The site for this project is an 18x100-foot lot, located between a curtain-wall glass building by Philip Johnson—which interrupts the sequence of town houses of a traditional Upper East Side street—and a Neo-Gothic church on the corner of Park Avenue. A town house by Paul Rudolph, back to back with the new building, completes this unusual architectural cluster.

The intention of the project is to establish a dialogue between the new building, the Neo-Gothic church, and the neighboring buildings. The bowed facade of the first six floors of this thin tower functions as a hinge between the Neo-Gothic facade of the church and the flat plane of its steel and glass neighbor. The building is another element in the already complex juxtaposition defined by the existing buildings.

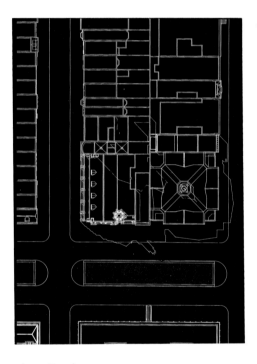

above: Site plan
right: Front elevation

The upper half of the building has been designed as a slender tower to express a typical element of the architecture of New York. In its duplication of towers it transforms the reading of the slab into two campaniles, acting as the missing campanile of the adjacent Neo-Gothic church.

Two towers, while reminiscent of medieval Italian towers, also refer to a sliver building, a typical element of the New York skyline. In one single gesture the original and the new referent are synthesized.

This project demonstrates the potential of resurrecting a building type that has been patently dismissed without considering the possibility to create anew within the interstices of the urban fabric.

The 18,000-square-foot structure is composed of one-bedroom floor-through apartments and two-bedroom duplexes on the eight upper floors.

The building is designed in a dialogue with the characteristics of its context, both in its fenestration (curtain wall and double hung windows) and its materials (brick and stone).

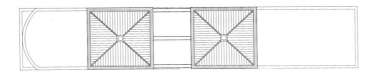

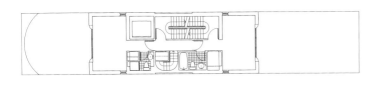

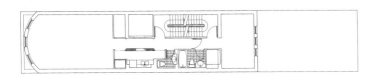

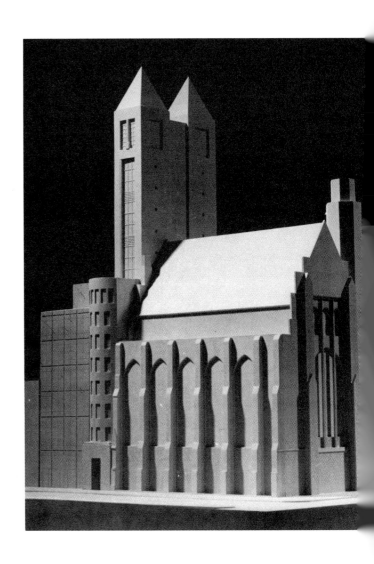

left, top to bottom: Roof plan; Two typical plans of tower duplex; Typical plan, floors 3–7; Second floor plan; Ground floor plan

above: View from Park Avenue

above left: West elevation

above right: South elevation

A CRITICAL READING OF THE URBAN TEXT

Les Halles, Paris, France, 1980

Mario Gandelsonas

Throughout history the Les Halles quarter of Paris has undergone continuous morphological transformations as a result of the successive construction of public buildings. This project proposes a different kind of transformation instituted through the construction, not of another public building, but of a public place. This change will displace buildings, which now occupy a privileged, prioritized position, in favor of the ensemble by which they are articulated. Buildings will function as boundaries of the enclosure of public spaces, as elements of transition between one space and another.

The two spaces proposed by this project take shape around a building-wall that defines and separates them. This four-sided building-wall, formed from existent and newly developed buildings, circumscribes a rectangular plaza and defines an adjacent, ring-shaped street. The street, in turn, separates the building-wall from the urban fabric, appropriates its contiguous edge as its external limit, and makes it into an urban wall. The interior, the building-wall, acts as an opaque, impermeable block, and confines a concentrated space, which can be perceived as a totality. The exterior, the urban wall, acts as a filter, permeable to the urban forces that distort and deform it, and defines a diffused, linear space, which can only be perceived sequentially. As the degree of resistance to the forces of the city is thus increased from the exterior to the interior walls, the stability of the space is also increased.

Finally, the innermost wall, the interior side of the building-wall that faces the plaza, defines the architectural qualities of this public space. This wall, planned to exceed the medium height of the other buildings of the quarter, emphasizes its own verticality. It is incised by windows that open out to the sky and by doors placed on the axis of the destroyed pavilions by Louis-Pierre Baltard. The wall splits at the intersection of the prolonged axis of the lateral door of the St. Eustache Church.

The project also proposes to intervene in the closed dialogue that now exists between the Bourse and the St. Eustache Church. As the Bourse is transformed, to accord with the elongated proportions of the interior public space, its relationship with the church can no longer be sustained. It becomes necessary to introduce a new monumental element, a third term, into this relationship. A tower modeled on the lighthouse in Jean-Nicolas-Louis Durand's nineteenth-century treatise is proposed. This shift initiates a new dialogue, which opens onto the register of the civic, between the Bourse and the tower, and displaces the church outside.

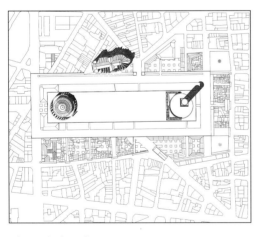

above: Shadow plan
right: Space as monument in Paris

Through the dynamism of its proportions (one unit in width to five in length) and the convex limits of its monuments, the space enclosed by the interior wall, containing the Bourse and the tower, proposes a transformation of the typology of the Place Royales.

The urban wall that surrounds this space is composed of existent urban blocks and newly developed blocks of the same typology. The wall has two opposing definitions—solid building-wall and open ring-shaped street. The two sides of this wall segment repeat Baltard's original design for the facade of the Les Halles pavilion: the side that faces outward, toward the city, reproduces the brick base of the design; the side that faces inward, toward

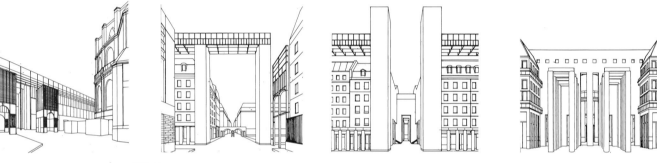

above: Vistas

the interior spaces and delimits the ring-shaped street, reproduces the cast iron superstructure. Once again there is a grading of the permeability of the wall surfaces and an increase in the force of resistance from the exterior to the interior. Similarly, as the converse placing of the two parts of the design resists the possibility of a totalized perception, the dispersal of space by a routing temporality is also increased at the exterior edges.

The corners of the urban wall are defined by four public spaces. The west, north, and south sides are marked by two cross-shaped commercial galleries carved out of the existing urban block. The eastern side is marked by two squares; the existing monument in the south-eastern square is transposed to the newly developed northeastern square, leaving a void as a mark of the south-east corner. Their four corners act as knots, by which the proposed space becomes stitched into the surrounding space of the city.

In addition, four crucial gates open the urban wall, by operating as points of ingress and egress between the spaces of the proposed project and those of the city. The western wall opens toward the Louvre, the northern wall toward the church and the markets, and the eastern, double-gated wall, pierced through by a window as well as a door, toward the new International Hotel and the Beaubourg center. The project, then, a construction of spaces, sets out its own spacing, releases its claim to autonomy, and becomes an interval along the urban passage.

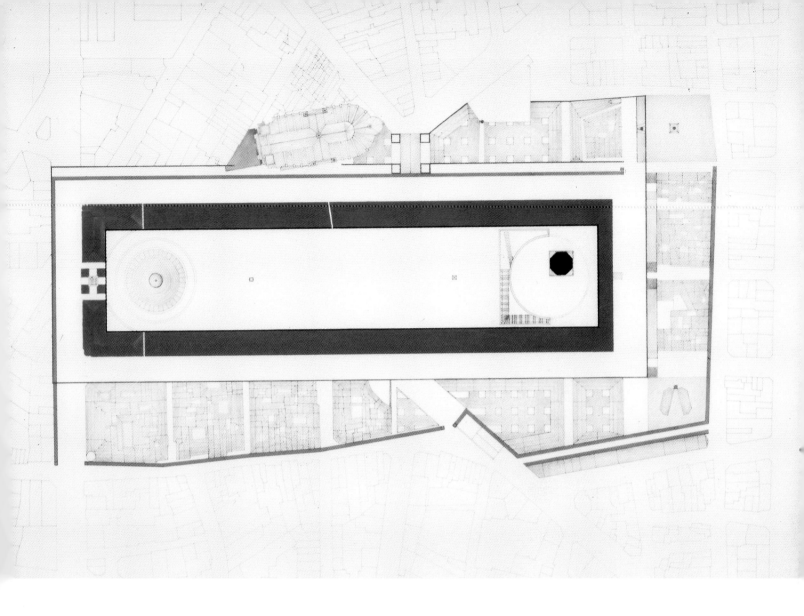

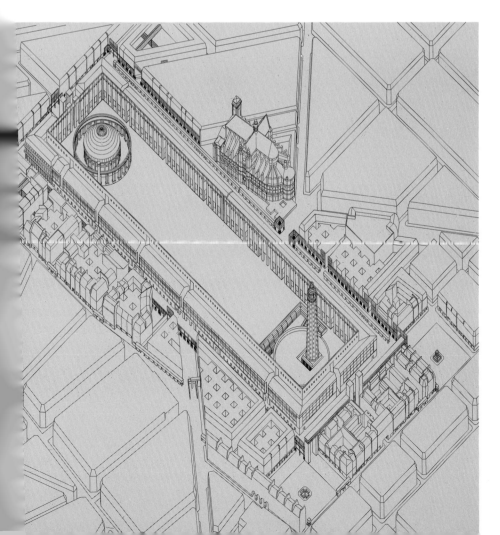

above: The three walls

below: Axonometric

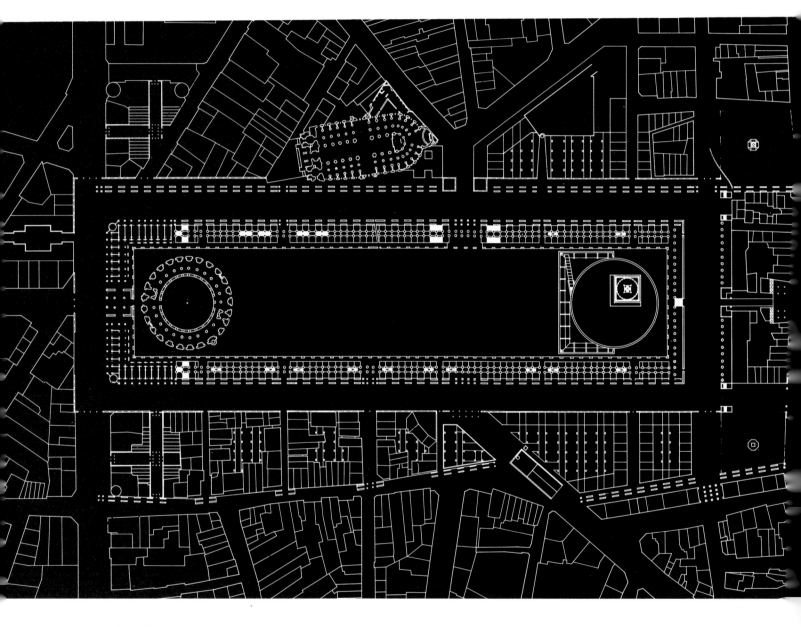

above: Plan
facing page: Sectional axonometric

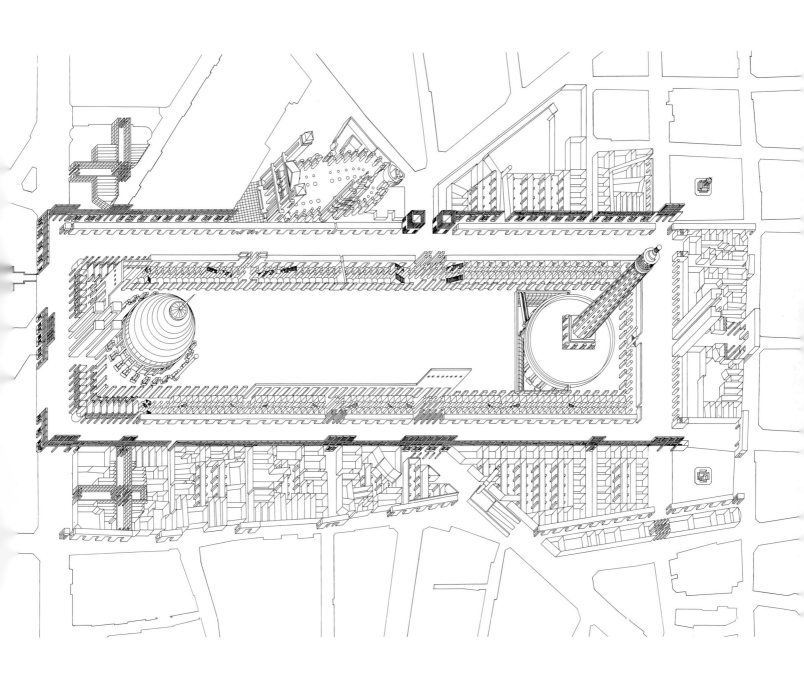

VARIATIONS ON A THEME

Office Building, New York City, 1981–83

In the design of three floors of offices in a Lower Manhattan loft building, the transformation of similar spatial sequences and their manipulation with light are variations on a theme.

The theme is developed within the existing confines of the raw loft space, which provides the framework for a progression of private and public spaces organized from front to back: private offices overlooking the streets, reception lobby off the elevator, a freestanding public room in the middle, and an open working area in the back.

The progression is organized to develop different degrees of openness and enclosure. The sequence of spaces and objects creates places that have a definition and identity while still being part of a larger perceivable whole.

This theme is varied by exploring the formal tensions between opposing conditions of symmetry versus asymmetry and room vs. open plan. In each floor these conditions are inspected and criticized in different ways through a series of related spatial permutations.

The lobby of the building is conceived as a confrontation between elements that define different notions of space: the grided slate wall and the granite walls and door frame. While the first wall, an abstract plane, suggests a flow of space, the second wall wraps the space, suggesting the enclosure of a room.

above: Street view
right: Lobby

AGREST AND GANDELSONAS OFFICES

left, top to bottom: Reception area;
Meeting room

above: Plan

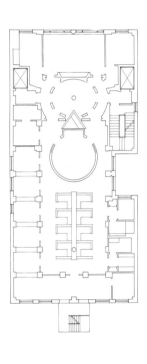

CF CORPORATION

left, top to bottom: Reception area;
Desk and volume of conference room;
Open office area

above: Plan

THE FORM OF THE PICTURESQUE

House in Georgica, Easthampton, New York, 1982–83

Shingle houses have been associated with picturesque architecture as opposed to an architecture based on a systematic approach to the organization of form. This house deals (as do our other houses) with the confrontation of opposites — classic and romantic, formal and picturesque — and with issues derived from their intersections and collisions. These collisions generate a set of transitional spaces that relate both to the inside and the outside, and acquire a life of their own.

This house studies the effect of a picturesqueness that is produced by a formal system. "Picturesque" is not seen as the opposite of "formal" but as an image produced by the conscious manipulation of form, not just in a purely pragmatic way.

The house is volumetrically organized as an intersection between a barn and two slab gates; this intersection generates four towers. While the two front towers make a finite set to create the front door, the two back towers with the addition of a fifth tower infer a sequence. The two front towers mark the organization of the interior of the house while the three back towers mark a new shifted symmetry that relates the house to the garden.

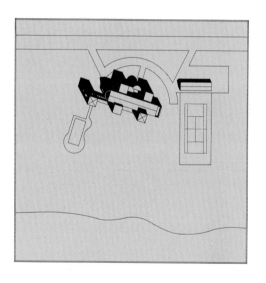

above: Site plan

right: Waterside view of model; Roof plan of model

A spatial canonic system is developed as a transitional sequence leading from front to back. This sequence is materialized in five deep planes. The first plane by the two front towers is articulated by a semi-circular canopy and the lobby space. The second is created in the upper level of the slab gates by the double stairs and the balcony/corridor linking both bedroom wings. The edges of this second deep plane are defined by a grid on one side and by a colonnaded balcony on the other side. The third is the space of the barn itself, where the transitional character is marked by an arcaded wall. The fourth is a compressed deep plane formed by the collapsed edges of the second plane, colonnaded gallery, and grid. The fifth is produced by the three towers, whose outdoor porches are linked by a continuous loggia.

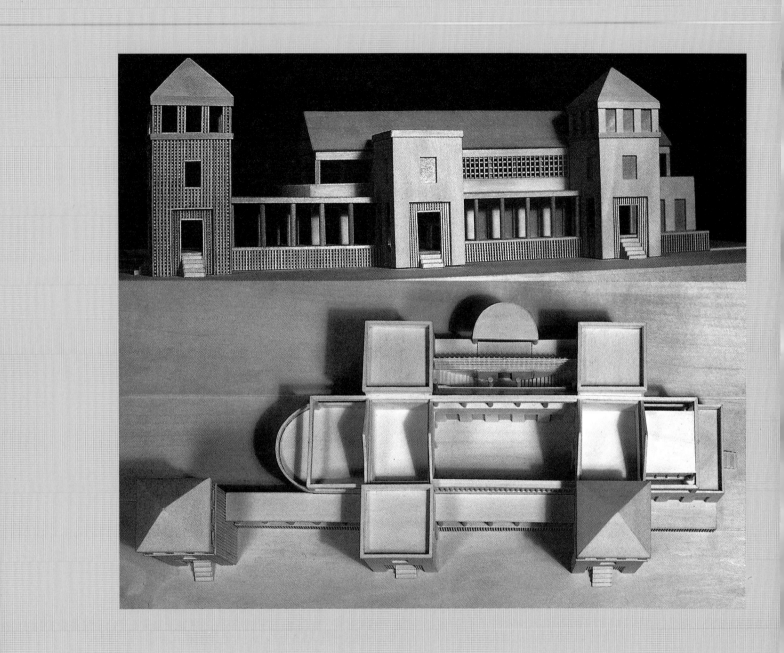

facing page: Axonometric section

this page, top to bottom, left to right:
South elevation; Section looking east;
Section looking west; Ground floor
plan; Second floor plan

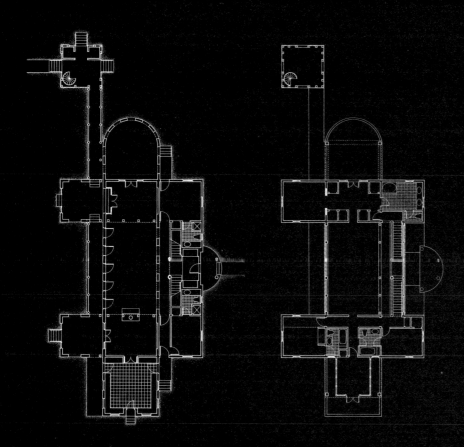

MONUMENTALITY WITHIN
AND WITHOUT THE CITY

La Défense, Paris, France, 1983

I. THE PROJECT WITHIN THE MONUMENTAL AXIS OF PARIS

The problem posed was to create a monumental symbolic mark in a monumental context in which large buildings without apparent order or organization would compete with one another.

Our initial gesture was to create an urban order as a counterpart to the lack of order that characterizes the context of La Défense.

Our project completes the symbolic axis that starts in the Louvre and culminates in La Défense by means of a sequence of public urban spaces and monumental buildings.

We are not attempting to create a building as an object of monumental proportions, but rather a group of buildings and public spaces that in their articulation generate a symbolic monumental presence at various levels of perception (We do not believe that big is necessarily monumental or that a monumental building necessarily has to be big).

Three main conditions have determined our approach: the site's history and its relationship to Paris, the preservation of the open view from different monuments along the symbolic east-west axis, and the theme of communication.

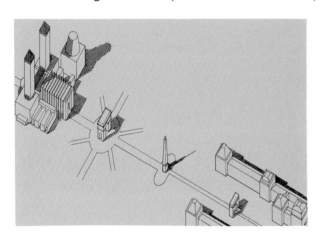

above and facing page: East-west axis

La Défense has been built without the support of a formal urban order. The organization is neither a composition of objects in a field, nor a collection of disparate objects located on a grid, as is the case in Manhattan. It is basically a collection of large buildings that are not organized in relation to a definition of public spaces or to the context of Paris.

Along the sequence of the east-west axis are examples of the history of the city and of urban ideology—from the Louvre to the Tuilleries to the Hausmanian incision of the Champs Elysees, from nineteenth-century urbanism to the post-World War II interpretation of "modernist" anti-urban urbanism of La Défense. The location of the Tête Défense is as crucial as a part of this historical sequence of urbanism as it is in the actual physical/symbolic east-west axis of Paris.

The selection of a grid operates in two ways in relation to that sequence. In terms of the history of urbanism, it represents the alternative modern city to the chaotic interpretation of modernist urbanism of buildings screaming at each other without underlying or explicit order.

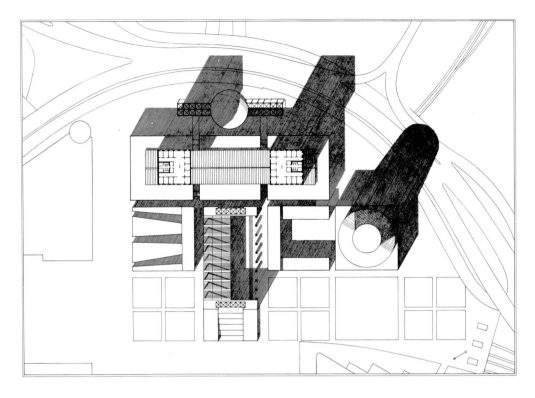

Roof plan

The grid, which is the epitome of American urbanism, is the foundation of "the other" city—the modern city that goes hand in hand with the development of modern types, such as the skyscraper. It is a rational system that may be imposed upon a neutral plane; it is an explicit order that is susceptible to an unlimited number of variations and transformations. It does not come from the erasure of the old historical city as postulated by the urban ideology of the modernist movement; rather it sets itself in a parallel and/or dialectical relationship with the old city.

II. THE SYMBOLIC SEQUENCE WITHIN
THE MONUMENTAL AXIS OF PARIS

In designing this project, a center for communication, we believe it is necessary to emphasize the contrasting and complementary natures of the two extreme modes of communication: interpersonal and informational. The former is eminently social and place oriented; the latter is more "punctual," is not place oriented, and situates the individual in the network of mass communication. The center itself is the focus of the informational and technological developments of communication.

The street, the locus of communication and trade, is a scene here. The group of retail buildings, which house shops and services, has been designed as a Palladian Teatro Olimpico in a monumental scale. The actual streets are treated as the perspective streets that open from the stage in the Teatro Olimpico; the metaphor of the street as a theater and that of the theater as a street have been synthesized.

The courtyard, a symbol of the most traditional type of French house—the *hôtel particulier*—is the foreground for the Ministry of Housing and the Environment.

The extended arch Agora, as it relates to the street and courtyard, materializes the interpersonal communication. The towers, in contrast, are only markers, framing an index to the infinity of the space of immaterial communication. The void in the center intends to emphasize this structural feature in the east-west symbolic axis. The towers are the articulation between the architecture of La Défense and the architecture of Paris. The towers in our project are a modern type; they are placed in a symbolic position, acting as a gate/obelisk/lighthouse. Only their tops, which are the most symbolic elements and are lit at night, will be seen from the Arc de Triomphe in the same way one can see La Place de la Concorde and the Arc de Triomphe from the Arc du Carrousel.

The copper-clad, spherical cinema, which is the culmination of the sequence, stands as the initial monument in the symbolic sequence along the road from the western suburbs of Paris.

right, top to bottom: Ground floor plan; +40m plan; +200m plan; -6m plan

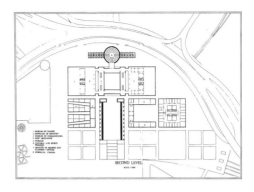

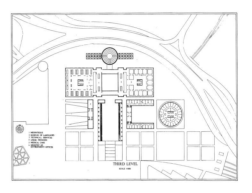

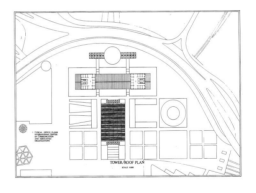

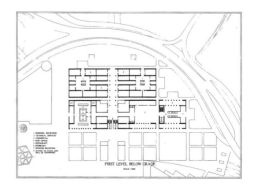

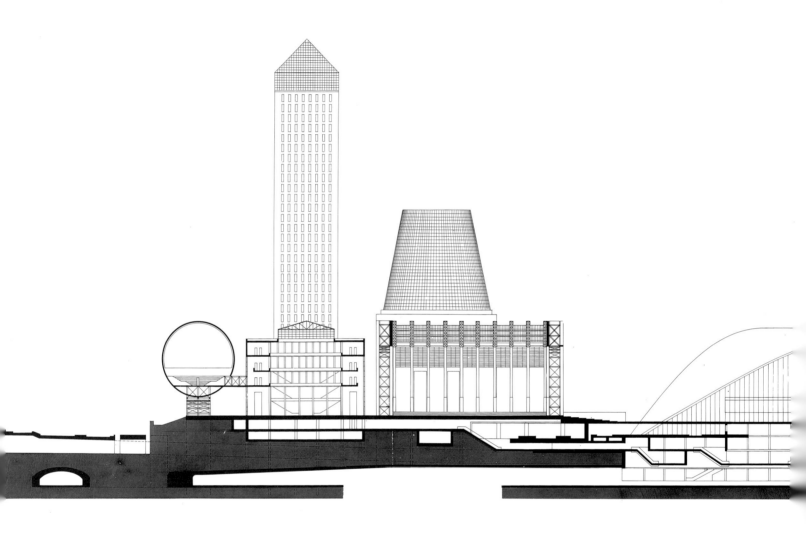

East-west section

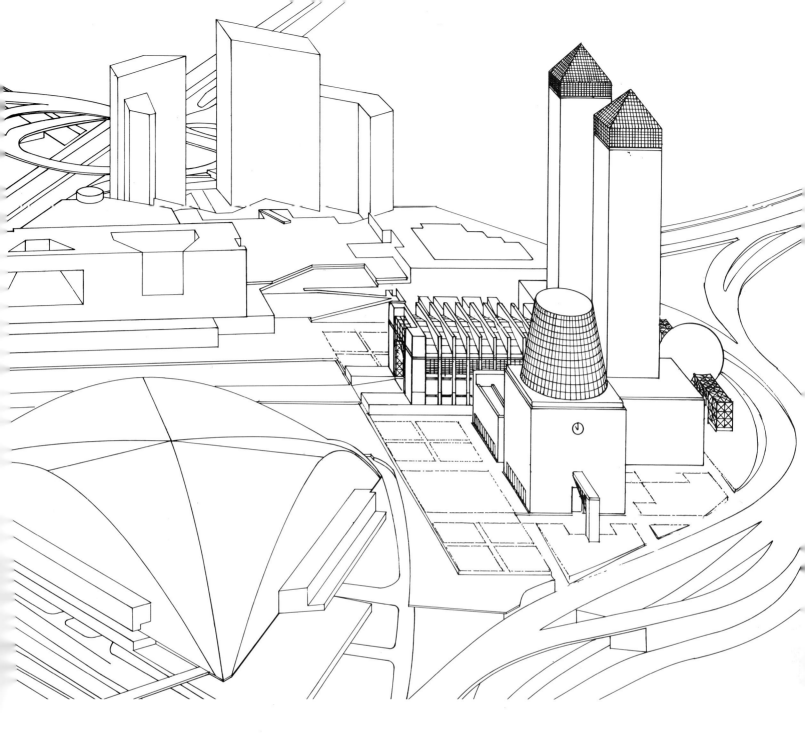

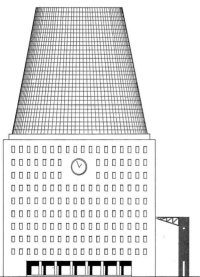

above: View looking south

left: Ministère de l'Equipement, elevation

DUPLICATION

House in Scarsdale, New York, 1982–1983

This villa for a family of six is designed as two pavilions linked by a gallery. This house becomes two houses, one for the parents and one for the children. The element common to both buildings is the gallery that allows the passage from the front to the back of the site without entering either house. This creates two kinds of entry: one to the whole house (the family's house), and one to each pavilion (the parents' house and the children's house). Formally it creates three sets of fronts and backs.

Varying degrees of outside and inside space are marked by the gallery: the front door is a solid within a translucent wall, and three glass garden doors are transparent within the rear translucent wall. The public space of the house is articulated both externally and internally in the vertical extension of the glass-block gallery to the pavilion roofs' lanterns, which light the staircases below. Internally, this places the drama of the project in the most public space of the house. A ritual of passage and entry is ultimately established in the separation of the two houses, each having its own door from the connecting gallery.

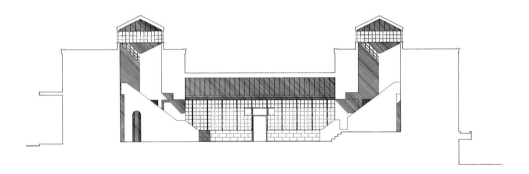

above: Section

right: Double entry from paintings gallery

This gallery, which is used for the display of paintings on easels, continues along either side of both stairs, and ascends in small skylit towers above. At the top of the stairs are the master bedroom suite in one house and the children's bedrooms and baths in the other. The gallery links, while the stairs separate. Along with the change in levels, there is also a change from the large scale of the public areas of the house to the smaller scale of the private room.

The decentralization and duplication of architectural form refer to the conflicting notions of sharing and independence within the family.

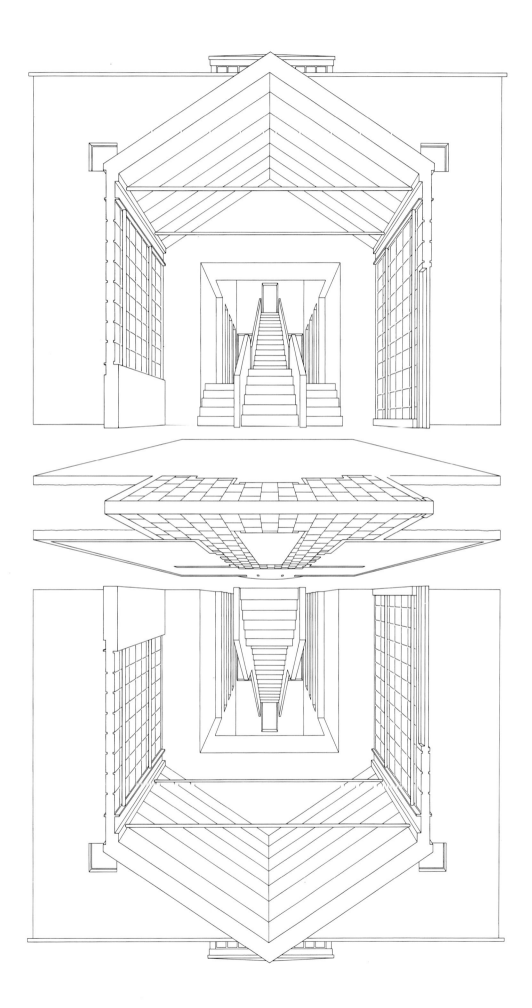

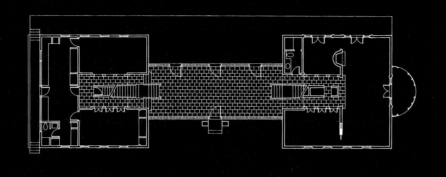

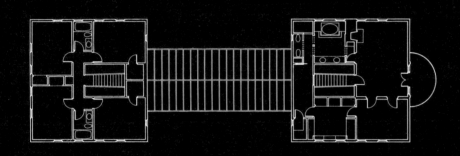

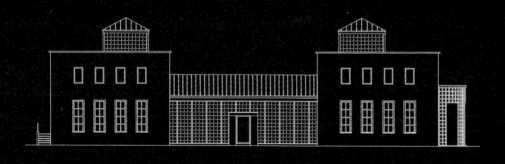

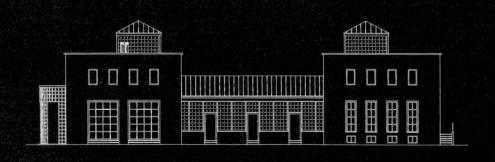

above, top to bottom: Model: Front view;
View of garage and kitchen side
below: Sectional axonometric

facing page, top to bottom: Ground floor
plan; Second floor plan; Front elevation;
Rear elevation

UPPER EAST SIDE TOWN HOUSE

Historic District, New York City, 1975

New York is a city that was made of town houses. The block where this building is located is one that has gone through transformations in scale and type. The site—part of the Upper East Side Historic District—is a very narrow lot (eighteen feet wide) located between two institutional buildings: The Russell Sage Foundation, formerly the Asia House—designed by Philip Johnson—to the left and a Presbyterian Neo-Gothic church to the right.

The different constraints that had to be dealt with were resolved by designing the building to act as a hinge between the two larger structures of opposite styles. While the first two floors are aligned with the church, the bowed facade of the upper floors links the building with the Russell Sage Foundation.

While the project resolves the "landmarks" status in its public face, the town house type has been transformed, both in plan and section. The building was developed using the stair—an ellipse with its long side perpendicular to the party walls—as a spatial organizer, creating a transverse vertical space. The typical section of the town house was inverted by locating the public areas of the house in the upper floors where the spaces generated by the stair are fully developed. In the lower floors, the stair is set within a rectangular figure dividing the plan in front and back. At the fourth floor, the stair volume starts to disengage from the box and is framed by a plane implying an elliptical volume. The eye of the ellipse creates an inner volume that projects through the roof in the form of a lantern.

left: Street view

facing page: North elevation

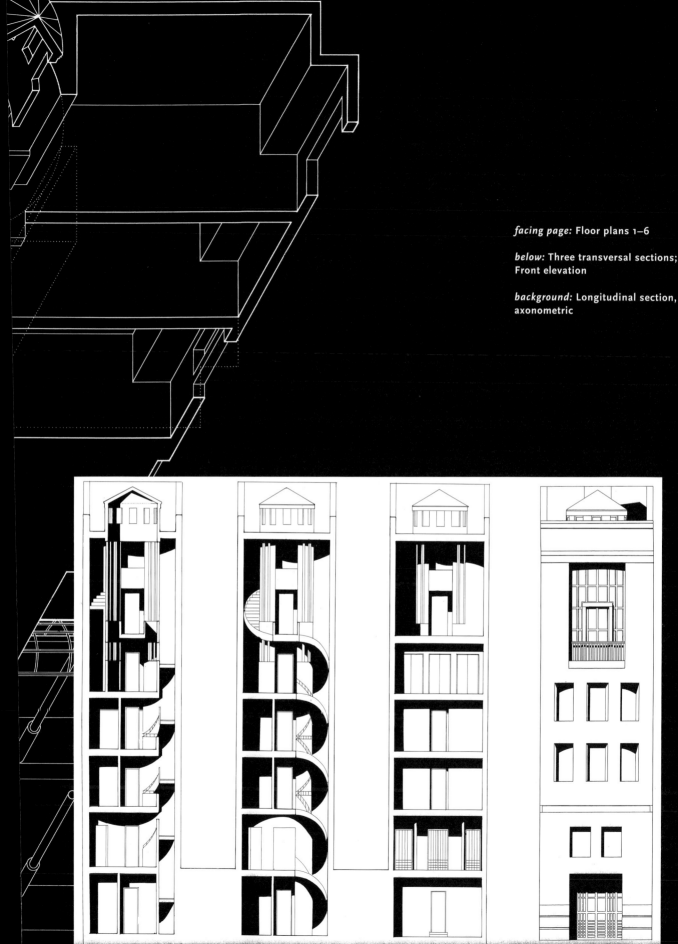

facing page: Floor plans 1–6

below: Three transversal sections;
Front elevation

background: Longitudinal section,
axonometric

THE FORMS OF A LEGEND

Follies, 1984

Whether the years of your life are 3,000 or ten times 3,000, remember that no one loses a life other than the one he lives now, nor lives life other than the one he loses. The longest and the shortest terms are thereafter the same. The present belongs to everyone. To die is to lose the present, which is only the briefest instant. The past and the future cannot be lost because that which belongs to no one cannot be taken. Remember that all things rotate, and rotate again, in the same orbit, and that for the spectator, it is the same to see them for one century, or for two, forever. — J. L. Borges, "El Tiempo Circular in Historia de la Eternidad" (1936), in *Obras Completas* (Buenos Aires: Emece Editores, 1974)

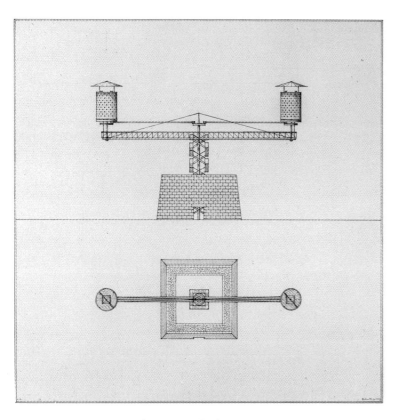

above: FOLLY 1, elevation

facing page: Box with model and oil painting background by Diana Agrest

Folly One:

THE CIRCULAR TIME

Two identical panoramas, held by a metal frame anchored within an outdoor stone room, revolve around a fixed column. The interior view is of a tropical garden. The panoramas, fixed to the center pole by chain and gear, maintain a static view, periodically entering one's field of vision as they revolve.

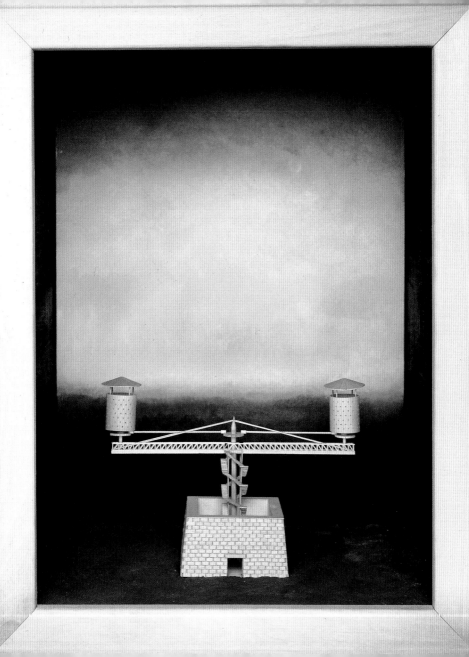

THE WALL AND THE BOOKS

I read not long ago that the man who ordered the building of the almost infinite Chinese Wall was the first emperor, Shih Huang Ti, who also decreed the burning of all books written before his time. Perhaps the emperor wanted to re-create the beginning of time and called himself first in order to be really first. We might also suppose that the burning of the wall and the burning of the books are simultaneous acts. And so, depending on the order we chose, we should have the image of a king who began by destroying and then resigned himself to conserving; or the image of a disillusioned king who destroyed what he previously defended. Perhaps the wall was a metaphor. "Men love the past and I am powerless against that love, and so are my executioners; but some day there will be a man who feels as I do and he will destroy the wall, as I have destroyed the books, and he will erase my memory and will be my shadow and my mirror and will not know it. Perhaps the burning of the libraries and the building of the wall are operations that secretly nullify each other.
— J. L. Borges, "La Muralla y los Libros in Otras Inquisiciones" (1952), in *Obras Completas* (Buenos Aires: Emece Editores, 1974).

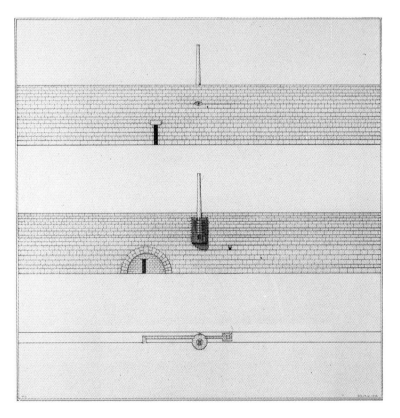

above: FOLLY 2, elevations and plan

facing page: Box with model and oil painting background by Diana Agrest

Folly Two:
SIX HUNDRED LEAGUES OF STONE

Within a fragment of a continuous stone wall, stairs lead up to a small pulpit where a book may be read or burned. At this point one oculus pierces the wall.

Folly Three:
THE RIGOROUS ABOLITION OF HISTORY

A stone arcade filled with books is sunk in a pool, dividing it in two. A diving board and a fountain spill into it.

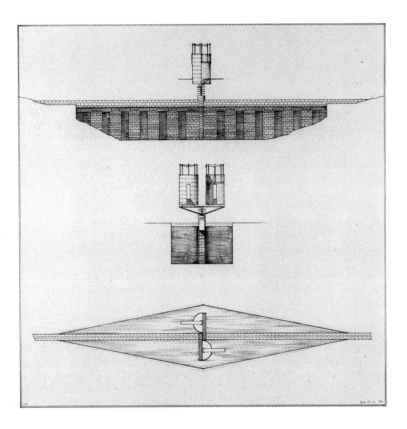

above: Plan and sectional views

facing page: Box with model and oil painting background by Diana Agrest

Folly Four:
PASCAL'S SPHERE

Perhaps universal history is the history of a few metaphors. Perhaps universal history is the history of the diverse intonations of a few metaphors. J. L. Borges, "La Esfera de Pascal" in *Otras Inquisiciones* (1951), in *Obras Completas* (Buenos Aires: Emece Editores, 1974).

Two columns: A wooden lighthouse is linked to a stone balloon-landing shaft by a mechanism that transforms the variable rotation of a windmill into the calibrated winding of a clock.

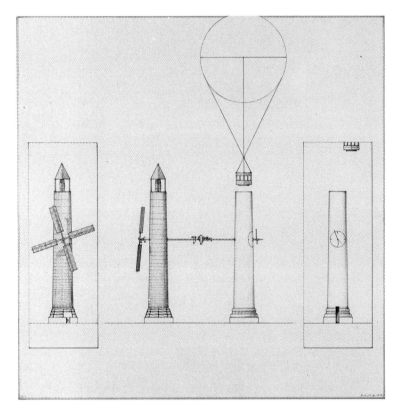

above: Elevations

facing page: Box with model and oil painting background by Diana Agrest

FRAMINGS

Bill Robinson Showroom, New York City, 1985

The showroom is an architectural statement on various modes of framing: perspectival space (theater) versus "accelerated" space (film), the contrast between the theatrical effect of suspense staged by the long "silent" gallery versus the cinematographic (unresolved) tension produced by the accelerated space of the main area. The pyramidal pivot articulating these two spaces through a change in axis acts as a shifter between different modes of framing.

This project for a 5,000-square-foot showroom for men's fashions is located in a Fifth Avenue office building. Two kinds of spaces were required: 3,000 square feet for public use, including a general display area and individual sales areas, and 2,000 square feet for private offices and the designer's studio.

The public space has been formally organized so that it serves as a place both for selling and for presenting fashion shows. In the reception area, a fifty-foot-long limestone and stucco gallery, three limestone benches are used for seating and as bases upon which models exhibit clothes during fashion shows. A truncated pyramidal volume articulates and mediates the entry gallery and the main space of the showroom. Clothes can be displayed in the corner spaces between the wood structure drum and limestone stucco volume.

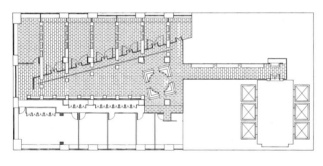

above: Plan

right: Axonometric views

following two pages: Display gallery

The main space is defined on the south with a wall of pilasters and columns and on the north by a series of receding brick parallel planes perpendicular to that wall. These planes define the sales area by creating an "accelerated" perspective, a very dynamic condition of movement as opposed to the "natural" perspective of the entrance gallery. The spaces between columns and pilasters on the south wall are used for photographic or actual clothing displays or as spaces where models or mannequins stand. Tongue-and-groove solid maple planes "cutting" through the brick walls further emphasize the perspective effect. These wood planes are doors that open to allow all spaces to be integrated for special events. Within the large doors there is a smaller door for everyday use.

The overall feeling of materiality, in particular the sensuous quality of the materials themselves, together with the lighting further emphasize the formal configuration of the space.

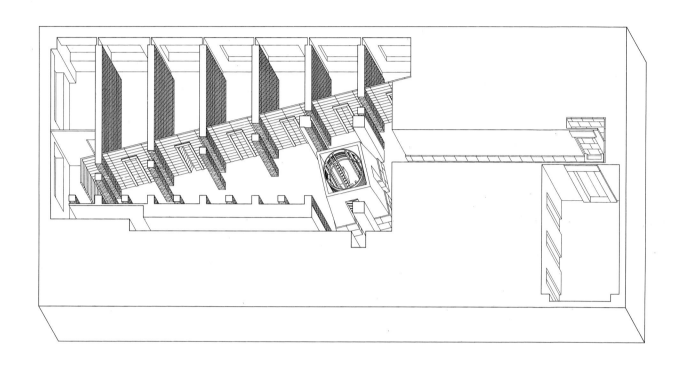

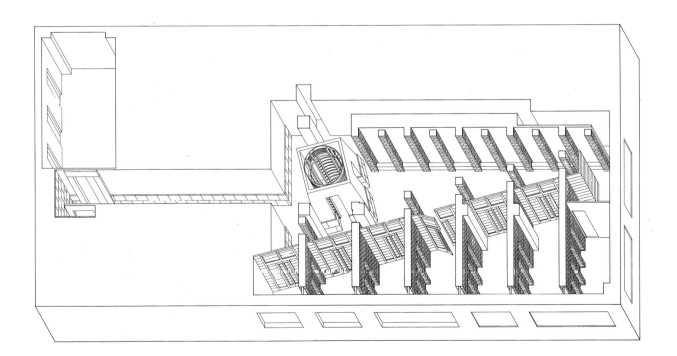

top left: Sales room with wood door within door

top right: Reception area

bottom: View of display gallery

facing page: Views of display gallery

THE RETURN OF THE REPRESSED

Deep Ellum, Dallas, Texas, 1986

Deep Ellum, a district adjacent to downtown Dallas, has been the silent witness to the intense development of the downtown area. Although its plan is in continuity with the downtown grid, its development has remained almost untouched by the changes that occurred in downtown, partly because of the physical barrier of the expressway. This set of conditions, along with the new zoning regulations restricting the floor area ratio (F.A.R.), establish the general background for the particular approach developed in our master plan for this area.

Our project proposes to create an urban environment with a strong identity in contrast to the character of downtown Dallas, both in terms of physical spatial configuration and programmatic organization.

For many years the focus of urban development and urban design has been on single-function buildings as isolated objects rather than on the heterogeneous programmatic nature of urban fabric. This has resulted in the destruction of streets and public places and the subsequent decrease in walking for pleasure. In cases where there had not been a pre-existing city life, that same approach made the development of an active urban life virtually impossible. Pervasive alienation and absence of delight are the effects of such a situation.

The creation of pedestrian public places is essential to the exchange that makes the culture of a city and that should be encouraged in the modern American city.

A premise in this master plan is that "master plan" is not synonymous with homogeneity. Formally unplanned, large-scale developments usually create chaos that is taken for "variety."

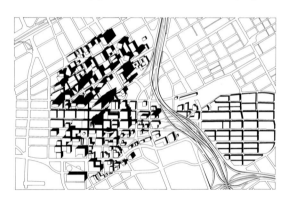

above: Downtown Dallas and Deep Ellum

right: Deep Ellum as the extension of downtown at the other side of the highway

In this project, we have produced the conditions for variety while avoiding chaos by establishing an urban structure and a massing. These will determine the general character within which the more idiosyncratic architecture will be developed.

A dense residential area is essential for the type of urban life we want to see developed in Deep Ellum. The master plan proposes the development of this district as a mixed-use area including residential buildings, retail establishments, offices, and small manufacturers. The creation of a residential neighborhood in the city is a rather unusual situation for Dallas. The project is an alternative to the prevailing solutions: the urban, isolated, high-rise tower; the suburban, single-family house; and the suburban, cluster housing.

Two interrelated aspects are of major importance in the implementation of the master plan: the urban morphological structure and the massing.

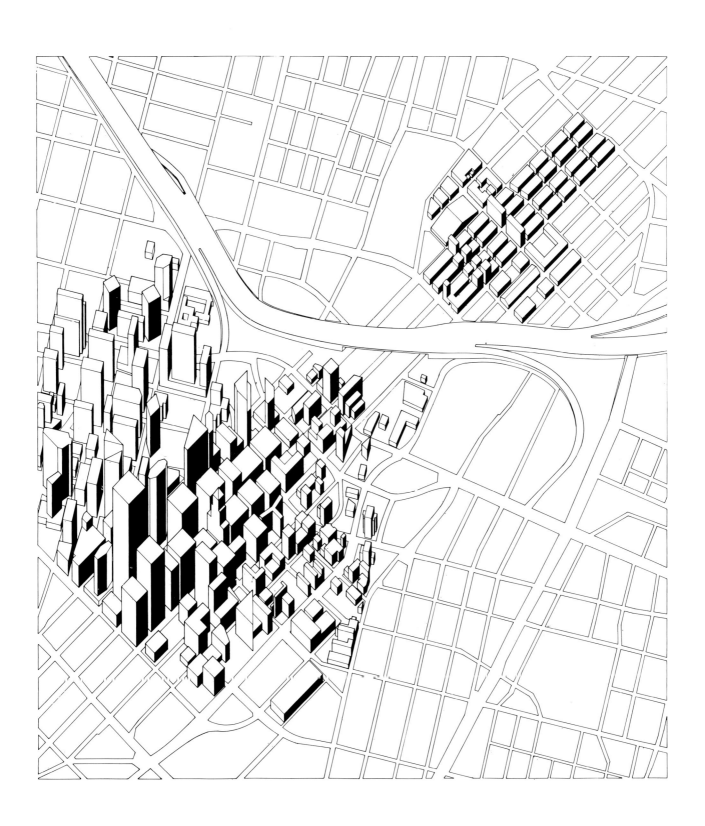

Concerning the morphological structure, the project is conceived as a network of vehicular and pedestrian streets and covered passages, creating blocks of a much smaller size than the present ones. By increasing the number of streets and the possible patterns of movement, the whole area is made more active. At certain points relating to the streets and particular buildings, such as a market or a tower, the plan provides parks of different sizes, allowing a variety of cultural or recreational functions to exist amidst the commercial and residential buildings.

Concerning the massing, this master plan proposes that one does not need to use high-rise, isolated buildings in order to achieve openness, views, and density. We achieve the maximum allowed density (F.A.R. 5) with only fifty-six feet of height in most buildings, and create more streets, squares, large courtyards, and a market without having to make economic sacrifices.

At the level of buildings, we provide a variety of building types such as the town house, the tower, the loft building, the courtyard, the market, and the

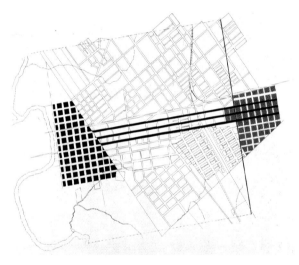

Return of original grid

passage. Another category of buildings is placed in a more symbolic position in relation to the site — for example, the gate buildings and the tower at the west end of Main Street, placed at the point of juncture between downtown Dallas and Deep Ellum to be clearly perceived from the expressway.

The market is a very important element in the development of this area. It is located in an area that, while being central to the whole development, is not in the physical center of Deep Ellum.

The project proposes residential buildings fifty-six-feet high, oriented to the street and the inner-block courtyard. Very few high-rise buildings are proposed, and these, not to exceed the 140-foot height limitation, serve as "punctuations," as points of reference within the urban fabric.

The project, while being very dense, preserves a feeling of openness and incorporates verdure into this urban fabric. Every residential block has a private green alley, which includes car circulation for tenants at the ground floor, and a courtyard on an upper floor. All residential buildings have retail use on the ground floor.

The plan makes the best use of the present ownership situation and limits further acquisitions for the first phase. It is designed in an octopus-like manner, proposing fragmented growth interlaced with existing buildings rather than a blanket solution. The project avoids the erasure of property lines, a typical result of building large, freestanding structures, and preserves the marks that uniquely affect the character of the American city.

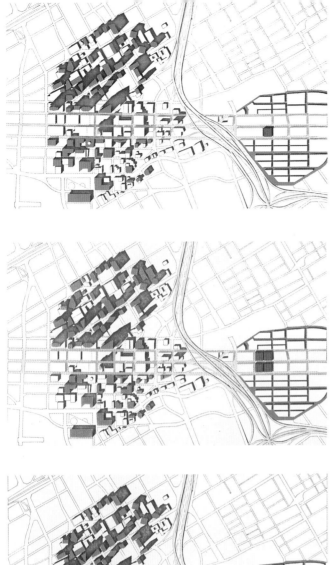

this page, top to bottom: Original square block; Four-square plan; Linear extension along Main Street; Fragmentation of blocks with service alleys; Transversal axis

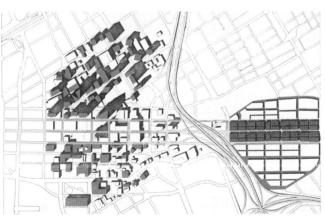

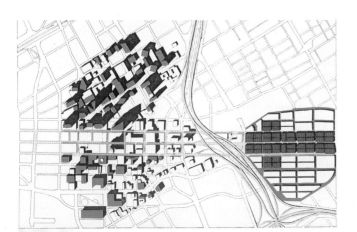

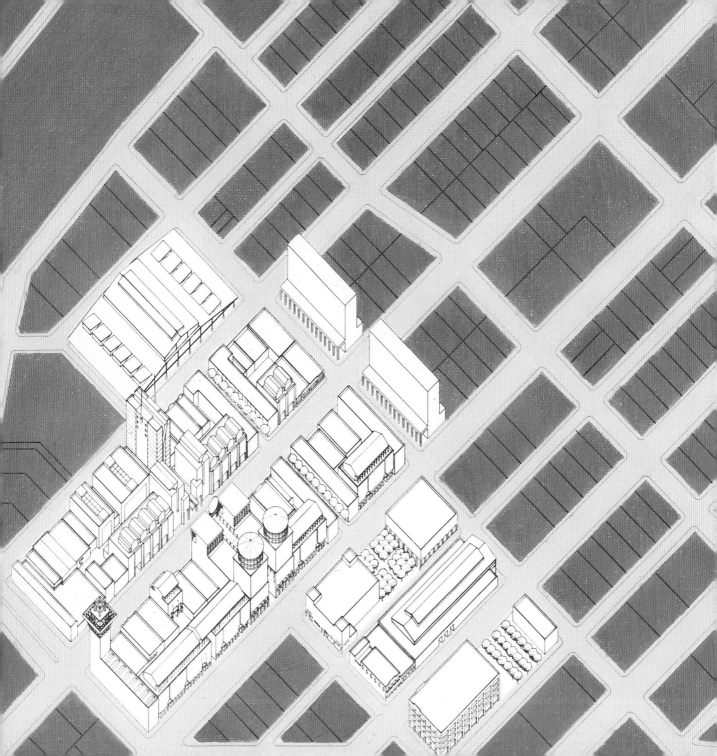

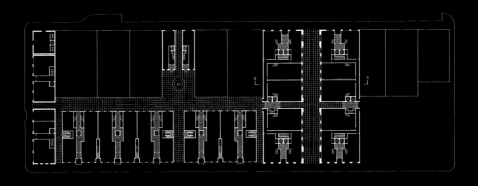

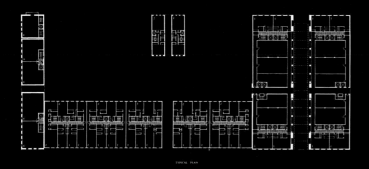

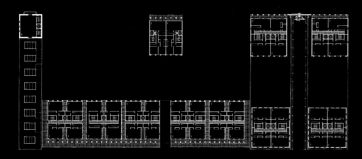

facing page: Axonometric view with lots subdivision

this page top to bottom: Street level plan; Typical floor plan; Upper floor plan; Plan with shadows

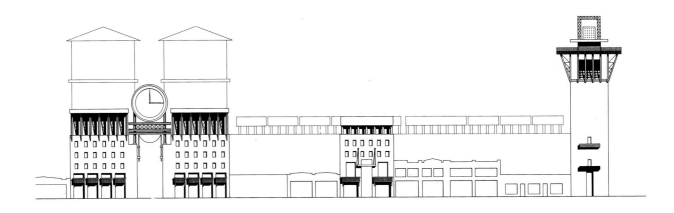

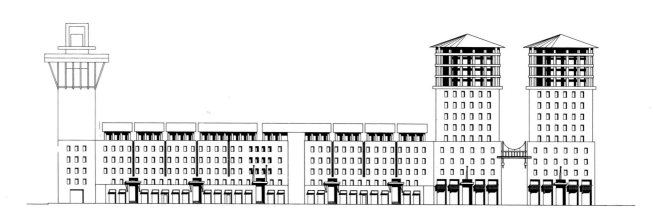

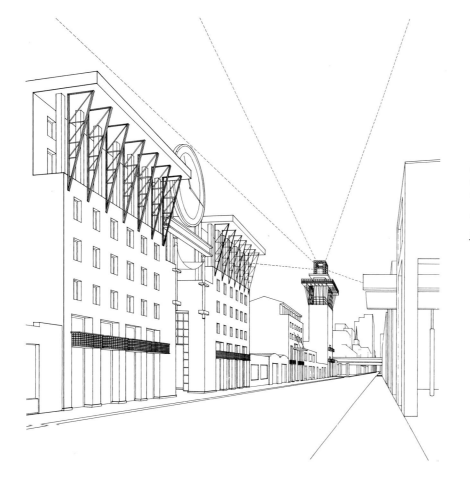

above: Main Street discontinuous
elevation; Elm Street continuous
elevation

left: Main Street perspective

facing page: Deep Ellum perspective

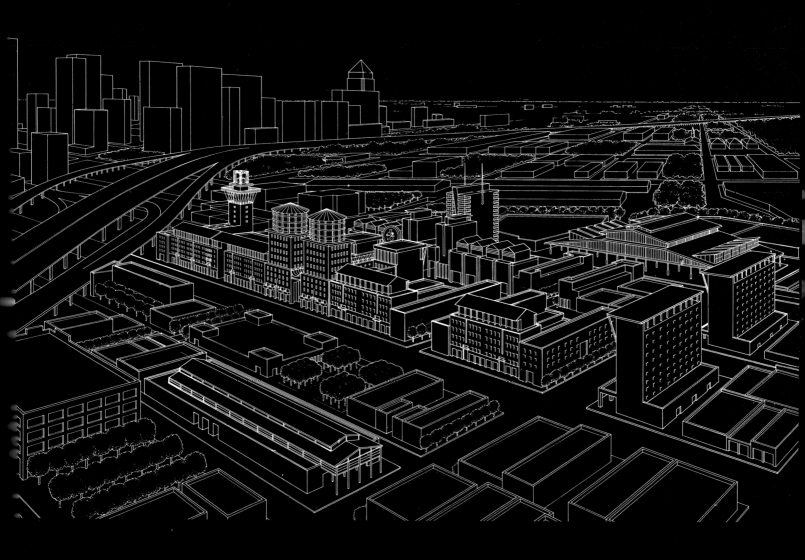

INTERIOR ON PARK AVENUE

New York City, 1986

This project establishes a sequence of spaces and rooms, marking transitions with a specific treatment of materials and surfaces.

Except for the bedroom, bathroom, and closet, the apartment is a continuous space entered through a steel-faced, oval hall.

Two maple columns linked by a thin, maple plane frame a gallery space and mark the entrances to the dining room and living room. Inlaid, flamed black granite—like that used in the oval entrance hall—marks the threshold to the dining room and announces that it is a room despite the lack of a literal door. This threshold is also marked with steel on its sides and top.

The column marking the entrance to the living room is "pushed" inside the space, so as to mark the transition to the private rooms.

The dining room is a small space that expands through sliding doors to a studio and through box-windows that project. A round window opens a corner of the living room to an outdoor terrace.

Different elements in steel throughout the apartment mark the significant design moments. The entrance hall itself is a steel "cabin"; one side of it opens into a closet that reveals the structure of the room. A semicircular bar is marked by a steel frame identical to the steel door with a porthole that indicates the transition to the kitchen. A steel slab mantlepiece sits above the living room's fireplace. Finally, a steel cone sink is the prominent object in the bathroom, where a landscape of objects serve as its background.

above: View of gallery from entry hall

right: Entry hall

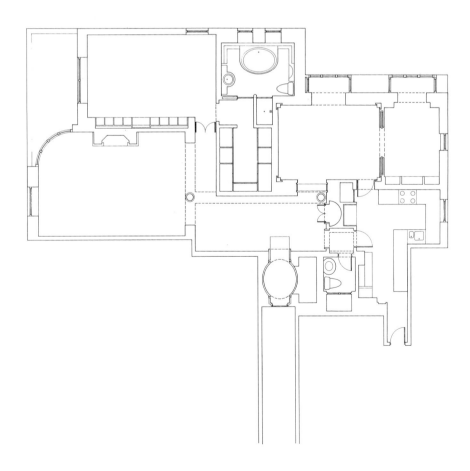

facing page, above left: Gallery space

facing page, above right: View of dining room with new bay window space from gallery

facing page, bottom: Plan

above left: Stainless steel bar

above right: Stainless steel mantelpiece

right: Stainless steel cone sink

OBJECT AS FABRIC

Porta Vittoria, Milan, Italy, 1986

Our project for the Porta Vittoria area of Milan proposes to regain the area acquired by the construction of the Passante railroad. The project addresses urban fabric, defining the area that is based on the strict cardinal-point grid of the 1912 Pavia Masera plan.

The plan develops a double reading of the area. On one hand it extends and transforms the grid. On the other hand the concentric structure of the historic center of Porta Vittoria is marked with buildings throughout the project.

The project proposes an answer to the central problem of modern urbanism—the dialectics between building, object, and fabric. Porta Vittoria is a laboratory where new public buildings and spaces are created, marking an edge between the old and the new city, between the early twentieth-century buildings and the late twentieth-century project.

Every building is subject to the dialectic between building and fabric; nothing in the project is entirely building or fabric. The fabric-like constructions have, in different degrees, building roles. The slabs and the monumental building have precise urban roles as street walls, park walls, and gates.

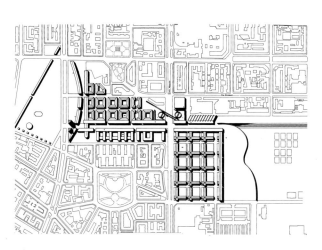

The project overlaps a series of slab buildings with commercial and public functions against a "background" of different residential fabrics that either suture the void left by the elimination of the railroad yards or are grafted into it. Public spaces permeate the project as the fabric unfolds from an ideal courtyard type to a double displaced grid of streets and buildings.

above: Site plan

right: Urban suture

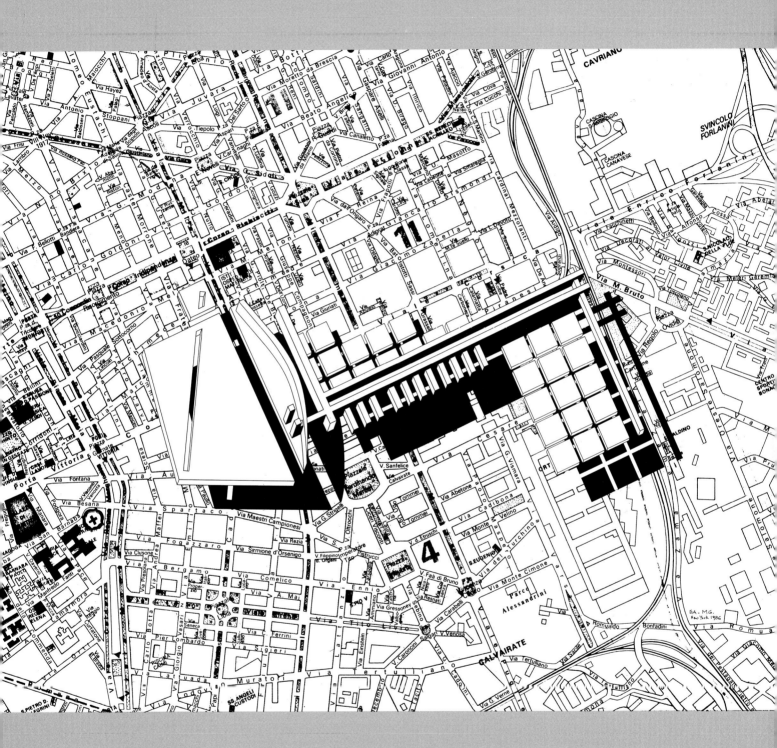

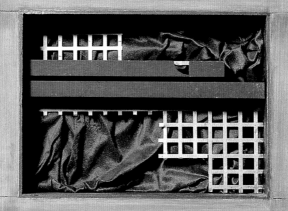

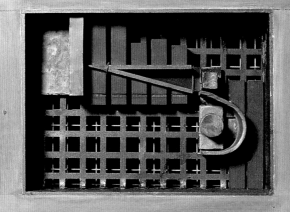

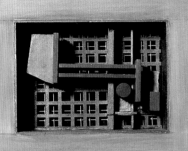
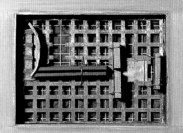

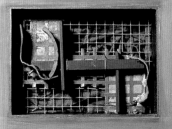

THE SLAB BUILDINGS

A parabolic bowed building defines the eastern wall of the Largo Marinai d'Italia Park.

A slab building running in the direction east-southeast of the park wall defines a commercial street at the scale of the new contiguous residential neighborhood.

Two slab buildings running east-west define a new boulevard, viale Porta Vittoria, from the Largo Marinai d'Italia to the new train station and bus terminals. The major commercial functions and public buildings are located on this Viale.

A slab separates the southern new residential area from the new proposed park east of this area.

THE URBAN FABRIC

Three different fabrics are based on a grid derived from the existing Pavia Masera grid:

Idealized courtyard buildings, extrusions of the regular gridded plan, represent a transformation of the existent residential building type (north of the Porta Vittoria Mall);

A grid that combines slabs and a street-wall structure that preserves the reading of the slab represent a transformation of the housing located south of via Monte Ortigara;

The new residential area grafted on the zone limited by viale Molise to the east, the new viale Porta Vittoria to the north, and via Cesare Lombroso to the south is an invention symbolic of the project. The overlapping of two displaced grids—one, the buildings; the other, the streets—produces a new housing type, which can be seen both as fabric and building object.

right: Model — transformations from
fabric to object
below: Axonometric view

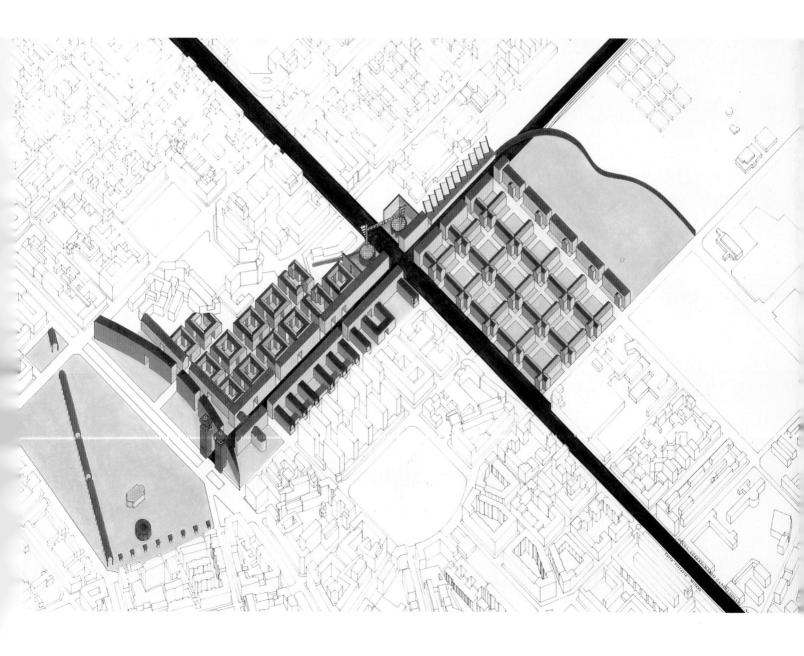

INTERIOR ON CENTRAL PARK WEST

New York City, 1987–88

This project undermines the stability of basic architectural concepts through a strategy that places modernism in the context of history, rather than in the immediate moment. The process of designing the project offers the inspection of meaning rather than the specious clarity of a manifesto.

The first floor plan includes movement. The pinwheel formal organization of the walls is reiterated by a curved stair implying a spiraling. The pinwheel plan produces an alternating reading: on the one hand, it appears as a figure in a neutral modern space, and on the other, it organizes volumes separating rooms that read as figures. This fluctuation of readings produces rooms coexistent with the spatial flow of the free plan.

The blurring of oppositions is carried through to detailing, where luxury and austerity are the alternating readings. The apartment works within the constraints of use, while at the same time it subverts the traditional notion of opulence, even as a modernist like Mies van der Rohe understood it. The quality of the materials and the level of detailing breaks down the separation between furniture and architecture.

Classicism is often an applied system of ornament that is a visual, representational structure rather than a "true" expression of structure or materials. The classic approach to detailing is exemplified by the molding, which conceals a joint between materials. In the modernist approach, a joint is treated as a separation, a reveal, allowing each material an independent expression of its own nature. Neither approach is used in this apartment; instead, materials butt each other. An aspect of modern detailing is retained, in that real materials — steel and wood — retain their own expression. But there is also the aspect of concealment; complex sleight-of-hand detailing is used to achieve the desired effect.

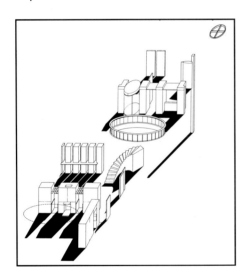

above: Conceptual framework

right: View through master bathroom screens

DOORS

FIRST DOOR: The entry door is a figural, massive, steel door and frame, quoting Adolf Loos.

SECOND DOOR: The door to the powder room is an abstract, steel plane affixed to the wall.

THIRD DOOR: The curved door to the kitchen literally disappears as an element of the wall.

FOURTH DOOR: The round, steel, sliding door to the pantry is conceived as a montage of a steel safe door, running on off-the-shelf library ladder hardware, with a commercial refrigerator door handle.

FIFTH DOOR: The winged, wood and steel door to the master bedroom hangs on a double-height steel flagpole.

SIXTH DOOR: The bar is a deep door.

SEVENTH DOOR: The two doors flanking the fireplace are defined by two vertical steel plates; a fragmented, alabaster lintel floats above.

EIGHTH DOOR: All other doors are "drawings" on the walls. The frames disappear and the doors become outlines.

above: View from master bedroom towards
living room

facing page: Bar within door space

Historically doors are conceptualized in different ways, from doors that are treated as frames to heighten the qualities of separation and passage, to doors that are played down or made to disappear in order to emphasize continuity of space and freedom of movement. The doors in this apartment oppose these two strategies and add a third. The entry door for example, is steel with a massive, steel frame. In contrast, the portals cut in the fireplace wall between the living and dining rooms are treated as punched openings through the thick wood plane. The waist-high steel plates on either side of the door are flush against the wood wall, as if they were leaning against it, and the alabaster lintel above it, treated as a floating plane that is almost dematerialized, emphasize the articulation of openings from the front view of the city. The door of the powder room, a steel plane "over" the wall, represents a third type.

Doors acquire meaning within a system of differences. As objects, they acquire characteristics that take them away from their specificity. As spaces, they are either semantically charged, as in the case of the bar, or syntactically placed in the overall sequence of spaces, as in the dining/living room doors.

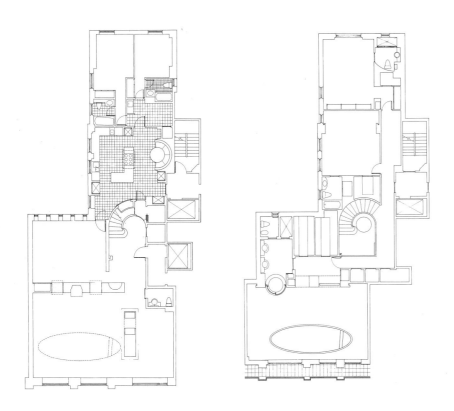

above left: First floor plan of duplex apartment

above right: Second floor plan of duplex apartment

facing page: View of living room, looking towards media/bar wall

left: Stairs looking to fireplace wall

below, left: Bathroom window into master bedroom

below, right: Stairs looking down to inlaid granite circle

above, left: Stainless steel pantry door

right: Master bathroom — TV and New York skyline

below, right: powder room

above: Fragmenting the view

left: Framing the view

WEST STREET
New York City, 1988

The western edge of downtown Manhattan has been radically transformed in the 1980s due to the development of Battery Park City and the continuous growth of Wall Street. Due to the resulting pressures, most of the old loft buildings and warehouses on West Street along the Hudson River were demolished. This renovation and conversion into offices of an existing loft building large enough to withstand the development pressures, is an exception to this rule.

The project takes into acount the location on the edge of Manhattan and the related questions of scale in the design of the skin of the building.

The facade, to be seen almost exclusively from the car, either from New Jersey or from the West Side Highway, is designed in relationship to the reading conditions established by those two different scales and speeds. The first scale, to be perceived from across the Hudson River, is addressed by a "belt" that divides the body of the building horizontally in half and holds (visually) an overscaled clock that can be seen from New Jersey while coming into Manhattan through the Holland Tunnel. The existing windows provide a rectangular shape that is used as a unit to develop a colossal staggered pattern throughout the entire facade of the building, which addresses the second scale. The pattern is materialized with black granite in the lower half of the building and with anodized aluminum panels in the upper half.

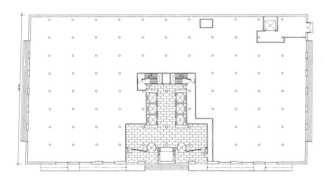

above: Entry level plan

opposite page: West Street elevation; South elevation

150 WOOSTER STREET
New York City, 1989

This interior for a Brazilian restaurant in downtown Manhattan presented the opportunity to inspect the possibility of generating formal arrangements and configurations that allow an exotic theme to be read without resorting to direct representation; instead a strategy of metonymic montage was used throughout the project.

Materials, primary colors, and abstract, minimal shapes have been selected so that they play in at least two symbolic "registers"; they propose a syntactic reading of the surfaces and at the same time recall Brazilian outdoor urban spaces. The syntax distorts the reading of the box by means of folded and overlapping walls, suggesting an urban space rather than the potential metaphoric reading of an outdoor room or courtyard. This is reinforced by the blue and yellow tile floor that recalls the sidewalks of Copacabana in Rio de Janeiro; the disruption of scale and the size of the floor tiles result in an image that is familiar but slightly distorted, as if it were on a computer screen.

The facade of the building, including the rolling garage door, is preserved, complete with graffiti. A glazed security garage door is the only addition.

above, top: New front window with existing garage door

above, bottom: Unfolded plan and elevation

facing page: Interior view

HOUSE ON SAG POND
Southampton, New York, 1989–90

Situated on a seven-acre lot facing Sagaponack Pond and surrounded by fields, Villa Amore suggests a cluster of "found objects" framing the agricultural landscape, rather than presenting itself as homogeneous.

Six idiosyncratic towers connected by bridges surround a 110-foot-long vault, creating a sequence of architectural experiences.

The house's formal structure is developed along two geometries. The vault is set at true north so that the facade of doors, to the west, captures the longest view of the pond. The towers and their bridges are rotated clockwise thirteen degrees following the edge of the pond.

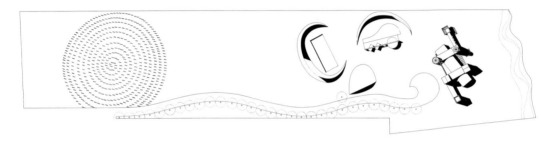

above: Site plan; *facing page:* Perspective

The vault encloses public living spaces while towers and bridges contain the private rooms. The towers and bridges create two independent wings on the second floor, one for the master bedroom suite on the south side and another for the guest rooms to the north, each wing with its own independent staircase.

The wedge between the two geometries generates a triangulated entrance hallway and is expressed in the anti-perspectival distortion of the staircase and the torsion of the parabolic roof. The overlapping of geometries also affects the volumes (of the twin fireplaces, the paintings cabinet, and the pantry/cupboard) that separate the main spaces in the vault.

The structure is always exposed: the laminated wood arches springing from the heavy timber columns of the vault and the diagonal trusses and steel plates of the bridges. The cylindrical greenhouse is the only tower in which the structure, composed of vertical steel columns and horizontal, laminated wood rings, is completely exposed. Fragments of structure are revealed within the private spaces.

The cluster of "found objects" is now assembled. Villa Amore resists stylistic, typological, or linguistic classification, drifting between the abstract and the figural, between convention and idiosyncrasy.

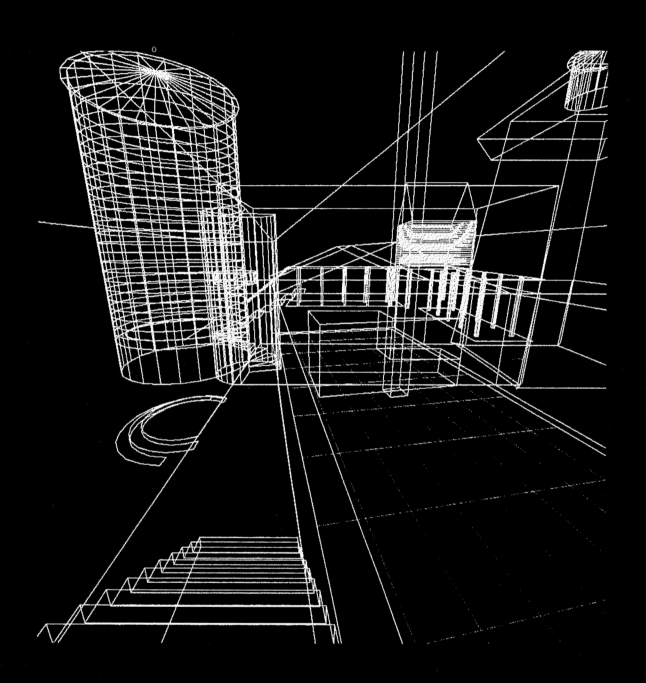

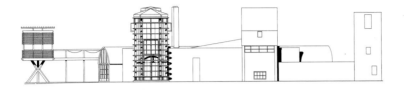

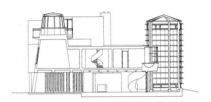

this page, top to bottom, left to right: East elevation; North elevation; West elevation; South elevation; Longitudinal section; Transversal section, Longitudinal section

facing page, top: First floor plan;

facing page, bottom: Second floor plan

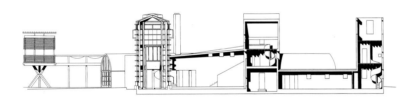

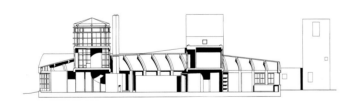

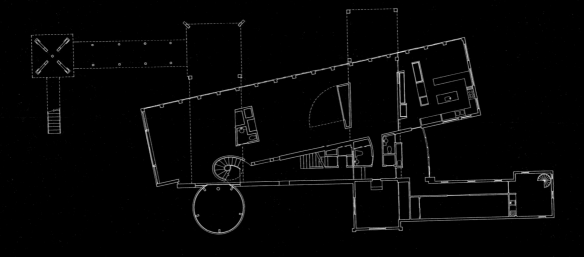

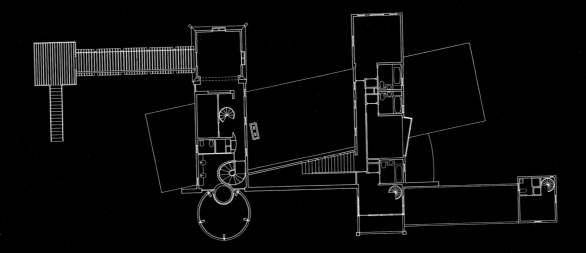

left, top to bottom: View from Bridge on Sag Pond; View from neighboring fields; View of house, entry side; View of north end and pond side

facing page: View of gazebo from south garden

top to bottom: Foundations; Two views of vault and bridges; Front wall

facing page, top to bottom: Guest wing; Front door; Greenhouse and sunroom at south end of living room; Viewing studio above master bedroom

following spreads: View of entry space framed by house and north side of pool house; View from south

POLOS
DESIGN
TO END

above: View from studio

facing page, top: Evening view from south
facing page, bottom: Roofscape

this page, top: View of master bedroom tower from gazebo

this page, bottom: View of gazebo from master bedroom

facing page, top: Entry hall seen from guest wing;

facing page, bottom: View of bar from sun room

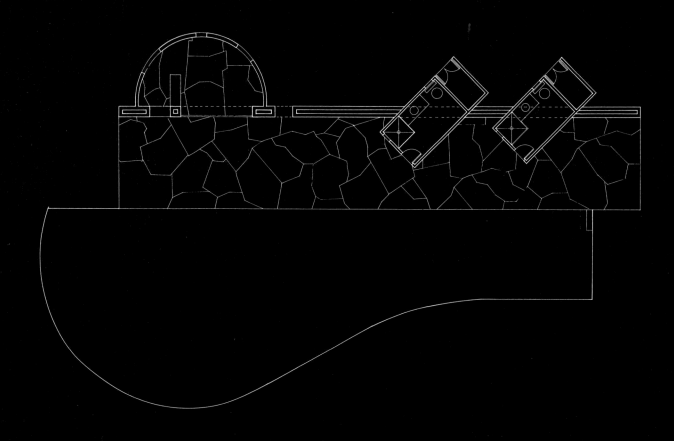

Pool house

this page, above: Wall cutting through cabins; *below, left:* North side; *below, right:* South (pool) side

facing page, top to bottom: Pool house — Pool side elevation; Garden side elevation; Plan

URBAN READY-MADES 1 AND 2

Goose Island, Chicago, Illinois, 1989

The question proposed by this project, "fabric as object," needs to be seen against the background of the separation between the historic city and the modern city. The classical European city of fabric and streets as figural voids opposes the modernist European city where building-objects sit on a (not always) green, neutral plane. One could say that the change from the conception of the city as a continuous fabric into the city as a collection of discrete objects represents one of the most dramatic events in the history of the city.

The American city has gone through this transformation as well, but in a different way than the European city. The American city's formal structure is based on the grid, and on a very unstable fabric in which individual buildings tend to preserve their "objecthood," defying the submission to a whole, as in the great nineteenth-century European capitals.

above: Goose Island in context

right: Reading Chicago

In the last third of the twentieth century, the American city has produced two situations that collapse the two terms of the opposition fabric/object.

The block, an essential element of gridded cities, has the potential to become an object. This happens when property boundaries of small parcels of land are erased so that a single large building can be built on an entire block, creating the building-object as fabric.

Another condition is produced by the erasure of fabric in contemporary downtowns, where enormous parking lots surround islands of fabric that look like objects on a field. This is the pragmatic situation that this project approaches from a formal/conceptual point of view.

In these ready-mades, the island is a colossal field upon which discrete districts—based on the notion of "fabric-as-object" as the basic structuring urban configuration—contrast with very large buildings. The pieces of fabric are either selected from various readings of American cities or from typologies developed by us from exploring the relationship between object and fabric. These urban fragments are not born from imitation or picturesque replication but from forms the city has historically generated. They are transformations of the result of an anonymous social, collective author, pieces of undesigned fragments of the city where streets and places are grafted. While the fabric is made up mostly of residential buildings, the immense building-objects are institutional.

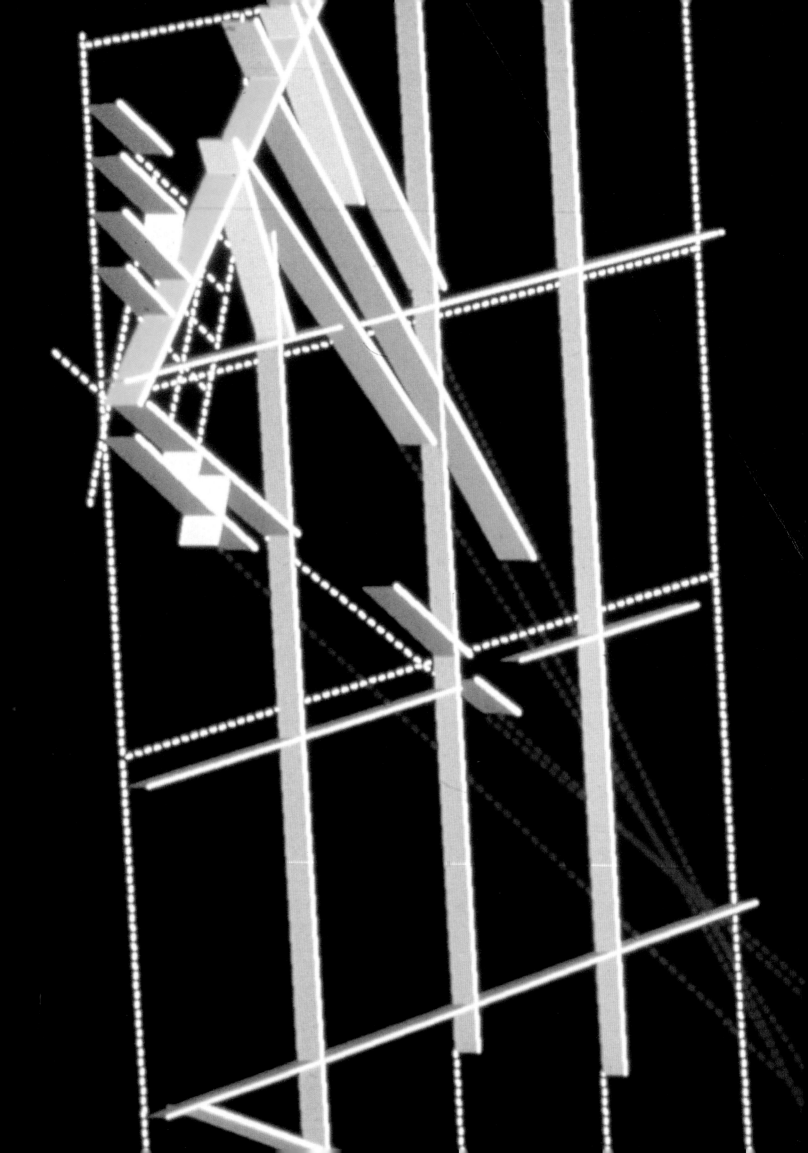

right, top to bottom: Le Corbusier's museum; Topographic disruption of the grid; One-mile grid and diagonal streets and grids

below: Huge buildings and existing axis

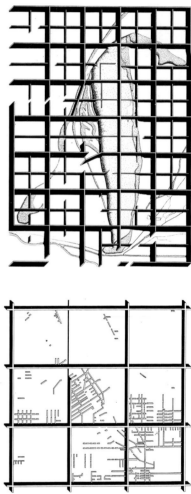

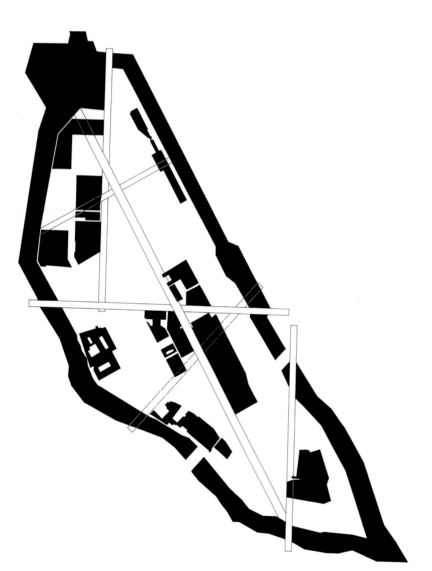

Ready-made 1: A bar of fabric splits the island in east and west parks.
Fragments of fabric-as-object and building-objects encroach on the island.

1. Planetarium
2. Museum of Architecture
3. Olympic Training Center
4. Recycled Building
5. Residential

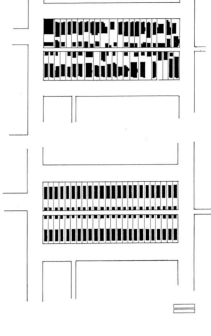

right, top to bottom: Typical Chicago block
with residential buildings; Chicago residential
typology; Beverly Hills streets

below: Tiny buildings with existing and
proposed axes

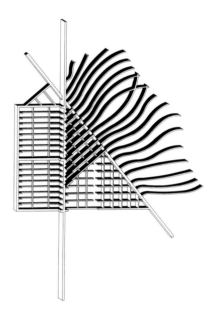

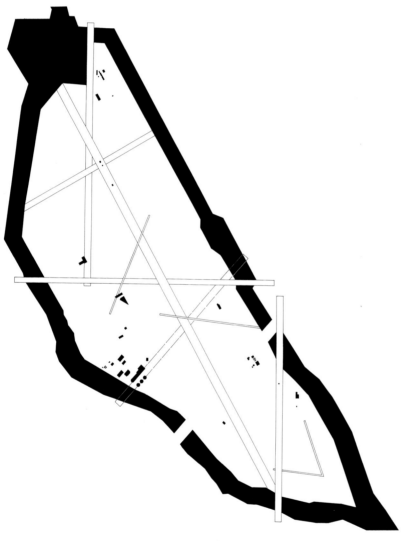

Ready-made 2: A cross formed by two bars of fabric, one with individual lots, the other framing and market place, divide the island in four fields or quadrants. Building-objects sit on or hover over the green.

1. Planetarium
2. Museum of Architecture
3. Residential
4. Recycled Buildings and Market
5. Residential
6. Subdivision in individual lots
7. Museum of Industrial Archaeology

VISION PLAN

Des Moines, Iowa, 1990-92

THE VISION PLAN: TOWARDS AN AMERICAN URBANISM

The Vision Plan is a new strategy for the theory and planning of architecture and for physical planning in the American city at the turn of the millennium. The Vision Plan is a design process based on an analysis of the specific form of the aesthetic conditions of a given city overlapped with an analysis of the specific economic development opportunities. One of the basic premises of this urban design process is our belief that the specific conditions that characterize the American cultural, economic, and political context imply the need for a radical critique of traditional urbanism. Instead of the traditional "Master Plan," the Vision Plan has developed a range of strategies that range from restriction to freedom, from determinate to indeterminate, from order to chaos, that focus on moments and not on a rigid plan. The Vision Plan does not establish an "image" of the city as a still life; rather, it is a continuous process involving a partnership between the city and the business community in which specific projects are developed and implemented. The traditional linear sequence of the stages of planning followed by the implementation and financing of specific projects is abandoned for a non-linear strategy in which implementation and financing are considered from the start, and in which projects are designed and developed simultaneously with the planning.

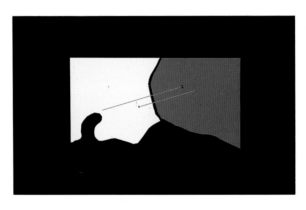

above: Twin axis defined by Capital (east) and City Hall (west)

right, top: View of downtown Des Moines from east

right, bottom: Aerial view of downtown and Des Moines River

The Des Moines Vision Plan began in 1990 as a physical planning effort that concentrated on the formal configuration of the city, with the objective to guide the physical and formal impact of future growth. As opposed to traditional master plans, where the physical city is approached as a totality and a formal whole, the Vision Plan purposed to establish a formal framework of urban planning and architectural point interventions — which we call "moments" — based on the reading of the city plan and on the specific geographic, historical, and cultural features of Des Moines as a guide to future growth. The term "moments" designates places with potential to generate development and design opportunities, derived from a formal analysis of the plan of the city and a list of available development sites. The Vision Planning process provides a menu of alternative design strategies and tactics that leaves room for market forces to influence the final, undecidable configuration of the projects; since the form of the city is determined by economic forces, its needs are unpredictable, it is subject to chance.

The continuing trend in most American cities since the 1950s has been to abandon the downtown for the suburbs. The Vision Plan attempts to reverse this tendency in Des Moines through a continuing process of revitalization, focusing on important areas downtown and proposing the development of new residential areas through significant point interventions.

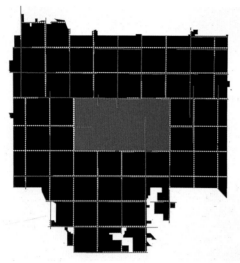

One-mile grid within city limits, framing downtown

The Des Moines Vision Plan was developed through a continuing dialogue with the local community, in collaboration with two local planners representing the private and public sectors. The "client," a joint partnership of the city of Des Moines, Iowa and the local business community, was represented by a ninety-member steering committee involving every sector of the community and chaired by the mayor.

A basic goal of the Des Moines Vision Plan is to promote a physical environment that reflects and contributes to the visual culture. The visual chaos of the metropolitan landscape is the result of the economic and political processes that generate cities through the accretion of object-buildings without any concern for the formal effect of their potential relationships. The planning disciplines could have an important role in the creation of a physical environment that reflects and contributes to the visual culture. However, planning has both focused almost exclusively on economic and functional issues and ignored the formal and symbolic aspects of the physical city.

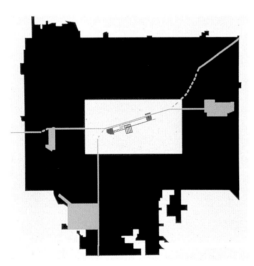

Downtown, airport, park, and fairgrounds

Another basic goal is to link the planning and design disciplines, and to promote the physical/formal planning of cities. A physical environment that reflects the formal-visual culture, and not only market forces, might become a reality if we re-establish the link between the planning and design disciplines that was broken in the 1950s. For this link to be re-established, both the urban disciplines (urban planning/urban design) and the architectural practice of the city will need to be re-examined and a new approach developed. The urban disciplines should abandon their exclusive attachment to the "scientific paradigm," opening up to the paradigm of artistic practices considered as laboratories in which the relationship between form/symbol and culture is explored. Architecture should abandon its "object-oriented fixation" and focus on establishing relationships between buildings and changing its formal strategies and heuristic tactics, from structure to process, from static to dynamic.

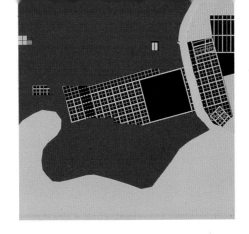

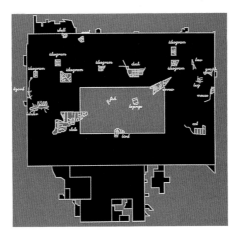

top to bottom: Formal structure of foundation plan; Topographic "constellations"; Downtown districts, existing and proposed; Buildings' footprints in "wedge"; Irregular elements in Des Moines plan

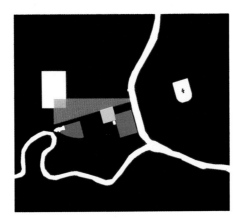

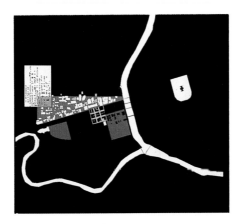

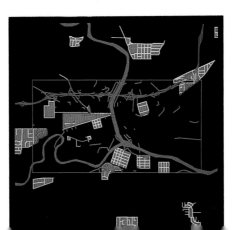

The final goal of the Vision Plan is to deepen the understanding of the specific visual and aesthetic character of the American city. The visual and formal elements discovered in the analysis overlapped with a list of potential development sites produce the final network of "moments." These drawings have played an important role during the Vision Plan process as a communicational and pedagogic tool in the public discussion about the form of the city.

It is also essential for both the planning and design disciplines to take into account the specific nature of the urban processes and the formal structures of the American city. These structures are determined by a political/economic context, democracy and the free market, which is radically different from the context in which the traditional European urbanistic theories originated.

The Des Moines Vision Plan was first approached in the context of teaching, as developed by Agrest and Gandelsonas over many years. It then became a subject of research, and was finally implemented in four phases, through a contract with the city of Des Moines.

1. CLIENT AND COMMUNITY INVOLVEMENT

The principal objective of this phase was to design a process to insure a continuous and productive exchange of information and views between the architect, the local coordinating team, including planners representing the city and business community, and a community-based steering committee for analysis/discovery of design moments. Analytical drawings of Des Moines, describing the actual and potential visual structure of the city and its specific aesthetic qualities, were produced. The visual and formal elements discovered were the basis for the development of a preliminary list of moments. Some of the results of this task were presented as images of alternative design and development opportunities.

Proposed Des Moines landscaping—
airport and downtown

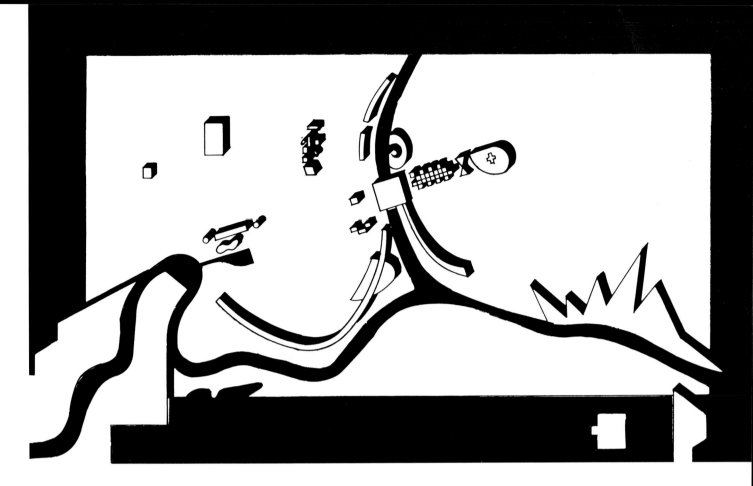

Downtown landscaping projects — residential districts and riverfront

2. VISUAL PLANNING STRATEGY

A vision plan never starts from scratch. On the basis of design moments discovered in the reading of and existing conditions in the Surrey City Center area, present or on the boards, a visual planning strategy was developed. A productive client review process resulting in mechanisms and specific strategies to foster a comprehensive stratum of urban design development was proposed. First, it was presented to the coordinating committee for comments and then shown to the steering committee once the comments had been incorporated, stimulating a dialogue that would provide the basic contents of the planning strategy. This visual planning strategy and general guideline materials were used to structure the designing of alternative visions. In more conventional planning this would be the master planning stage. In a vision plan there is no one "correct" answer, instead, a visual armature is developed to generate alternative strategies that are eventually selected not by the urban architect but by the social, cultural, economic, and political forces that cause the city to grow.

3. DEVELOPMENT OF DESIGN ALTERNATIVES AND GUIDELINES

The visual alternatives and design guidelines for future development were generated, refined, and expanded. During the course of this phase, alternative design guideline strategies for selected project areas were developed and reviewed. Working meetings and presentations were conducted with the different committees and other officials and citizens. Finally, the alternative visions developed by Agrest and Gandelsonas were reviewed and evaluated against the development goals and planning objectives through public discussion.

4. MOMENTS

The conditions of Des Moines are ideal for the Vision Plan: symbolically, Des Moines is the heartland of America; formally, it is set in the Jeffersonian grid; culturally, its population is sophisticated and very educated (having the highest level of education in the country); economically, it is based on an advanced service industry and sophisticated technology for agricultural development.

The Vision Plan process detected and proposed a network of the following moments: Fleur Drive, Riverfront, Gateway, and Civic Center; residential neighborhoods downtown: Court Avenue, Lakefront, Hillside, M Drive, Living Legend, East side, Airport, Cultural Crescent, Skywalk System; transportation: Central Business District (CBD) loop, bicycle paths and monorail along the freeway, north-south and east-west shuttles. In the last two years, moments one through five have been developed.

Fleur Drive establishes the link between the Des Moines Airport and downtown Des Moines. It provides the first impression of Des Moines on arrival. The drive is characterized by its variable surroundings, which range from a mediocre strip to a beautiful green double edge, composed of the Arie den Boer Arboretum on the west side, Grey's Lake and the Wakonda Golf Course to the east, and residential areas of houses and gardens in between. This axis is treated as a sequential condition in time and space.

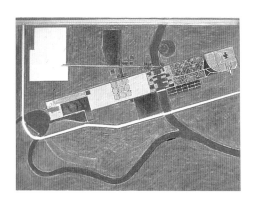

Downtown moments

Several intersections are identified as possible points for emphasis in this sequence. It is proposed to continue the green along the entire drive interrupted only by intersection points. The point of arrival to downtown Des Moines is not presently marked, but the conditions for a ceremonial gateway exist and its development is proposed in the riverfront plan. Raccoon River intersects Fleur Drive at this important point of entrance to downtown. Because of the lack of character of the river and road, an otherwise relevant condition is unnoticed. One of the proposals for the riverfront is to exploit its destructive potential for flooding. The Vision Plan proposes to flood the area creating Fleur Lake, which will also serve to control future flooding. The road is proposed to eventually engage with the CBD loop and create a triple bridge condition, the physical manifestation of a gate.

Another point of intervention proposed is the Civic Center in the sole area that contains some of the buildings and bridges built during the City Beautiful movement in the nineteenth century. Several proposals were presented to emphasize the point of intersection between the linear downtown bar and the Des Moines River as a connector between the east and west sides, thus modifying the separation that exists today. This area is to become a public place for cultural and civic activities by implementing several formal strategies that will project the nineteenth-century structures into the twenty-first century: enlarging the river into a square lake, eliminating the bridge, extending existing buildings into the water with places for public gathering, "floating" some of these buildings, and adding new structures for public spaces.

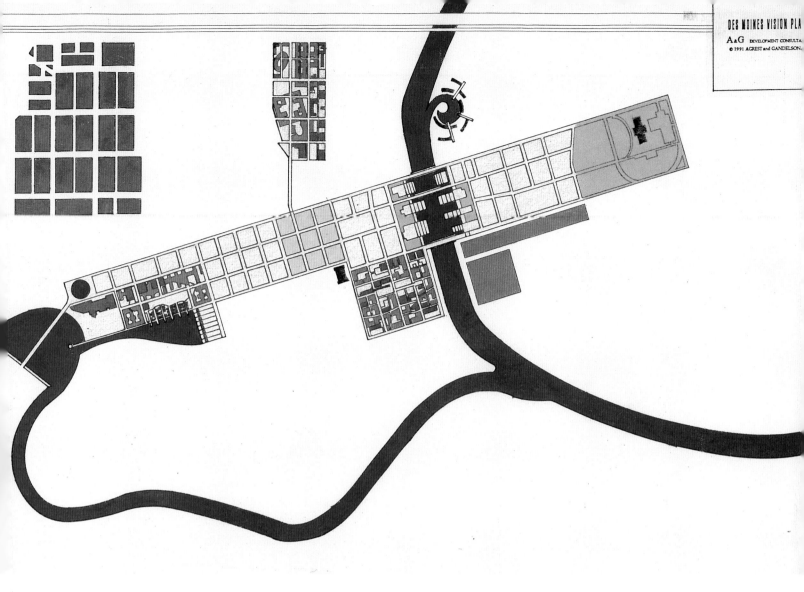

Proposed downtown moments with
residential neighborhoods

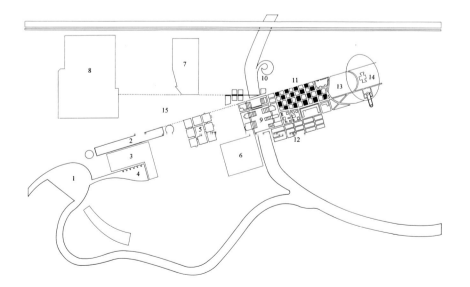

Downtown moments:

1. Gateway/Lake Fleur
2. Central Park
3. Riverside residential neighborhood
4. Lake riverside
5. Skywalk
6. Court Avenue district
7. Hillside residential neighborhood
8. Sherman Hill residential neighborhood
9. Civic Center
10. East side Marina residential neighborhood
11. Red Brick City
12. East side neighborhood
13. Capitol Park
14. Capitol
15. Wedge

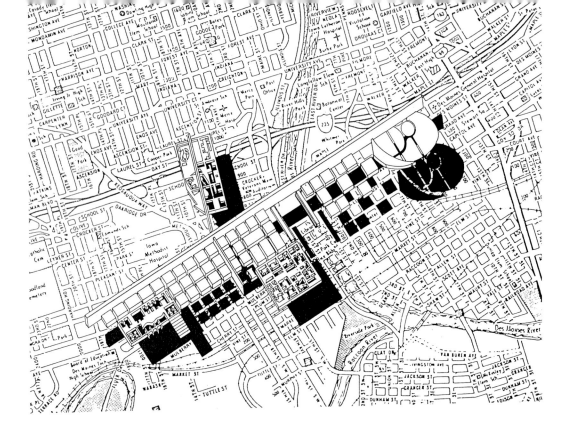

Downtown corridor and residential neighborhoods

RESIDENTIAL NEIGHBORHOODS

Several areas were identified as possible new residential neighborhoods downtown. In order to create a vital downtown, the Vision Plan proposes to replace the migrant nine-to-five population with twenty-four-hour residents. The intention is to reverse the present "flight to the suburbs" with a "flight to the city." This urban growth must be based on some form of concentration and not on limitless outward growth that wastes infrastructure and energy. The young population and the older "empty nesters" feel completely alienated in the suburbs. In order to compete with the suburbs, the principles of air, light, and green are essential (as great contributions to modern urbanism), but these should not be gained by the sacrifice of urbanity.

It is proposed to create edges, multiply streets, and create different types of housing to superimpose and juxtapose. The Vision Plan advocates that the incompleteness and impureness of the city are positive qualities. A planning ideology was implemented during the sixties that involved the extensive demolition of old buildings. Formally, the downtown became a combination of freestanding buildings and open spaces, creating a combination of grid and *tabula rasa*, a condition with great potential for the exploration of the American city.

Two different formal strategies are proposed: object as fabric and fabric as object. This proposal opposes both the approach to urban design as all fabric—the historical approach of classical European cities—and the approach in which urban buildings are seen as freestanding objects—proposed and realized in post-World War II Europe and America.

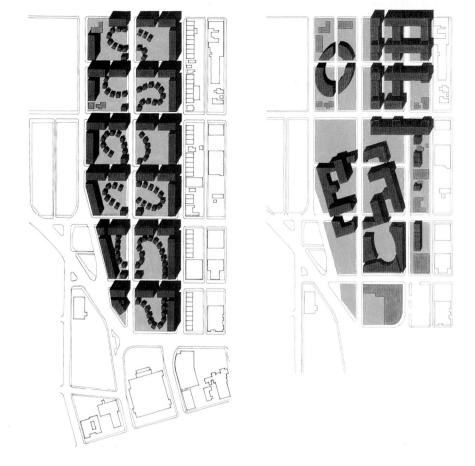

above: Hillside neighborhood alternatives 1 and 2
below: Riverside neighborhood alternatives 1 and 2

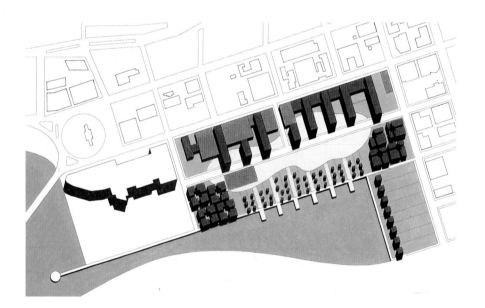

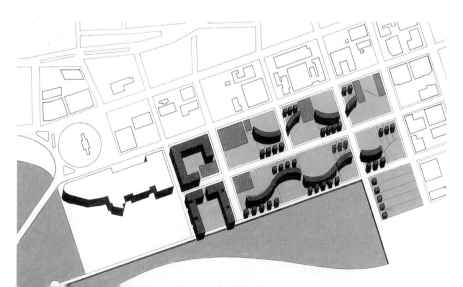

EAST SIDE

The east side, ranging from the riverfront to the capitol, is characterized by the strong presence of the capitol high on a hill, surrounded by a park and a number of government buildings. It is otherwise a very eroded zone. The Vision Plan proposes to treat the east side as a low-density, mixed-use area. The low density is considered an important element in the case of object as fabric. A series of design alternatives are presented based on two conditions: sequence and integration of green as part of a fabric condition. Taking advantage of the grid (with Savannah as a reference), a checkerboard becomes the main formal device in several versions ranging from basic all-checkerboard configurations to complex sequential transformations of discrete fabrics.

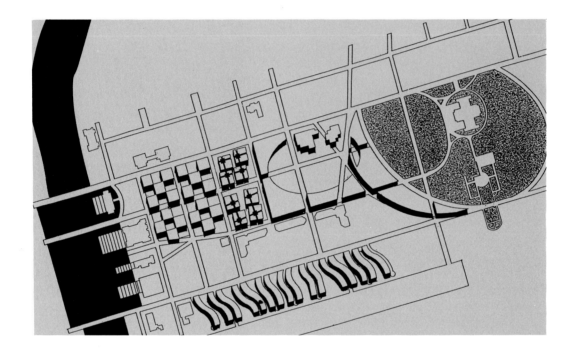

above: East side—Red Brick City alternative 1

facing page, top to bottom: East side alternatives 2–5

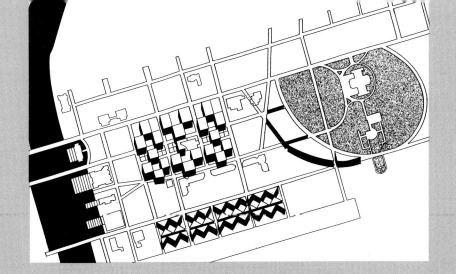

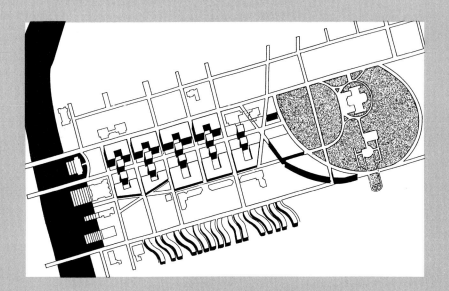

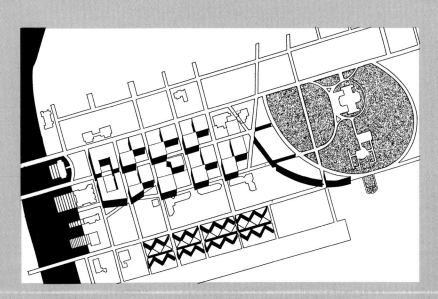

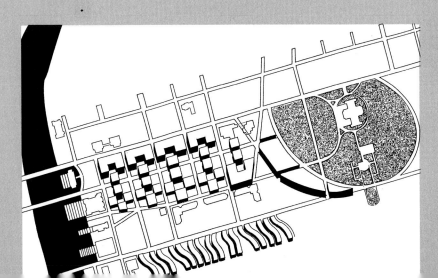

PRINCETON CAMPUS CENTER

Princeton University, Princeton, New Jersey, 1990

preliminary study

The Princeton Campus Center is a renovation of the East Pine Cafeteria and Chancellor Green Building as well as an addition of new dining and meeting facilities facing Nassau Green. From a programmatic point of view, the challenge was to maximize the use of existing spaces and to create a fluid communication between all spaces in the new organization. From a symbolic point of view, the location of the building was of major importance. The site is very prominent, located between the Nassau Street entrance to the campus next to the Firestone Library and the Nassau Green, the oldest and historically most significant area of the university.

The project presented a contradiction and therefore a challenge: the design was to project an identity and a symbolic presence and at the same time avoid direct competition with the existing buildings.

The Princeton Campus Center was conceived as a cluster of garden elements that is never perceived as a whole object. These elements perform two different roles: they supplement the existing structures and places and they propose movement sequences that flow from the existing to the new.

The project proposes to change the datum of the entrance level from a hyphen that links the Chancellor Green to East Pine to a kiosk placed at the level of the existing basement of the Chancellor Green building. The new structure produces a totally new reading of the entry.

The kiosk is the first of a sequence of garden elements that organize the new building. A "neck" links the entrance of the kiosk to a greenhouse that acts as a second hyphen between Chancellor Green and the new Campus Center. A stone wall articulates the greenhouse with the dining and meeting facilities. The stairs inside the greenhouse provide a connection to the existing cafe in Chancellor Green; a new bridge links this cafe to the roof garden of the Campus Center. A monumental stair opens up this garden to the green, both for a natural promenade and a place to sit and watch graduation ceremonies or other special occasions. The facade of the building facing Nassau Street defines a new garden connected to the roof by a ramp.

above: Model—view from Princeton Green

right: Site plan

A student restaurant and cafe currently occupy the first floor of the East Pine Cafeteria and the Chancellor Green Building. The new building is to house an expanded restaurant, smaller private dining and meeting rooms, and a new kitchen.

The different sequences of enclosed private to more open public places overlap in section and at the same time maintain separate identities.

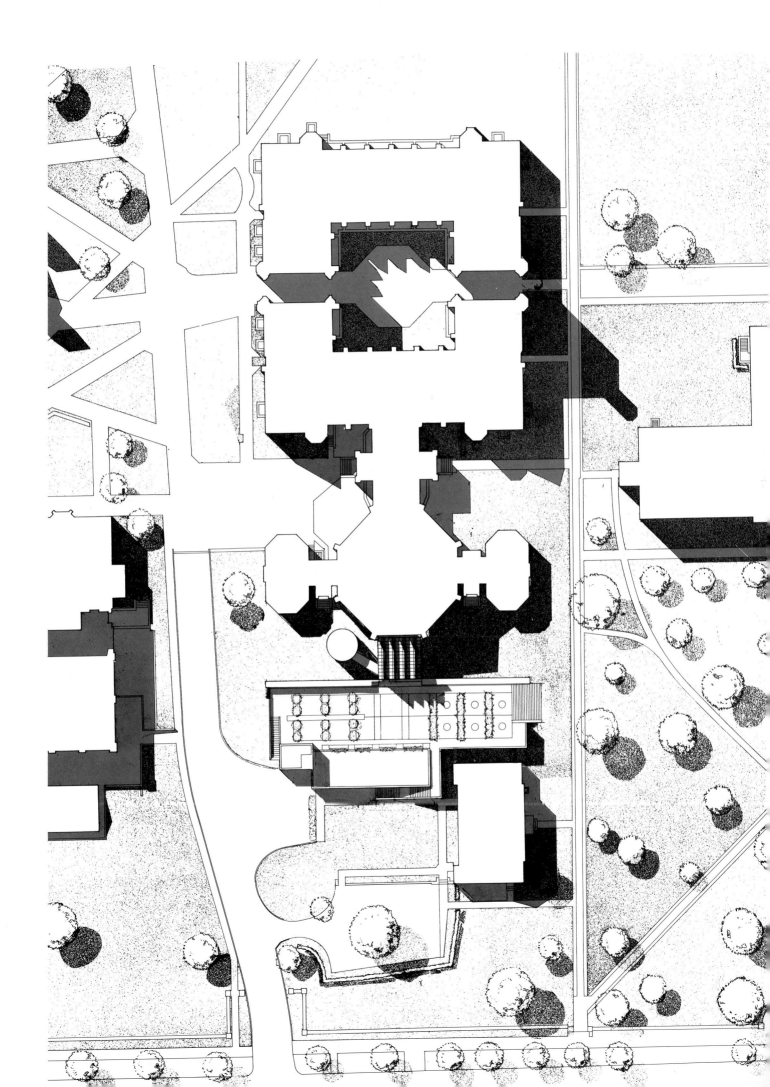

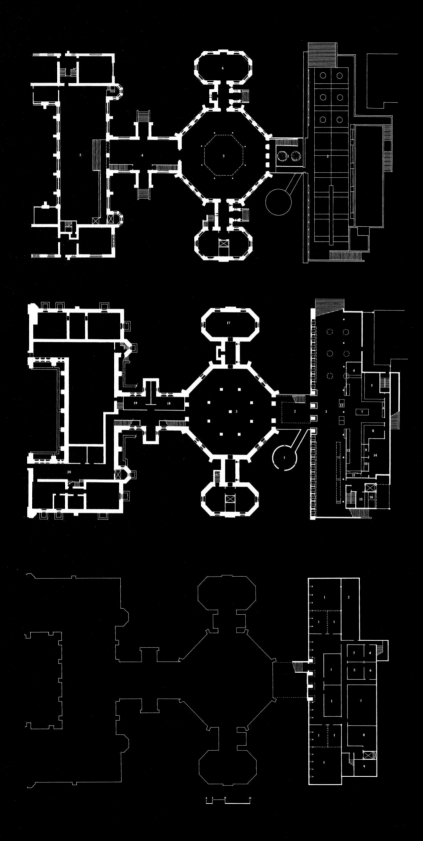

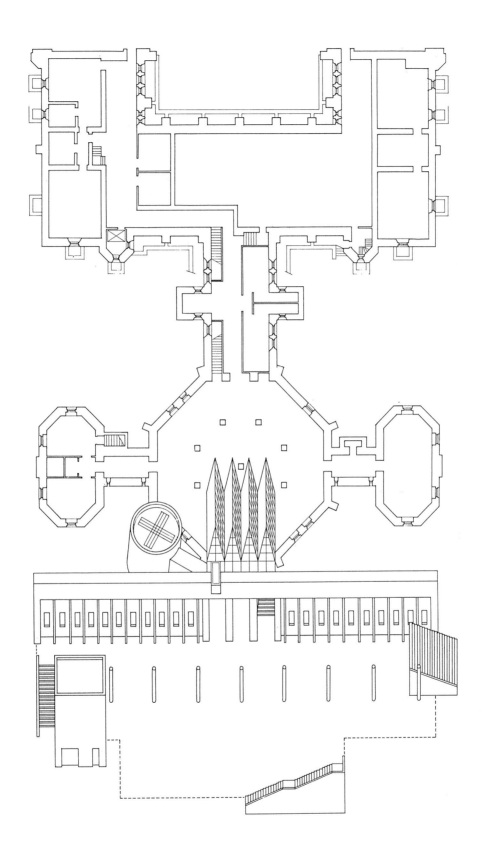

above, top to bottom: Plan of existing renovated buildings with axonometric of new Campus Center

facing page, top to bottom: Roof garden level; New entrance level; New underground level

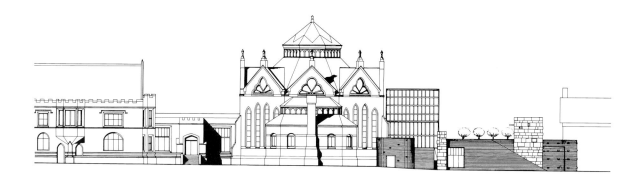

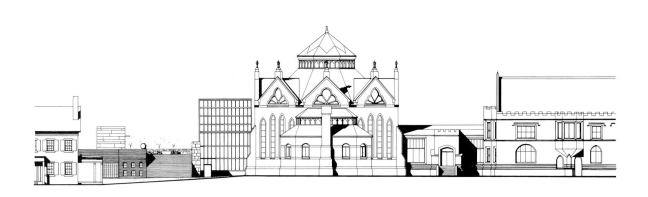

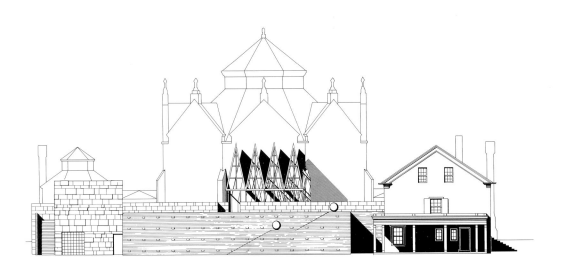

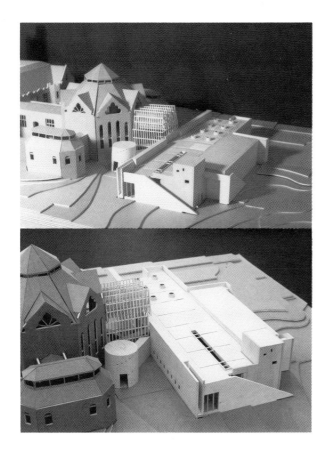

facing page, top to bottom: East elevation with new entry; West elevation with stairs connecting roof garden and Nassau Green and glass interchange; North elevation

this page: Model views

GATE

Cranbrook Academy, Bloomfield Hills, Michigan, 1991–92

The gate choreographs a minimal arrangement of architectural forms that announces the Cranbrook campus in both its material and symbolic dimension. A new designation of gate needs to be conceived of for this moment in history in which gates are made of cybernetic codes, in which non-physical communication pervades and forms modes of contact, where accessibility is independent from proximity, where the non-place opposes the place-specific urban realm. Instead of a frame holding a gate we propose a roof. Instead of accentuating the vertical plane and the recording of a passage, we privilege the horizontal. The place at the empty center of the gate is occupied by a wall and thus denies accentuating the movement in both directions. The gate becomes more than an "object" in the landscape; it "frames" the landscape and creates a place.

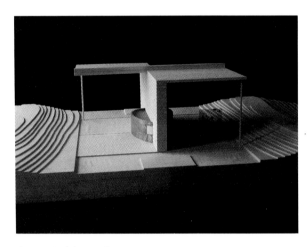

above: Model view from entrance

facing page: View from the car

The gate to Cranbrook is not a static barrier: its forms are derived from the movement of cars coming and going in opposite directions. It is designed for the drivers, both those passing by on Woodward Avenue, and those entering and leaving the community. It represents the effect of speed on a built threshold. It is not just about space, but also fundamentally about time. It is not just about inside/outside or private/public, but about before and after, about coming to a stop and moving again, about sliding by a wall and about traversing the shadow of a roof.

The gate echoes the formal economy of the buildings and spaces of the Cranbrook campus. The double scale of the feature (in the booth and gate) refers to the two scales of Cranbrook's buildings and spaces: the grand scale of the classicist library and art museum, and the picturesque scale of the early buildings. At a syntactic level the gate opens up a rich symbolic field that slides through the twentieth century, focusing on the contemporary issues of time and speed. Finally, the galactic formations represented in the literal gate are given the symbolic role of linking its expression to the Arts and Crafts education while its content refers to the Institute of Science.

The four-foot-thick masonry wall is constructed of reinforced concrete and bears on a "fixed" foundation system capable of withstanding tremendous forces and clad in four-by-four-by-twelve-inch brick. The roof slabs are poured-in-place concrete supported on one edge of the wall, at a perpendicular edge by a one-by-two-foot steel I-beam, and on one corner by an eight-inch-diameter steel column. The roof system is comprised of a four-inch, lightweight concrete slab spanning fourteen inch-deep concrete beams at seven feet on center. This is designed as a spanning "T-beam." The primary support at the center line of the wall is a seventy-foot-long, twenty-one-inch-deep, steel girder supported on a steel concrete composite column at the wall. This girder cantilevers out thirty-five feet to each side of the wall to support two edges of the roof plane. The remaining two edges of the roof planes are supported by concrete beams spanning to a steel column support at the outer corner. Slabs slope out to drain and be heated. The masonry walls of the booth are clad in copper panels two-feet-three-inches square. Curved glass at the window openings is recessed in a metal frame structure. A display cabinet for leaflets, maps, and other information is located on the entry side of the booth. Magnifying mirrors for viewing rear license plates are located as required. Red and gray, square, granite pavers (cobblestone type) are placed in opposite quadrants of the ground plane. Gates are of forged steel frame and galactic pattern on steel mesh, to be raised and lowered by a hydraulic lift system.

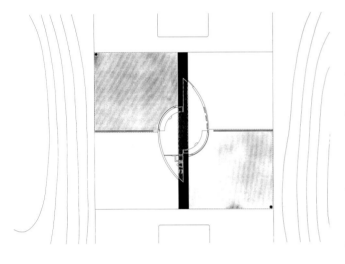

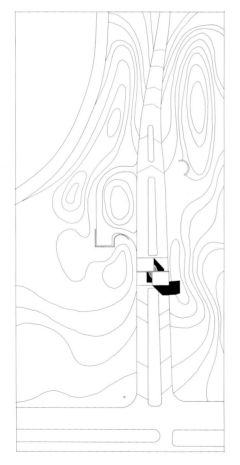

above: Plan

left: Site plan

facing page, top to bottom: Entry side elevation; Orientation elevation

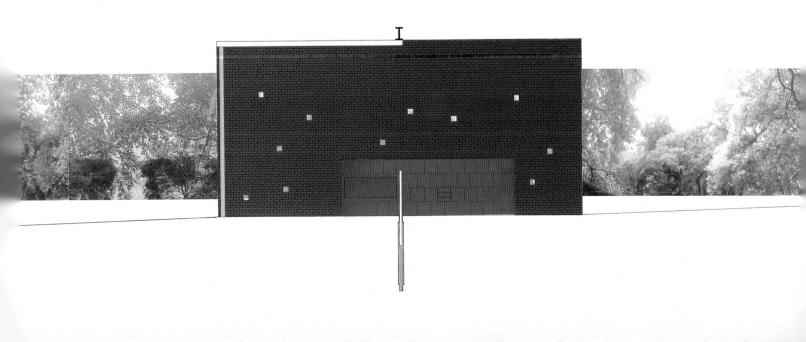

HILLSIDE

Des Moines, Iowa, 1992

Hillside is one of the four downtown neighborhoods proposed by the Des Moines Vision Plan as a way to restore living downtown and reverse the late 1950s flight to the suburbs that created the current vacuum of residential buildings and uses in downtown Des Moines. Hillside is located on a site that slopes one hundred feet north-south from the expressway to the edge of downtown.

Hillside is structured as a checkerboard urban morphology of contrasting green blocks and walled precincts. At the same time, this formal strategy is overlapped with the concept of a sloped park, with interconnected, landscaped, public spaces that promote pedestrian-related activities. A variety of building types sit on top of parking structures from which the vistas of downtown Des Moines can be enjoyed.

Plan and terraces

STREETS AND BLOCKS

The project deals with two different conceptions of the street, first as space defined by urban street walls and second as non-spatial markings on a field (as a way to introduce the notion of the "exurban field of green with objects" into the urban context). This is produced with a checkerboard of superblocks defining street walls and blocks conceived as fields with building objects.

By establishing a checkerboard of city blocks, formed by perimeter blocks defined by street walls contrasted to blocks where free-form buildings or setback buildings allow for green, every building faces green area, bringing one of the advantages of the suburbs — the abundance of green, open space — to downtown.

LANDSCAPING

Our project proposes five concepts for landscaping the sloped park. The first is the overall site concept of terraces, using the existing topography and the alternation of the terraces between hardscape and planted areas. The second refers to the identity of the public and semipublic interior block courts; in every block a major court, with defined access points, is provided. The open space includes the provision of an activity (recreational or cultural) that is unique to that block. The third refers to the network of pedestrian paths that link all the public spaces. A fourth concept is the distinction between deep and shallow planting areas, which results from the location of the lower-level parking structures. The final concept deals with orientation, using trees to accentuate the slope, and hedges to accentuate the terraces.

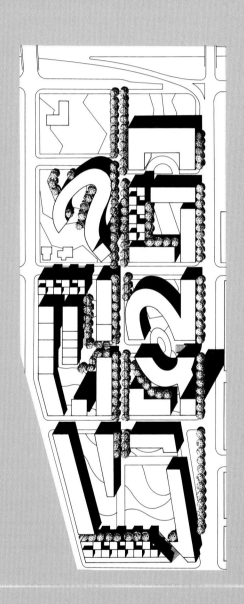

RESIDENTIAL TYPES

Hillside has been designed with a mix of residential types to provide for a variety of different conditions and situations, multiple entrances, and different apartments on top and bottom floors of buildings that take advantage of those conditions. The different residential types are juxtaposed to form hybrid buildings; as part of the overall building footprint, they define an open court or a street. The residential buildings are designed to bring a new scale to downtown. A variety of building and unit types, ranging from three to seven floors, are used independently or combined with other types to constitute the basic building fabric of the neighborhood. A few high-rise buildings with small footprints act as landmarks in contrast to the fabric. The hybrid buildings contain at least two of the following types:

Aerial view of model

Townhouse: a unit with private direct access from grade that has its own vertical circulation and is at least two stories high.

Maisonette: a one-story unit with private direct access from grade.

Apartment building: a building where a maximum of twenty-five units share a lobby from grade.

Penthouse apartment: located on the top level of a building at least two stories high; alternates with equally large private open space.

Duplex apartment: a two-story apartment with its own vertical circulation; may be located on any level of a building.

This list is not restrictive of other types including single-family or single-family attached units as long as they are a minimum of two stories high and are located where such height is allowed.

SCALE

The existing blocks too big (300 by 600 feet) to promote pedestrian use are fragmented with new internal streets to a smaller size and scale. These internal "streets" are intended to downsize the regular blocks to a scale more appropiate to residential use. The intersections, which create corners vital to the life of the street, occur every 200 to 300 feet. The pedestrian circulation system, a network of walkways linking public and private spaces throughout the neighborhood, transforms the scale of the existing Des Moines block structure.

MIXED USE

Although Hillside is a predominantly residential neighborhood, the establishment of commercial and professional uses and retail appropriate to its scale is encouraged. Sidewalk cafes and restaurants are proposed for the blocks adjacent to the downtown commercial buildings. Commercial use is allowed at the first or second levels from the lowest grade in some areas. Public as well as private uses are encouraged in the commercial/office areas. Commercial use is divided into two types: at the scale of the city on the southern edge and at the neighborhood scale in the core of the residential district.

PARKING

Parking has been conceived as a "base" for the buildings and public spaces (under-building and under-plaza parking) to serve residential units as well as downtown parking needs. The sloped site also allows for the implementation of a new parking strategy that makes parking structures under the buildings a possibility on much of the site, and a new type of grade-level connection to the existing skywalk system. The direct access from residential units to parking is considered essential for the success of Hillside in its attempt to compete successfully with the suburbs

THE URBAN GAZE

Seeing and being seen is another reason to encourage the "stepped" approach to building and landscape that allows for a maximum of units with views toward downtown and the capitol. At the same time, Hillside, in particular its roofscape, will become an object of viewing for the downtown high-rise buildings.

top: Model looking south

middle: Model looking north

bottom: Model looking east

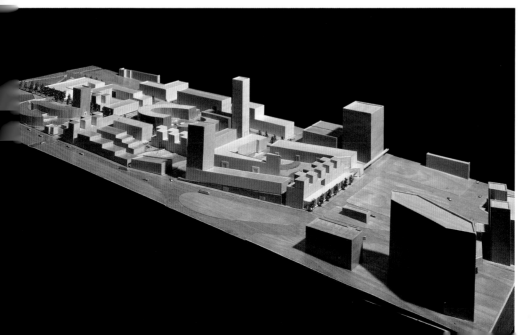

DES MOINES INTERNATIONAL AIRPORT

Des Moines, Iowa, 1992

The Des Moines International Airport is the major airport facility in central Iowa. It serves the state's capital city and provides the region with most of its aviation services.

Our project develops one of the basic concepts proposed by the Des Moines Vision Plan: the airport as the national and international gateway to Des Moines, as a sequence of architectural events that will provide travellers with an initial impression of the city.

The various landscaping and architectural interventions in the construction of this initial reading of Des Moines take place on Fleur Drive, the road that links downtown Des Moines to the airport via the airport forecourt and parking, the airport infield and the large agricultural fields that frame it, and the airport building.

The various "green" strategies developed in this project relate to three different viewing positions: the pedestrian inside and outside the terminal building, the automobile driver in the streets and highways adjacent to the terminal, and the airplane passenger when landing and taking off. The specific tactics are therefore developed in a variety of scales from the interior spaces of the terminal building to the colossal scale of the agricultural fields marked by the continental grid.

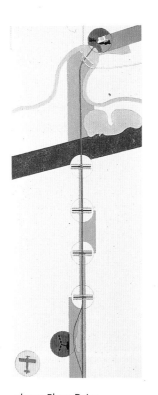

above: Fleur Drive

facing page: The large frame

FLEUR DRIVE

Fleur Drive is a major gateway into the city from the airport, and as such it provides one of the visitor's first impressions of Des Moines. While there is a large amount of open, green space between the airport and downtown along Fleur Drive, especially the Arie den Boer Arboretum adjacent to downtown, the street in the proximity of the airport is a typical suburban strip. Our project proposes to turn Fleur Drive into a continuous greenway, a green, commercial boulevard from the airport to downtown with commercial development concentrated in the major street intersections that occur at half-mile intervals along the way, which are to be designed for the view from a moving car.

AIRPORT FORECOURT AND PARKING

One of the most beautiful assets of Des Moines is the Arie den Boer Arboretum, a repository of over 300 varieties of crabapple trees set against a background of evergreen and deciduous trees. The project suggests the extension of the arboretum as a continuous link from the airport forecourt to downtown Des Moines.

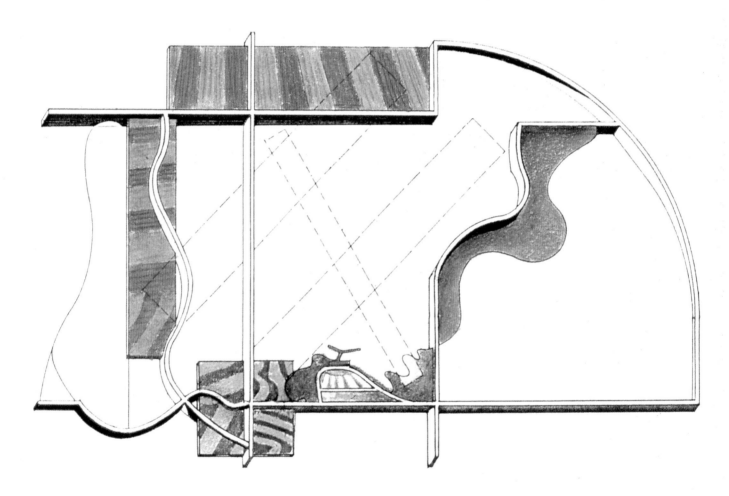

The design of the forecourt, which fades into a meadow landscape, establishes a contrast with the arboretum. The parking is conceived as a warped two-dimensional composition. The area is graded up and down to protect the view from Fleur Drive, hiding the vehicular parking. Trees are added to the meadow, creating a pattern to be viewed from the air, just before landing. A three-to-four-foot-high elliptical burm frames the plaza as a transition between the terminal building and the parking area while it also serves as a green screen for the parking area.

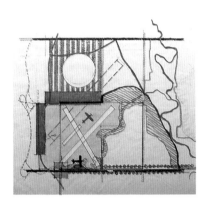

The infield/the large frame

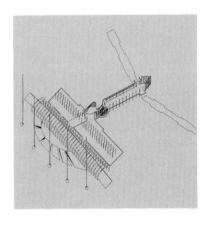

Plan of new central spine

THE INFIELD/THE LARGE FRAME

The infield, where the planes take off and land, is comprised of strips of mown grass located between the runways. By mowing this area at different heights, a pattern is created to be viewed from the air.

This pattern becomes a formal element within the large frame developed to define the edge of the airport through a number of landscape and architectural strategies. Agricultural fields designed to be perceived from the air, as well as from the car, as a large-scale landscape device play as a counterpoint to the arboretum. A smaller-scale pattern is used to emphasize the unbuilt areas at the intersections of Fleur Drive and the avenues that delimit the airport.

AIRPORT TERMINAL BUILDING

The major elements included in the project involve improvements inside the existing airport terminal building, the central circulation from the gates to the baggage and ticketing area, and a new canopy and a plaza in front of the terminal building.

Our project proposes to restructure a "central spine" of public spaces, including a double-height waiting area adjacent to the main entrance, a restaurant, a bridge linking the restaurant with the gate-access gallery, and a cafe with a viewing area at the end of the stem past the security checkpoint.

A large-scale canopy becomes the new three-dimensional facade for the terminal building. The new canopy will cover the sidewalk, the roadway in front of the terminal, the two taxi lanes, and the median separating them. The canopy, seventy feet high and seventy feet wide, creates a vaulted space for the entire length of the airport terminal building. The vault is formed by ribs made of metal plates that taper at the bottom, and is enclosed by a translucent, fabric, tensile canopy made of Kevlar. Lighting the canopy from below makes the vault a major element in the Des Moines landscape at night.

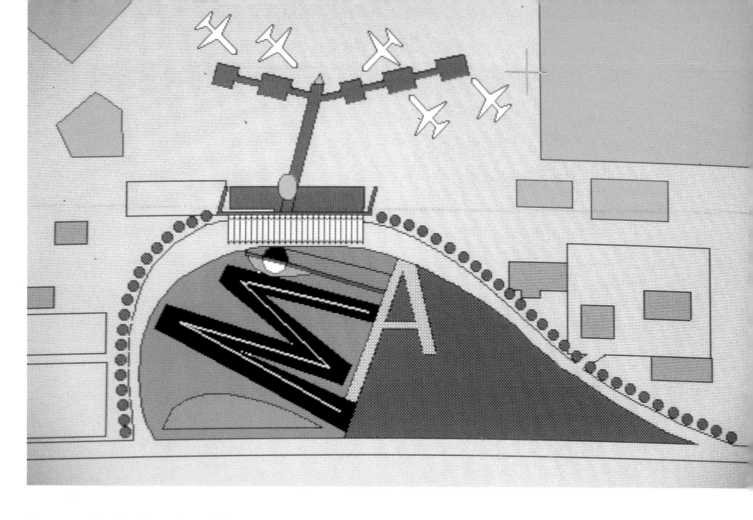

Forecourt and parking alternatives 1 and 2

THE MACHINE IN THE GARDEN

China Basin, San Francisco, California 1989–91

Diana Agrest

This work explores the conditions that articulate the notions of nature and architecture in the ideology of modernist urbanism. It focuses on the *American city,* a city that regulates (suppresses or generates) pleasure through the presence of *object buildings,* indicating the repetition of a symptom that goes back to the original urban scene/sin, the violation of *nature* by the *machine.*

Nature had always been a referent for western architectural discourse from the age of Vitruvius through the Renaissance. Beauty, the most important property of buildings, was supposed to result from the representation of nature. In the twentieth century, nature reappeared in the urban discourse not as a part of an architectural metaphoric operation but as an element in an urbanistic metonymic construct, as in Le Corbusier's Ville Contemporaine and Radiant City. Since the aftermath of WWII, nature has been absent, though unnoticed, from the urban discourse. However, we can better see the question of nature and the city in relation to the American city.

The American city developed through time on a conflictive opposition between nature (the rural country) and culture (the city). The city was first seen as a negative, while nature embodied everything positive (God). When the fontier line started to move westward and the wilderness became something to be conquered, the city became the positive term of the conflict. Nature, now representing the danger of the unknown, became the negative sign. This conflict between city and country became explicit with the discovery of the great potential of the machine, which altered rural life and thus the pastoral ideal.

The conflict between nature and the city can be better understood in light of the conflict between nature and the machine—with the locomotive representing the machine that interrupts the peacefulness of the idyllic countryside, that slashes the virgin land leaving its scars behind, paradoxically destroying what it wants to discover.

Together with the machine, the train crossing the land generated another phenomenon, that of the appropriation and subdivision of land and the concomitant plans for towns and cities. The Jeffersonian rural, one-mile grid became an urban footprint cancelling the opposition between country and city.

The gridding of America should be seen as the creation of the real modern city, an abstract Cartesian grid with no past, traced on virgin land, a condition that Le Corbusier claimed for his Radiant city.

From a general opposition nature/culture, another opposition develops more specific to architecture: nature/city or nature/architecture. This new opposition is articulated in the form fabric/object entering the architectural urban discourse as the historical city—fabric—versus the "modern city"—object—on a green plain. In its application what remains of the opposition is only object, while the green plain (nature) disappears.

Nature is represented in the imagery of modernist urbanism as an artificial construct or as mechanized nature. For Le Corbusier, architecture starts by establishing an artificial ground. "Machinism," as scientific ideology, instrumental in the political and economic realm, is at the base of the architectural and urban ideology that results in its development in the supression of nature.

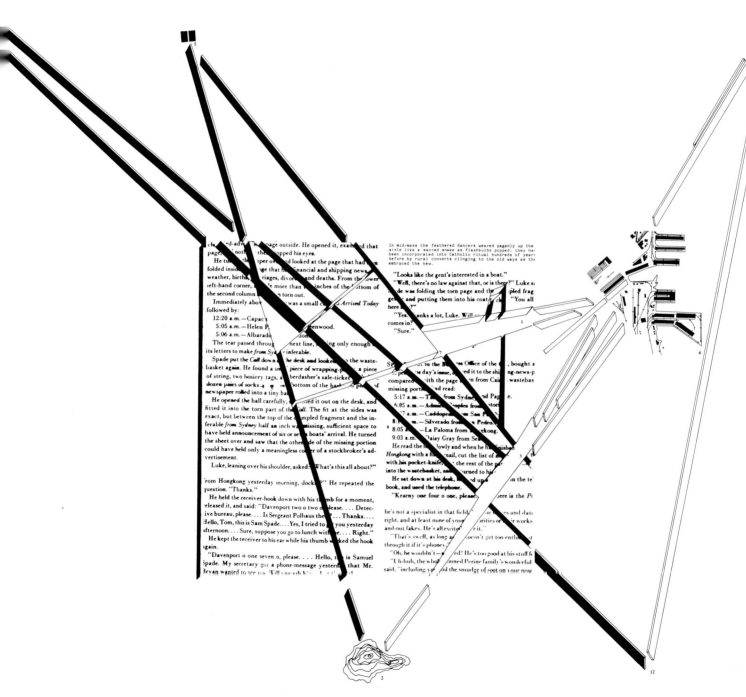

In mid-mass the feathered dancers weaved paganly up the aisle like a sacred snake as flashbulbs popped; they had been incorporated into Catholic ritual hundreds of years before by rural converts clinging to the old ways as they embraced the new.

cha___ed-adv___ __ _age outside. He opened it, exam___ed that page, __ noth___ the___ opped his eyes.

He tu___ ___per ov___ ed looked at the page that had ___ folded insid___ __ge that _is ___nancial and shipping new_, weather, birth_, ___riages, divor__ _nd deaths. From th___ower left-hand corner, __ __e more than __ inches of the ___ttom of the second column __ __ n torn out.

Immediately abo___ _ was a small c___ _ _a Arrived Today followed by:

    12:20 a.m.—Capac__ __
    5:05 a.m.—Helen P__ ___enwood.
    5:06 a.m.—Albarado ___ __dom__ __

The tear passed throu___ _next line, ___ing only enough __ its letters to make from Sy__ _inferable.

Spade put the *Call* down on _he desk and looke___ __ the waste-basket again. He found a sm___ piece of wrapping-p___ _ a piece of string, two hosiery tags, a__ berdasher's sale-ticke__ _ __ dozen pairs of socks _ __ ___ottom of the b___ __ p___ of newspaper rolled into a tiny ba___

He opened the ball carefully, ___ _med it out on the desk, and fitted it into the torn part of the ___ *oll.* The fit at the sides was exact, but between the top of the ___mpled fragment and the in-ferable *from Sydney* half an inch w___missing, sufficient space to have held announcement of six or se___ _s boats' arrival. He turned the sheet over and saw that the other___de of the missing portion could have held only a meaningless co___ _r of a stockbroker's ad-vertisement.

Luke, leaning over his shoulder, asked: "What's this all about?"

_rom Hongkong yesterday morning, dock___?" He repeated the question. "Thanks."

He held the receiver-hook down with his th___mb for a moment, ___eleased it, and said: "Davenport two o two o __ lease. . . . Detec-_ive bureau, please. . . . Is Sergeant Polhaus the___ . . . Thanks. . . . Hello, Tom, this is Sam Spade. . . . Yes, I tried to __ you yesterday _fternoon. . . . Sure, suppose you go to lunch with __ e. . . . Right."

He kept the receiver to his ear while his thumb w___ked the hook _gain.

"Davenport o one seven o, please. . . . Hello, t___ is Samuel Spade. My secretary got a phone-message yesterd__ that Mr. Bryan wanted to see ___. _Will ___ ___ ___ ___ _ __ ___

"Looks like the gent's interested in a boat."

"Well, there's no law against that, or is there?" Luke sa___ _de was folding the torn page and the ___pled frag-ge___ and putting them into his coat __ ch___ "You all here ___ _?"

"Yes ___anks a lot, Luke. Will ___ _ _ comes in?"

"Sure."

S___ ___ _ut to the B___ ___ss Office of the ___, bought a ___ pr___ __s day's issue, o___ ___ed it to the shi___ng-news-p___ compared ___ ___ith the page ___ __n from Cair__ wastebas missing port___ __ad read:

    5:17 a.m.—T___ from Sydney ___ d Pap___ _e.
    6:05 a.m.—Adm___ ___oples from ___ _ _tor__
    ___:37 a.m.—Caddope___ ___om San F___ __
    8:___ _.m.—Silverado fro___ __n Pedro__
    8:05 a.m.—La Paloma from ___ __tkong.
    9:03 a.m.—__aisy Gray from Se___

He read the l__ _lowly and when he h__ ___nished *Hongkong* with a f__ ___nail, cut the list of ___ __ _ with his pocket-knife, __ _t the rest of the p___ __ __ into the wastebasket, an__ ___urned to hi__

He sat down at his desk, ___ ___ed up___ __ __ n the te___ book, and used the telephone.

"Kearny one four o one, please___ __ ___ere is the P___

he's not a specialist in that field__ ___ the ___es and date_ right, and at least none of you___ ___orities o__ _ r works __ and-out fakes. He's all excite__ __ er it."

"That's swell, as long a__ ___ doesn't get too enth___ _t through it if it's phones_ __ __ __

"Oh, he wouldn't—__ __ _ed! He's too good at his stuff f__

"Uh-huh, the who___ __mned Perine family's wonderful___ said, "including y o___ __d the smudge of soot on your nos__

CHINA BASIN

This work takes place in the urban realm, where the city as object of desire is transformed into the city as the place where the forces of desire are set free.

Nature and machine join in the creation of collective territories. Residues of the forces that traverse the subject—the memories, the emotions, the rationalizations, the history, the stories, the assumed knowledge—are fixed by lines, by marks that project the forces of desire. The survival of an experience.

An urban realm discloses the historical role of the notion of "nature as female," a key in the struggle for power and the engendering of power. The conception of the world as a machine in fetishistic architecture allows the double domination of nature and woman. Throughout the design, the unconscious, conscious, and physical relationships between body, nature, and machine are examined.

In China Basin, the smooth fabric of nature replaces the striated fabric of the city, which in turn is buried under the site in the form of various street grids—a seamless continuity of activity (of program) flows under the smooth surface of nature. A continuous flux without delimitation.

This project addresses and encourages active production rather than passive consumption, and, in so doing, also redefines the creation of public place. The China Basin project is not intended as a global resolution for future cities, for we do not believe in an all-encompassing urbanism but rather in partial interventions. The project serves as a unique opportunity to examine and ask some pressing questions concerning place, role, and form of urban development at this moment in time.

The China Basin site slopes down from the Embarcadero Freeway towards the water. The scheme assumes the creation of a new natural datum plane related to that of the existing freeway, which in turn is rendered obsolete and transformed into a residential structure. The freeway both defines one edge of the site and indicates the highest point above sea level. The China Basin Canal bounds the northwestern edge of the site. The San Francisco Bay and a field of thirty solar panels supplying power to China Basin facilities lie to the east. An undulating blanket of nature covers the site and is punctuated by curvilinear courtyards varying in function and depth.

Zones of programmatic superimposition and interrelation radiating out of each courtyard are created, thus defining a public place. The boundaries determining various social functions are left in suspense, indetermined, creating areas of programmatic instability, dissolving barriers of institutionalized practice, and reflecting the chance process of urban change in time.

This project proposes to explore the possibilities of using geometries other than the Euclidean, which is at the core of the Cartesian grids of both the American city and early twentieth-century urbanism.

An intermediate level provides most of the movement routes. Horizontal, vertical, and diagonal movement is modeled on an intricate system in which rotating, interlocking reels and platforms allow pedestrians to displace from one place to another. At other levels, more traditional communication routes are present.

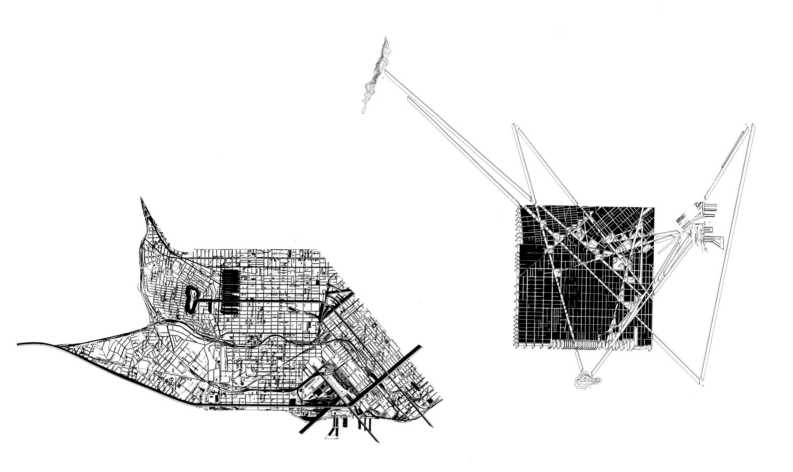

above: Mapping the city through text — (*left*) Locations of narrative; (*right*) Characters and actions

below: Garden China Basin — The machine in the site plan

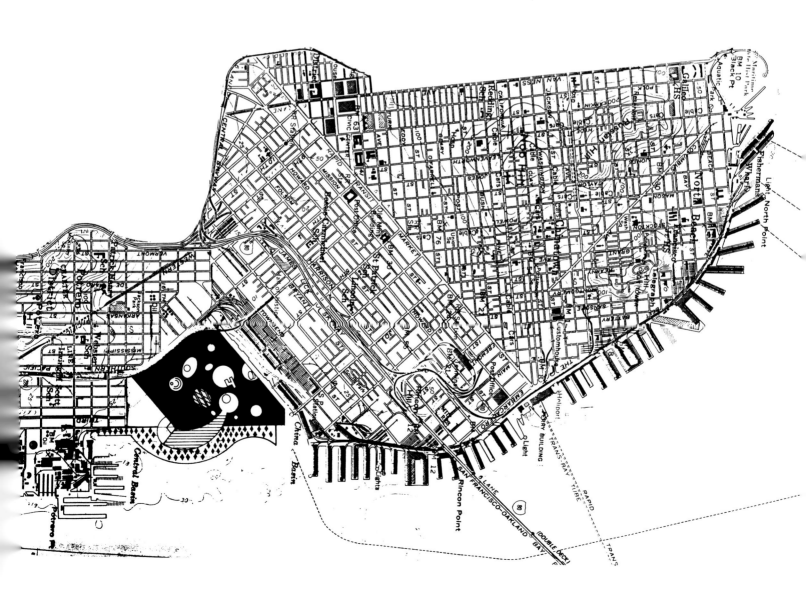

PROGRAMS

1. AMPHITHEATER

2. GENETIC RESEARCH CENTER
Here, a place for the Genome Project, the body as machine is scrutinized on the most scientific and analytic levels.

3. MUSEUM OF THE TWENTIETH CENTURY

4. OLYMPIC TRAINING CENTER
The Olympic Training Center is organized in linear fashion for swimming, running, jumping, skating, etc. The machines for exercising the body further elaborate the relationship between body and machine.

5. RADIO TOWER

6. WORKSHOP
The workshop is a center for production. Space is available for individual or group work in disciplines ranging from the fine arts and literature to cooking and computer animation. Spaces are oriented radially, with the most concrete of physical activities—those requiring the most space—occurring closest to the center. Moving outward, the space becomes more limited and the activities more abstract and conceptual. Sectionally, each discipline occupies an L-shaped space. The individual spaces are stacked vertically while the horizontal space is maintained as a communal area for the exchange of ideas within a discipline. Acting as a two-way panoptic device, the workshops accommodate visual interaction between different disciplines.

7. SEAT-IN SCREENING
The screening studio is a dual "seat-in" open-air film theater with screens oriented back to back. The occupants are protected from the elements and earphones are provided at each seat. The studio is intended to present sporting events and those films not shown in the popular commercial cinema, including experimental films, documentaries, foreign films, and low-budget films.

8. MARKETPLACE
The marketplace is a "mega-automat," where a structure rotates within a series of walkways. The structure itself is composed of four levels where the exchange of merchandise may occur. The consumer travels exclusively along the peripheral walkways, while the central structure rotates around its own axis, thereby making products accessible to the public. Adjacent to the marketplace are agricultural fields and workshops, where items are collected and produced for sale. Only those items produced on the China Basin site would be sold at the marketplace.

9. AQUARIUM AND OCEANOGRAPHIC RESEARCH CENTER

A semicircular wall with a diameter of 500 feet defines the entire site of the aquarium and oceanographic research center, which is composed of three major elements: a primary research tank connected to the China Basin Canal, an elevated aquarium tank, and, adjacent to the primary tank, a three-dimensional grid of pathways giving access to research floor space.

10. BATHS

The notion of *depense* underlies the program and the pleasure of free bodies is able to express itself. The baths symbolize the intentions of the project as a whole. In this natural forum for the discourse on the body, the public is encouraged to develop a new vision for the twenty-first century.

11. BASEBALL

12. FIELDS

Here, activities of agricultural experimentation take place, generating products that may be obtained at the market.

13. FIELD OF SOLAR COLLECTORS

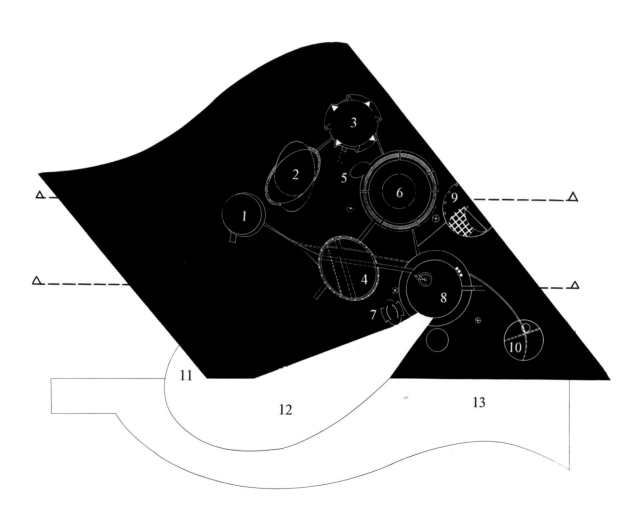

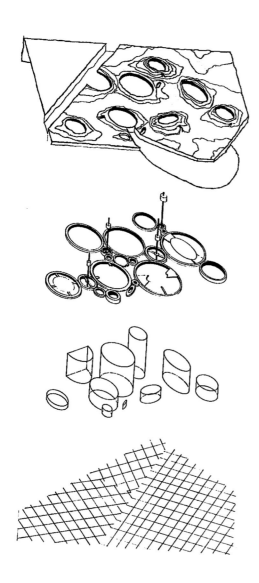

left: Layers of components of project

below: Circulation mechanism model

facing page, top to bottom: Plan movement mechanism; Section through Genetic Research Center workshops and movement system; Section through Olympic Training Center; Section through marketplace

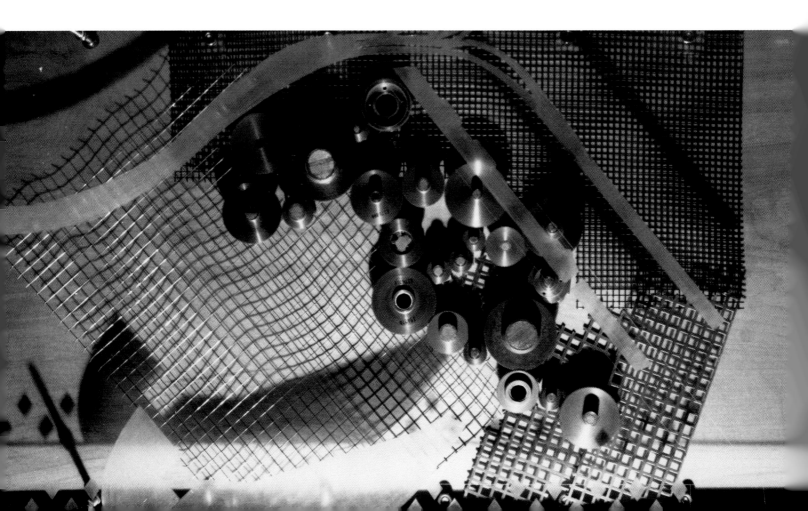

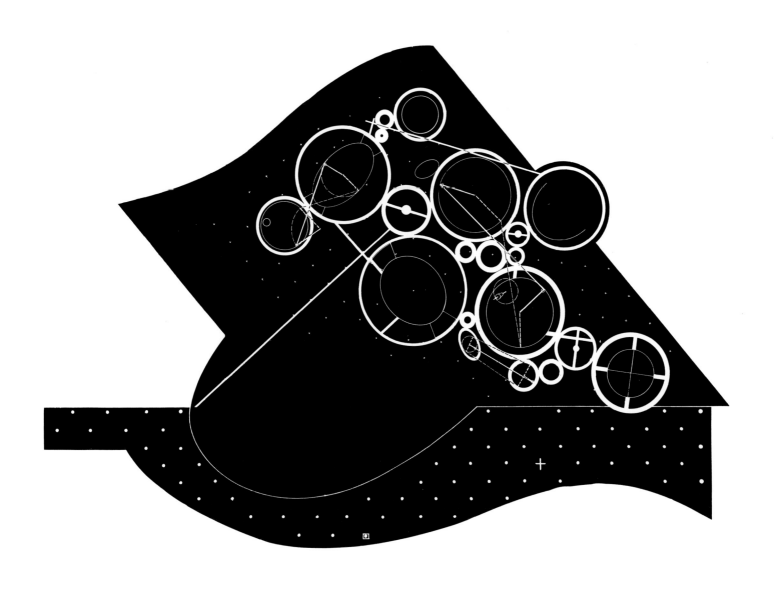

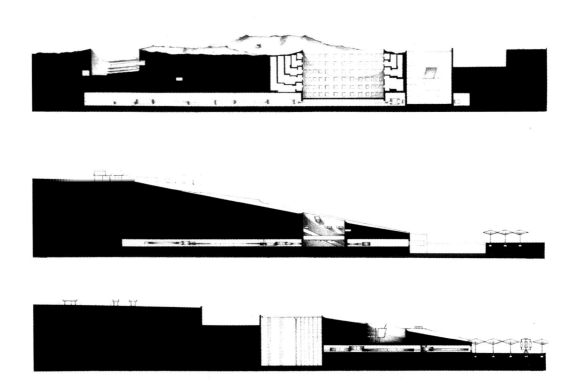

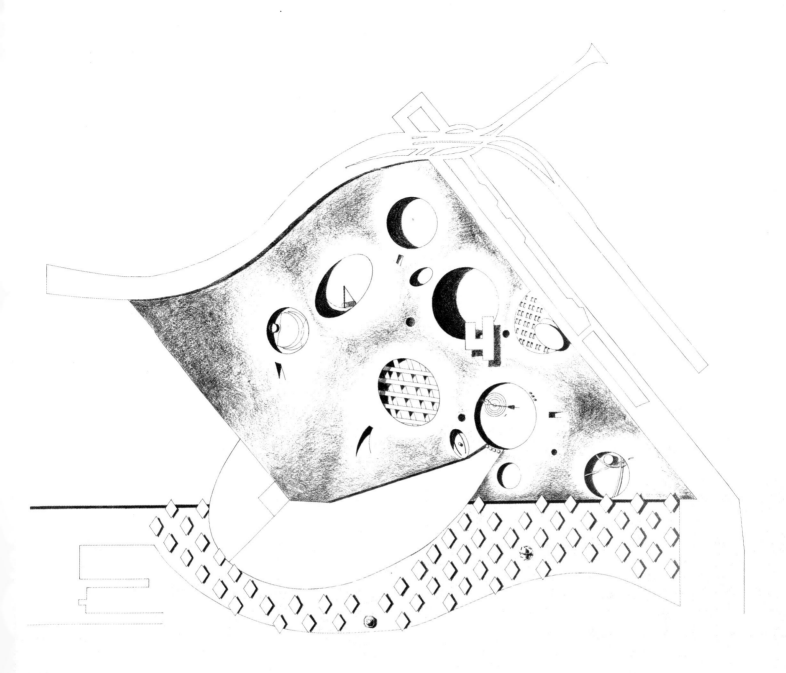

left: Model view

above: Plan at ground level

right: Seat-in screening

Nature and machine join in the creation of collective territories. Residues of the forces that traverse the subject, the memories, the emotions, the rationalizations, the history, the stories, and the assumed knowledge are fixed by lines, by marks that project the forces of desire—"the survival of an experience."

A movement flows through earth and body, reaching through the gaze and into the depth of the universe, in the framing of infinitude, in the folding, collapsing of the sky onto the earth, through edges, borders, the borders of the body. Orifices and borders are the makings of a body.

Border, edge, and frame capture and lose focus in an oscillating movement between the recognizable and the unknown.

The window, border, and frame protect the interiority of the subject from the collective outside, while allowing the eye as shifter to bridge both worlds, while the mirror reflects the gaze back (to us).

A seamless continuity of activity (of program) flows under the smooth surface of nature—a continuous flux without delimitation.

The natural machine— the point where nature, body, and the machine intersect— places the subject and object on the same plane.

The traces of a body of a woman that embodies desire is itself and the other. Woman as gender constructs a new nature.

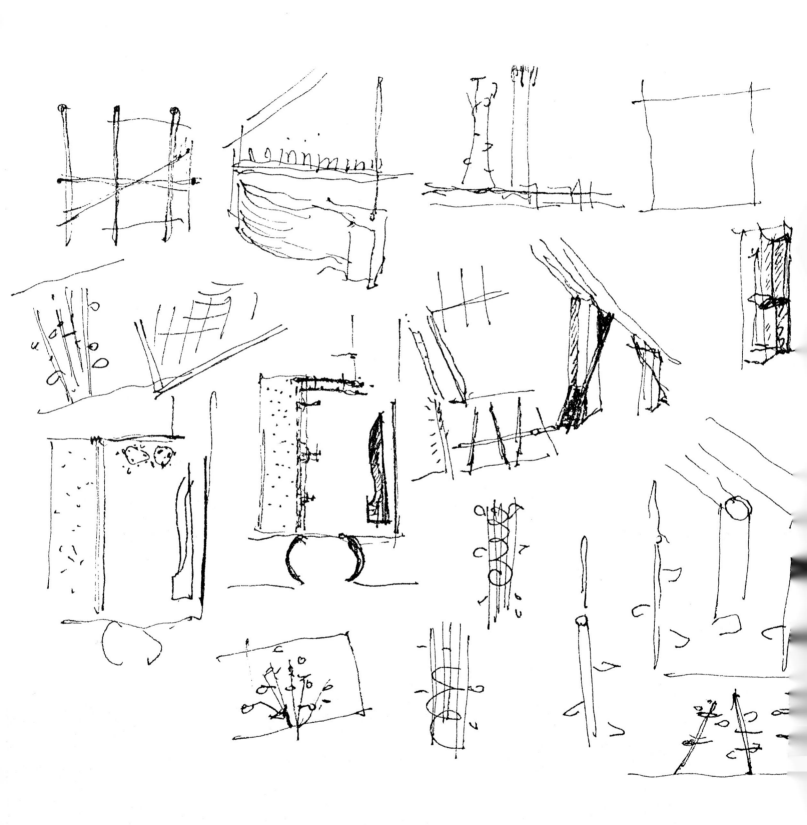

FURNITURE AND OBJECTS

CENTRAL PARK WEST, 1988

top row: Cone Chair (three views) and
Cone Stool, 1989, part of the Cone
Line started in 1985 with the Cone
Sink, stainless steel and leather

bottom row: Mannequin Chair and
Ottoman, 1989, pear wood and leather

left, top and center: Flamingo Table,
1989, stainless steel and mahogany

left, bottom: Central Park West
Settee, 1989, silk velvet

above: Central Park West Chair (three
views), 1989, silk velvet

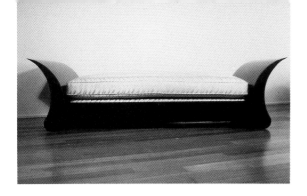

CENTRAL PARK WEST, 1988

top to bottom: DIA Daybed, 1989, makerai and silk; Suspended Elliptical Table, 1989, crutch mahogany and hot-rolled steel; Suspended Circular Table, 1989, crutch mahogany and hot-rolled steel; Coffee Table, 1989, stainless steel and glass; Side table, 1989, mahogany and hot-rolled steel

facing page: STOPPAGE BAR, 1988

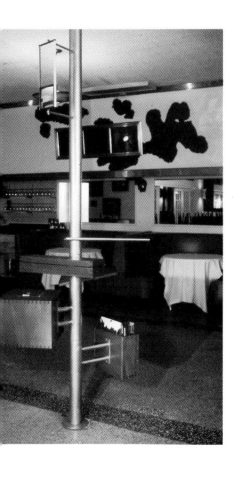

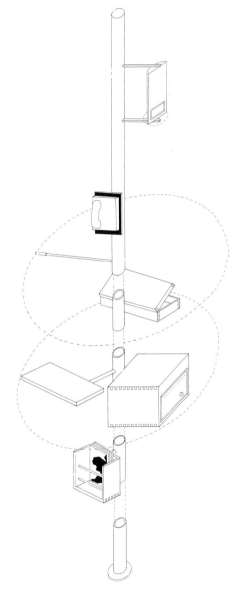

above: CANAL BAR, 1988
Maitre d' station, stainless steel and mahogany

top to bottom: Menu holder, stereo control, appointment book support,
tape/cd holder, light for maître d', phone, rearview mirror

facing page: BEACH STREET LOBBY, 1988
Reception station in steel and granite

SCREEN, 1990

The screen, made of cherry wood structure and parchment panels, filters the light coming from the windows. It is meant to work with the geomantic evaluation of the space. A plane on the entrance hall disengages itself from the wall and becomes a free-standing screen.

The screen is composed of three sections that move 360 degrees. Each section in turn is formed by three vertical units, holding seven staggered parchment panels each, which also move so that they may vary from creating a continuous flat plane to more diverse combinations of formal organization.

As a film screen, it works with the light as a rear projection so that shadows insinuate bodies in movement behind. The screen is to the body as the fan is to the face. They are objects of seduction through modesty.

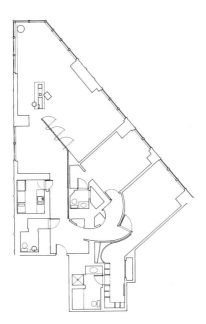

left: Apartment plan

right: View of screen from dining area in a planar configuration

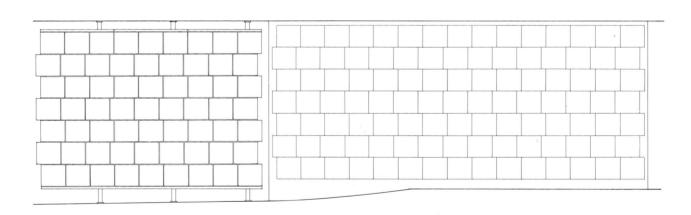

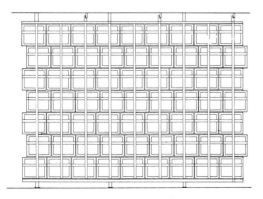

top left: View of parchment panel wall in hallway and screen with rotated panels

top center: View of bar station and screen from living room

top right: View of screen dividing living room from dining area and entry hallway

facing page: Screen structure and bar

Oro Azul Temporary Exhibition Pavilion for a domestic appliance company, Buenos Aires, Argentina, 1969

~~architecture~~ ARCHITECTURE

The term "architecture" refers to a set of more or less systematized representations and beliefs about the built world and the practices related to it historically, defined within Western culture as "classical architecture" or "modern architecture." We will refer to it as "architecture." The term "Architecture" refers to the production of knowledge about that built world and those related practices. Architecture as production of knowledge is developed as critical work on architecture.

This text, as part of a more general theoretical work on architecture, is placed in an eccentric position within the field delimited by "architecture," and at a certain distance from the rules that constitute its core. From this position we intend to confront a number of questions, to break the monolithic appearance of architecture, to disarticulate the illusion of unity sustained through the rhetorical structures of the architectural discourse. The present historical moment demands a radical change in the practice of architecture. Instead of adding architectural products to the already existing ones, we should produce knowledge about "architecture" and its effects.

THE WRITTEN TEXT

This written text is part of the critical "deconstructive" work on architecture. Its function is to indicate the place of this production in relation to "architecture" and the impossibility and uselessness of its recuperation by "architecture," to unearth the repressive mechanisms within architecture that obscure the conditions that determine the architectural discourse and its practice, to disclose through their subversion the mechanisms that preserve its limits, and to produce knowledge on architecture as a historically defined class ideology.

THE ~~SYSTEM OF RULES~~ INDICATION

If by architecture we mean the (conscious or unconscious) system of rules used by architects to produce form, as well as to recognize these objects and buildings as architectonic—and distinguish them from those that are not—our work is an attempt to indicate the prescriptive and conventional nature of that system of rules: to make it explicit, to produce knowledge of it, not to work blindfolded within it, and to undermine it.

Some of the implicit rules of the system of architecture are:

1. The constructive "truth" that requires the exhibition of structure, of the "soul" of the building and devalues both "surface" and "ornament," both disavowed but necessary as "sin" is necessary to define "virtue." The function of this constructive truth is to hide the formal work of the architect, to hide the conventional nature—which is culturally determined—by subordinating it to building systems and technology. Its effect is the naturalization of form as the simple result of technology.

2. The correct "fit" to functional requirements implies seeing the building as something to be "used" (its function) at the point when we read its signification. This reading of the object as linked to a function is one of the typical ideological mechanisms in our culture. "We believe in a practical world of

uses, of functions, but we live in a world of sense, of reasons." (Barthes) The function of fitness to use is to hide the symbolic aspects, the work on meaning, which is thus associated with art, with the "irrational." Its effect is the naturalization of form as simple result of utility or use.

3. The "expression" is rendered by means of a repetition through transformations and variations of a formal system by means of rules that are never made explicit. The function of expression is to hide the conscious-unconscious work on form and meaning, which is seen as the product of intuition or inspiration. Its effect is the naturalization of form as a simple result of the artist's expression.

Work within Architecture does not define itself by constructive truth, utility, or expression; rather it is a work of indication and production of knowledge. At the present time we should raise the question of the object (and the subject) of architecture, and architecture itself as a signifying practice, as production of meaning.

Is it possible to think with objects? No, if they are considered as product and result of architecture; yes, if they are considered as one of the texts embodying a particular theoretical work.

~~THEORY/PRACTICE~~ PRACTICES

Architecture is an ambivalent activity, a resolution of the contradiction between design and building, theory and practice.

"Theory" is defined in architecture as everything related to this activity except building, that is, design and written texts. "Practice" is applied to the building of the object—as a final goal, as the only practice.

We believe that in Architecture both aspects are to be considered as practice. Practice will be defined in this text as a process of transformation on a given primary matter whose result is something new, something different from the given elements of the initial primary matter. This work of transformation subverts the ideological reproduction or repetition of the primary matter. The theoretical work as part of Architecture is to be considered as practice even without effective design or buildings. Instead the design or building are not to be considered as practice if there is no production of knowledge through them.

The distinction between theory and practice as it has been understood up to now—projects or texts on one hand, built objects on the other—is no longer pertinent. Instead, another distinction should be established: The ideological practice of architecture as it relates to an overall ideology should be distinguished from the practice of Architecture, which constructs an "analytical zone" where the rhetoric and ideological systems of architecture are criticized and radically transformed.

At this juncture, the production of knowledge on architecture is crucial—a work that implies an eccentric position, a certain distance, a displacement of architecture, and its inscription in history and the social.

~~CONSUMPTION~~ READING

Architecture should not be consumed only by the sight or the feeling of space. The deciphering of Architecture is only possible through understanding, through the work of reading at various levels. Instead of a single unitary reading we propose multiple readings. The multiple readings proposed subvert the double consumption imposed by the system: that of the architect and of the layman. In both cases these readings propose a work on meaning. Objects in isolation

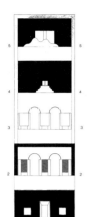

above:
Pierre Cardin 1,
isonometric

left:
Pierre Cardin 1,
plan

below:
Pierre Cardin 2,
axonometric

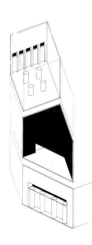

present known meaning, but in context they present other meanings as well, sometimes even contradictory among themselves.

But to work with the meaning of objects is not to say that we attempt to create new symbols or new rhetoric systems—we are interested in the objects' potential for indication, for the dissemination of sense, and not to "communicate" systems of meanings responding to a historically defined logic (ideology).This work does not attempt to refer to an established code; it rather points at the deconstruction of the "oppositions" created by the system.

~~OBJECT-PRODUCT~~ PRODUCTION

The object of architecture is the formal-physical construct designed by the architect to fit a function (technical, of use or aesthetic). In this system the work of design is only a means for the architect to produce a building, a production that is eclipsed by the object-product.

From this operation we are left with two remainders: the drawing and the building. They represent precisely the two places where the work on signification takes place. A work is hidden in architecture by the set of notions indicated before—truth, fitness, expression, theory/practice, form/function—and by the complicity between rhetoric and ideology, by the circulation and repetition of form that hide the reproduction of the same ideology.

The specific dynamic of the production of architecture can be defined by the articulation of three texts: the written text (writing), the graphic text (drawing), the physical text (place). None of these texts represent the other two. There are points of similarity but they allow the accentuation of the differences and heterogeneity that separates them.

~~FORM/FUNCTION~~ SIGNIFICATION

Instead of looking at objects exclusively as a physical form adjusted to a certain function, they will be considered as symbolic production, as produced by a practice that through them or their design-construction manipulates meanings. They cannot be thought outside their condition of carriers of meanings as the effect of a complex writerly practice or of a reading that organizes that meaning. As a static effect, as a presence, the object hides the signifying practices related to it, replacing them by a pseudo-correlation with function. Both terms of this relationship appear as naturally linked. They are reciprocally defined in a tautological circularity. It is from this tautology that we propose to get away in order to understand that both forms (objects, buildings) and functions should be considered as one of the possible choices out of an infinite range of possibilities. The form-function relationship in architecture allows us to articulate objects within the system of social action, as mediators between man and action, between man and the world, but at the same time it forbids the understanding of another deeper systematic organization of objects that goes beyond mere formalism or economism. As the introduction of the problem of meaning into the consideration of objects and the environment takes the place presently occupied by the form/function relationship as the subject matter of architecture, it necessitates the reorganization of that activity. Architecture is thus transformed from a mask that hides the real functioning into a practice of Architecture as demystification, as production of a specific knowledge. The task of Architecture consists in clarifying the place of architectural ideology within general ideology, within history, and thus its linkages with a mode of production, a social class, and a given social formation.

ON PRACTICE, 1978

THE CRITICAL PRACTICE

A critical practice is developed as a process acting both at the level of architectural ideology, that is, on architectural and other related ideas and notions, and at the level of projects (forms) and buildings. This process sets up a confrontation between the discourses and buildings that persist within architecture and other discourses and buildings that exist external to it.

We confront the current architectural ideology and discourse with the discourse of linguistic theory. We confront the current architectural lexicon and syntax with the vocabulary and syntax belonging to the urban realm, the city. We begin this confrontation by marking out a space, a distance between architectural discourse and other, foreign discourses, between architectural buildings and spaces and built forms and spaces that are not considered architectural.

Architectural discourse and buildings have always been seen, until the arrival of the Modern Movement, without distance, that is from an architectural point of view or, in other terms, from a point of view located within architectural boundaries and definitions. Within such a situation, a truly critical approach is impossible. The Modern Movement's successful contestation of classical architecture is due in part to the introduction of external, sometimes foreign, discourses and models—the discourse of abstract geometry as opposed to architectural geometry, the discourse of industrial imagery, of the machine. These external discourses and forms are still viable as challenging instances, but their nature must be reassessed.

We begin a reassessment through the challenge of two other discourses, linguistic theory and the city, by which we criticize both the lack of a distanced position characteristic of architectural discourse that accepts and works within the ideological limits historically imposed on it without questioning them, without a critical attitude; and the isolated position that divorces architectural from cultural issues and rejects a consideration of socio-political contexts.

We propose: 1) that the theory of language, as a critical discourse, and the urban realm, as a critical configuration, allow an understanding of the way a practice of architecture may be articulated within the present ideological and political conjuncture, the theory of language allows the systematic and critical "demontage" of the different varieties (behavioral, sociological, cybernetic, or communicational) of the present functionalist discourse, which implies an architectural practice completely dependent on external forces or meanings and reflecting unproblematically a pregiven order; 2) that the urban realm as a "storehouse" of unexplored configurations allows the critique of the notion of an architectural practice completely detached from political and economic determination, that is, an architecture postulated as an autonomous practice; and 3) that the theory of language and the urban realm introduce into the practice of architecture a recognition of the preeminence of the social through which it exists.

While the linguistic theory provides an abstract model of the social activity par excellence—language—the city provides a physical and symbolic place where the social drama is played out. We propose to build our theoretical practice at the site of this intersection, in relation to the movement of this play of forces.

THE FUNCTION OF THEORY

The theory that we propose is a critical discourse that confronts the most vital forces of architecture—the symbolic force, the forces of meaning production. It is critical because it does not pretend to be purely neutral or descriptive; it does not attempt to naturalize its object. It is a discourse that makes explicit its own rules, questions its own basic assumptions. It is a discourse that confronts formal and symbolic architecture with the conditions of its historical determinations. It confronts architecture with other discourses, establishing a distance from which the fiction of the unitary system of architecture loses its hold.

This new distance allows us to see beyond the simple and unproblematic separation of theory (discourses, drawings) from practice (buildings) to an understanding of the interpenetrations of their multiple and heterogeneous texts. We contest the simple exteriority of practice to theory that tends towards the homogeneity of the sensible against the sense, the subject against the social. Architectural drawings are not simple, completed texts, ideas to be more or less fully realized in completed buildings. Nor are buildings simple texts that completely embody ideas and thus eclipse the need for drawings. Theory and practice, designs and buildings, do not relate simply and directly the one to the other. Rather they relate through subjects (as they are) formed within a social context. We propose a critical theory that investigates three sources of symbolic, formal energies. We investigate not only architecture as subjectivity and architecture as an autonomous institution, but also the formal systems that configure the political, economic, and ideological determinations of the urban realm, and that implicate the other two forces in the investigation.

ON READING

The linguistic and urban models are not reproduced or syntactically recombined in our critical theory. They are read as texts that traverse the architectural discourse and buildings and are at the same time rewritten by them. They provide architecture with an opportunity for abandoning its autonomy and redefining its specificity. Architectural texts are always part of a larger set of texts with which they are designed to engage in a dialogue.

Reading, in the sense that we are using it, is not just a passive consumption of texts, a silent, listening attention, but is an aggressive participation and active appropriation of them. Architectural writing is a reading that has been transformed in actual production. Architecture does not begin at any instant, is not inscribed on a blank page, but continues to rewrite an already written text. The rewriting affects not only the content, but also the form, and the form of dealing with the form, that is, the structure of the text and its relation to ideology.

We call our approach to the design process "design-as-reading"—a reading-transformation of existent architectural texts.

With the exception of the period in which the Modern Movement broke away from classical language, architecture has always been an art of transformation. Elements, and the arrangement of the elements have been transformed in relation to the architectural problems with which they were contemporary. These transformations, however, have moved within certain limits. Beyond these limits one confronts plagiarism or illegibility. In between, the stylistic changes mask the continuity of a deeper conceptual and formal nucleus. We attempt a more critical transformation that acts on the iconic logic in the relationship between image and text. We attempt to test and force these limits not only in order to expose their ideological functioning, but also to forge new symbolic experiences.

THE TRANSFORMATION OF THE ARCHITECTURAL PRACTICE

The consideration of architecture as a text and its practice as writing affects the theory and practice of architecture. Criticism and design have been for a long time distinct and separate practices representing the consumption and production of architectural ideas and forms; that is, they have been considered as opposed instances in the production process. To propose that criticism and design become equivalents of reading and writing is to propose the recognition of a transformation in the practice of architecture—a transformation that erodes the boundaries that separate criticism from practice, the purely theoretical from the purely technical and pragmatic. *We propose, in short, a transgression of boundaries.*

THE QUESTION OF LANGUAGE

The theory of language poses a problem for architecture. The problem is not that of architecture as language, but rather of language in the practice of architecture. We confront the apparent paradox of the situation defined by the impossibility of language and the inevitability of language—"apparent" because, in fact, this is not a simple contradiction. The term "language" that appears in the two phrases names two different referents. When we speak of the impossibility of language, we refer to the specific notion of a natural language, language in the strict sense. When we note this impossibility, we criticize the utopian belief in the possibility of creating a totally structured architectural language and the objective rationalism that presupposes the possibility of a diaphanous communication between the architect and the public. When we speak of the inevitability of language, we refer to the more general notion of language as a system of rules institutionalized through history. Language in this sense is unavoidable and reveals the belief in the possibility of a purely subjective architecture ecstatically expressing itself, as an idealist illusion.

Not to address these issues of the relationship of architecture to language is to avoid the complex problem of elaborating the relationship between the forces that are constituent of the history of architecture as a cultural practice—that is, the relationship between subject and history, between the forces of desire and the forces of the social, between the forces of poetry and the forces of language. To undertake an understanding of the way these forces are sutured in architectural production is to begin an active "writerly" practice of architecture.

THE ORDER OF THE CITY

There was once an urban vision that recognized the cities of Europe and America. European cities were seen as the markings of the development of a civilization. American cities were seen as visions of a new start; their plans resembled those plans for cities that the Renaissance produced—endless grids running from south to north and from east to west.

But modern architecture has forgotten the city. The Modern Movement has attempted to raze the European city that now represents a blind spot in its architectural vision. The American city and its suburbs are perceived as mere hallucinations and their inherent challenge to both classical and modern formal and visual ideology is disavowed. A fetishistic culture is erected on the foundations of the denial. In both cases, the cities represent images of chaos, the one as a residue of the past, the other as a symptom of future disorder. They are held by eyes that do not see the underlying order, the emergence of new typologies that do not exist as part of the history of architecture. The new mode of thinking that the city proffers has no precedent in any part of our memory.

The city is a public place, a place with no function, a place that cannot be consumed. Our design practice takes the city as a point of departure for the development of new critical concepts that reveal the limits and weaknesses of both the urban ideology of the Modern Movement and the simple reversal of this ideology. We use the city as the source for a new vocabulary and a more powerful syntax of architecture.

ON READING THE CITY

Traditional notions of typology propose a complete repertory of types and mechanical formulas for their combination. Within such a system combination is conceived as simple juxtaposition rather than articulation and the elements themselves are left virtually unchanged.

We introduce, through the process of reading that we described, another aspect of types, a dimension that has been repressed by exclusive concentration on structural analyses. We introduce a consideration of symbolic performance. In symbolic performance, the types themselves are transformed and articulated in the confrontation between different languages or systems. Change is motivated by confrontation and not merely arbitrarily, that is, formally, induced. Elements are shifted and recast to produce meanings in a process analogous to that involved in dream production.

Our work exhibits examples of symbolic performance. The French hotel transformed into housing takes advantage of the potential for its public context to invade its private space (Projet Architecture Nouvelle). The column towers in the Roosevelt Island project read as a colonnade. Where the building wall behind and the spaces between are read as fragments of a Greek temple designed in a colossal order. The articulation in these works becomes more important than the types themselves. Entities give way to relations; structures open up, unfinished.

It is a reading of the city that explodes the metaphorics of wholeness inherent in traditional notions of type and traditional notions of architecture as a language system. The city produces the difficulty of (acts as an obstacle to) the static conception of systems. It is the body in excess of its inertia.

The city is an inconsistent multiplicity of discourses figured out simultaneously on its syntagmatic and paradigmatic axes. Its types are an anagrammatic configuration of signifiers. This criss-crossing of axes interrupts the unity of objects within the city. A building within a city cannot be read as an isolated sign or symbol. Rather, its meaning is dispersed along the chains of its relations. Its *mise-en-sequences*, the linear narration of its sequential visions, are violated by other relations that are independent of the syntagmatic logic.

As site of the social drama, the city reveals the implication of metaphoric substitutions in the metonymy of desire. The urban subject is not an isolated, unified individual but a process and a construction of heterogeneous intentions. The Modern Movement's critique of classical language falls short of the idea of unity that this language presupposes. It is this failure that causes the Modern Movement to misrecognize the radical heterogeneity that characterizes the logic of the urban order, and accounts for the lack of theoretical and iconic development, for the impasses at which the final third of this century finds itself.

FRAGMENTS

We distinguish our approach from a simple historicism and from a complex and contradictory picturesqueness by attempting to use a logic of contradiction, through the denial of an originary order and simplicity, through a textual density that is always related to the development of an architectural problem. Moreover, our work is always critical; that is, it always presupposes a parallel theoretical development. Since our designs work within and against classical and modern language, the resulting tensions lead to an explosion of languages and previous texts, to the subversion of the notion of unity, and, as a result, to the notion of "fragments," which might be the starting point or the final stage of the design of buildings and places.

AMNESIA

The actual limit of the process of transformation is the point where the invariant aspect that allows one to recognize an architectural text as a transformation of a previous text—written, drawn, or built—is no longer recognizable, where the memory or reminiscence of the past is lost. *Design implies the transformation of sense, of memory of the known.* It is not only *memory,* but also *amnesia.*

BIBLIOGRAPHY

WRITINGS BY DIANA AGREST AND MARIO GANDELSONAS

"On Practice." *Akshara* (April 1982): 7–15.

"On Practice." *Architecture and Urbanism* 114 (March 1980): 33–38.

"Architecture as Cultural Practice." *Architecture and Urbanism* 114 (March 1980): 39.

"On Practice." *International Architect* 1 no. 1 (1979): 50–51.

"Semiotics and the Limits of Architecture." In *A Perfussion of Signs*, edited by Thomas A. Sebeok,
pp. 90–120. Bloomington: Indiana University Press, 1977.

"Architecture." *L'Architecture d'Aujourd'hui* 186 (August–September 1976): 73–74.

"Semiotics and the Limits of Architecture." *Architecture and Urbanism* 67 (July 1976): 57–70.

"Semiologia e Architettura: Consumo Ideologico Lavoro Teorico." *Controspazio* 1 (October 1975).

"Semiology and Architecture: Ideological Consumption or Theoretical Work."
Oppositions 1 (1973): 93–100.

"Critical Remarks on Semiology and Architecture." *Semiotica* 9 no. 3 (1973): 252–271.

"De La Semiologia, los Objectos Perversos y los Textos Ideologicos." With J.C. Indart.
Summa 32 (1970): 73–74.

WRITINGS BY DIANA AGREST

Architecture From Without: Theoretical Framings for a Critical Practice. Cambridge: MIT Press, 1991.

Memories and Places (catalog on photographic work of Roberto Schezen). Edited and introduction by
Diana Agrest. New York: Rizzoli, 1988.

"Architecture From Without: Body, Logic and Sex." *Assemblage* 7 (1987): 28–41.

"Architecture of Mirror/Mirror of Architecture." *Oppositions* 26 (1984): 118–133.

"La Arquitectura de Espejo/Espejo del la Arquitectura." *Summa* 202 (July 1984): 42–47.

"Architetttura di Specchio." *Rassegna* 13 (March 1983): 55–61.

A Romance with the City: The Work of Irwin S. Chanin. Edited and main essay by Diana Agrest. New York:
Cooper Union Press, 1982.

"Notes on Film and Architecture." *Skyline* (September 1981).

"The City as the Place of Representation." *Design Quarterly* 113–114 (*City Segments*) (January 1980): 8–13.

"Cansado de Gloria" (interview with Aldo Rossi). *Summa* 114 (December 1979): 81–86.

"The Architecture of the City" (interview with Aldo Rossi). *Skyline* (September 1979).

"Design Versus Non-Design." *Communication* 27 (1979): 79–102.

"Towards a Theory of Production of Sense in the Built Environment (1968–1972)." In *On Streets*,
edited by Stanford Anderson. Cambridge: MIT Press, 1978.

"Architectural Anagrams: The Symbolic Performance of Skyscrapers." *Oppositions* 11 (Winter 1977): 26–51.

"Notes Critiques sur le Concours pour Roosevelt Island" (with A. Latour). *L'Architecture d'Aujourd'hui*
186 (August–September 1976): 22–25.

"Form Diggers of 1976: Charles Moore." *Architecture d'Aujourd'hui* (March–April 1976).

"Sviluppo Urban e Forma Della Citta a New York: Note Critiche Sul Concorso per Roosevelt Island"
(with A. Latour). *Controspazio* 4 (December 1975): 4–7.

"The Sky's the Limit." *Architecture and Urbanism* 60 (December 1975). 47–60.

"Le Ciel est La Limite." *Architecture d'Aujourd'hui* 178 (April 1975): 55–64.

"Designed Versus Non-Designed Public Places." Paper presented at the *First Congress of the International
Association of Semiotics*, Milan, Italy, June 1974.

"Les Infortunes de la Theorie." In *Histoires et theories de l'Architecture*, edited by P. Lesterlin. Paris:
L'Institut de l'Environment, 1974.

"Epistemological Remarks on Urban Planning Models." *Institute for Architecture and Urban Studies,
Working Paper* 9 (1972).

"Ideology of Urban Planning Models." University of Buenos Aires, Internal Publication, 1971.

WRITINGS BY MARIO GANDELSONAS

"Not the last word." *ANY* 1 (July–August 1993): 62. *The Urban Text*. Cambridge: MIT Press, 1991.
"Conditions for a Colossal Architecture." In *Cesar Pelli, Building and Projects 1965–1990*, p. 9–12.
        New York: Rizzoli, 1990.
"New Haven." In *Order 1987*. New Haven: Yale University School of Architecture, 1988.
"Analytic Drawings of Boston." *Assemblage* 3 (1987): 63–71.
"Interview: 24 October 1985." *Journal* (School of Architecture, University of Notre Dame) (1986): 3–9.
"Banco de la Ciudad de Buenos Aires, Head Office." *Global Architecture* 64 (1984).
"From Structure to Subject: The Foundation of an Architectural Language." In Peter Eisenman, *House X*,
        p. 7–31. New York: Rizzoli, 1982.
"Despues Del Modernismo." Interview with Mario Gandelsonas, *Summa* 178/179 (Sept. 1982): 25–36.
"From Structure to Subject." *Architecture and Urbanism* 112 (January 1980): 53–57.
"From Structure to Subject." *Oppositions* 17 (1979): 7–29.
"Neo-Functionalismo." *Arquitecturas Bis* 22 (1978).
"Theoretical landscapes." *SD* (March 1978): 55–56.
"On Reading Eisenstein, Reading Piranesi." In *Oppositions* 11 (1978).
"Editorial" (with Peter Eisenman, Kenneth Frampton, and Anthony Vidler). *Oppositions* 9 (1977).
"La Architectura entre la memoria y la amnesia." In *Projecto y Ciudad Historica*. De Galicia, Spain:
        Colegio Oficial de Arquitectos, 1977, p. 117–122.
"Neo-functionalism and the State of the Art." *Oppositions* 5 (1976).
"Richard Meier's Douglas House." *Architecture and Urbanism* 64 (April 1976): 81–86.
"Theoretical Landscapes." *Lotus International* 11 (1976): 57–63.
"Semiotics and Architecture." *Architecture and Urbanism* 64 (April 1976): 21–26.
"Linguistique, Poetique Theorie de l'Architecture." *Histoires et Theories de l'Architecture*. Paris:
        L'Institut de L'Environment, 1975.
"Oppositions." *Architecture, Mouvement, Continuite* (April 1975).
"Linguistics, Poetics and Architectural Theory." *Semiotexte* 1 no. 2 (Fall 1974): 88–94.
"The Architectural Signifier." Paper presented at *The First Congress of the International Association of
        Semiotics*, Milan, Italy, 1974.
"On Reading Architecture II" (on the work of Peter Eisenman). *Architecture and Urbanism* 38 (Feb. 1974).
"Semiotics and Architecture: Ideological Consumption or Theoretical Work?" *Oppositions* 1 (1973).
"Semiotics, A Tool for Theoretical Development." In *Environmental Design Research, Volume II*, edited by
        Wolfgang F.E. Preiser. Dowden, Hutchinson and Ross, 1973.
"Linguistics in Architecture." *Casabella* 374 (1973): 17–31.
"On Reading Architecture." *Architecture and Urbanism* 21 (September 1972): 41–64.
"On Reading Architecture." *Progressive Architecture* (March 1972): 68–87.
"El diseno en la utilizacion del tiempo libre." *Summa* 34 (1971): 27–29.
"Un enfoque teorico de la Arquitectura." *Summa* 32 (1970): 69–73.

WRITINGS ON DIANA AGREST AND MARIO GANDELSONAS

Giovanini, Joseph. "Haus der sechs Turme." *Architecktur & Wohnen* (January 1994): 35–41.
Moonan, Wendy L. "House of Lights." *Harper's Bazaar* (August 1993): 179–181.
"Charivari Store." *Oculus* (November 1992).
Slezin, Suzanne. "Village, Sweet Village." *New York Times*, 23 July 1992.
Arcidi, Philip. "Filling in Princeton." *Progressive Architecture* (April 1992): 127–130.
Arcidi, Philip. "Work in Iowa." *Progressive Architecture* (February 1992): 98–99.
Architectural Desk Diary for 1992. New York: Rizzoli, 1992.
Gallagher, Mary Lou. "Des Moines and the Vision Thing." *Planning* (December 1991): 12–15.
"Image Update Eyed for D.M. Airport." *Des Moines Register*, 1 November 1991.
"'Farm Art' is Part of Vision Plan for Airport." *Des Moines Register*, 26 October 1991.
Zingsheim, Patricia. "Work In Iowa." *Iowa Architect* (Fall 1991): 30–35.
Popper, Ellen. "Hampton Houses." *New York Times Long Island Weekly*, 23 June 1991.
Zingsheim, Patricia. "The Des Moines Vision Plan. The American City: An Architectural Continuum."
        Iowa Architect (Winter 1990): 10–15.
"Old World Concepts for Downtown Housing." *Des Moines Register*, 9 November 1990, Real Estate p. 1–3.
Andersen, Kurt. "Masters of New York Material Culture." *Architectural Digest* (November 1990).
Viladas, Pilar. "Revisionist History." *House and Garden* (November 1990): 162–169.
"Looking Back to the Future." *Des Moines Register*, 8 October 1990, p. 1–2.

Stephens, Suzanne. "Architect Abuse." *Oculus* 52 no. 8 (April 1990): 10.

Goldberger, Paul. "Agrest and Gandelsonas." *Architectural Digest* (April 1989): 94–97/114.

Schmertz, Mildred F. "Homage to Loos." *Architectural Record* (Mid-September 1989): 50–57.

"Agrest and Gandelsonas." *Architectural Digest* (April 1989): 94–99.

Lipstadt, Hélène, editor. *The Experimental Tradition.* New York: The Architectural League of New York and
    Princeton Architectural Press, 1989.

Stephens, Suzanne. "Ad at large." *Architectural Digest* (November 1988).

"On the Drawing Board." *Avenue* (November 1988): 132.

"Architectural Study Could Give Des Moines Ideas." *Des Moines Register,* 17 October 1988.

"Des Moines Chosen for Major Architectural Study." *Business Record* (Des Moines), 10 October 1988, p.1.

"Two Urban Proposals for High-Rise Residential Buildings." *Summa* 251 (July 1988): 27–41.

Giovanini, Joseph. "Un-Design, Out with Aggressive Decor." *New York Times,* 22 June 1988, p. 61.

Pelli, Cesar. "Agrest and Gandelsonas." In *Five Choose Five.* Saint Louis: Saint Louis AIA Convention, (1988).

Benedikt, Michael. "Realness and Realism: A New Edition." *Center: A Journal for Architecture in America*
    (University of Texas at Austin) 4 (1988).

Stephens, Suzanne. "The Architects vs. the Critics." *Avenue Magazine* 12 no. 3 (November 1987): 136–151.

Bethany, Marilyn. "Whats Modern Now: Fire and Ice." *New York Magazine,* 28 September 1987, p. 58–63.

Nicolin, Pierluigi. "Le Citta Immaginate." *Nove Progetti per Nove Citta* (Milan: Electa, 1987).

Muschamp, Herbert. "Ground Up." *Art Forum* (March 1986).

Nicolin, Pierluigi. "On the Traces of the American City." *Lotus International* 50 (1986): 5.

Jakobson, Barbara. "Deep Ellum Project." *Lotus International* 50 (1986): 46.

Malieu-Viennot, Isabelle, and Philippe Robert. "The Gramercy Park Condominiums, New York."
    Creer dans le Cree, (Paris, 1986).

Timmermann, G. "Ideas, Work and Trajectory of Diana Agrest." *La Razon* (June 1985).

"Architetti, USA, Portrait." *Vogue Italia* 422 (April 1985).

"Theme and Variations." *Architectural Record* (April 1985): 124.

Oechslin, Werner. "The Beautification of the City." *La Ricostruzione della citta* (Milan: Electa, 1985): 284–285.

Ancker, Andrew, Mark Kessler, and W. Scott Clark, editors. "Autonomous Architecture, Diana Agrest—
    Mario Gandelsonas." *Harvard Architectural Review* 3 (Winter 1984).

Colquhoun, Alan. "Creative Design and Critical Discourse." *Architecture and Urbanism* 167
    (August 1984): 44–47.

Forster, Kurt. "A Sense of Building." *Architecture and Urbanism* 167 (August 1984): 40–44.

"Folie per Paesaggi del XX secolo." *Casa Vogue* 148 (January 1984).

Forster, Kurt. "A Sense of Building." *Lotus International* 41 (1984): 90–100.

Colquhoun, Alan. "Creative Design and Critical Discourse." *Lotus International* 44 (1984).

Hammer, H. W., and J. P. Kleihues "Idee Prozess Ergebnis." *Die Reparatur und Rekonstrunktion der Stadt
    catalog* (Berlin: Internationale Bauausstelung, 1984).

Boyer, Christine. "Architecture of Fragments in Detail." *The Special Task.* New York: AIR Gallery, 1984.

"Metamanhattan." *Whitney Museum Catalogue.* New York: Whitney Museum, 1984.

Colquhoun, Alan. "On Writing Architecture." *Progressive Architecture* (June 1983): 81–85.

"Manhattan Additions I." *Art Press* (June–July 1983): 22.

Suarez, Odilia. "Edificio para Viviendas Buenos Aires." *Summa* 186 (April 1983): 49–51.

Rossi, Aldo. "On 22 East 71st Street." *Skyline* (April 1983).

Simmonetti, Giannini Giuilo. "L'Architettura BiFronte, Relazioni di Progetti, Diana Agrest and Mario
    Gandelsonas." *Gran Bazaar* (March 1983): 110–115.

Portoghesi, Paolo. *Post Modern: The Architecture of the Post-Industrial Society.* New York: Rizzoli 1983.

"Edificio Para Viviendas." *Summa* 178–179 (September 1982): 22–36.

Lewis, George. "Chapter Active on Upper East Side District." *Oculus* 43 no. 8 (May 1982): 5.

Brody, Samuel, John Hejduk, Jacquelin Robertson, and Anthony Vidler. "Letter to the Landmarks
    Preservation Commission in support of A & G project in Manhattan Additions 1."
    Architectural Design 52 (May–June 1982).

Viladas, Pilar. "Right Building, Wrong Block." *Progressive Architecture* (January 1982): 31.

Lampugnani, Vittorio Magnano. *Architecture of the 20th Century in Drawings.* New York: Rizzoli, 1982.

Stephens, Suzanne. "Tradition of the New." *Skyline* (December 1981): 4–5.

Portoghesi, Paolo. "Un Omaggio a New York." *L'Espresso* (November 1981).

Goldberger, Paul. "Debate Over Proposed 71st Street Tower." *New York Times,* 10 November 1981.

Huxtable, Ada Louise. "State of the Art." *New York Times,* 28 August 1981.

Filler, Martin. "Harbingers Ten Architects." *Art in America* 6 (Summer 1981): 114–123.

Miller, Robert. "Designs for Living." *Ambassador* (TWA) (April 1980): 38–41.

Shapiro, David, and Lindsay Stam. "On Intensity." *Window, Room, Furniture*. New York: Cooper Union and Rizzoli, 1981, p. 29.

Vidler, Anthony "The Texts of Typology, Diana Agrest—Mario Gandelsonas." *Exhibition Catalogue*. New Haven: Yale School of Architecture, 1981, p. 4–5.

Ranalli, George. "Foreword, Diana Agrest—Mario Gandelsonas." *Exhibition Catalogue*. New Haven: Yale School of Architecture, 1981, p. 3.

Friedman, Mildred S. "Editor's Notes, City Segments." *Design Quarterly* (1980): 113–114.

Stephens, Suzanne. "Beyond Modernism, Playing with a Full Decade." *Progressive Architecture* (December 1979): 49–54, 59.

Grossman, J. "A Different Project: Three Buildings in Buenos Aires." *La Nacion* (Buenos Aires), 21 November 1979, p. 2A, 1–2.

Grossman, J. "IAUS: New Roads in the Theory and Criticism of Architecture." *La Nacion* (Buenos Aires), 14 August 1979.

Staat, M. "The New Architecture: Houses to Human Scale." *Quest* (February–March 1979).

Forster, Kurt. "Between Memory and Amnesia." *Skyline* (January, 1979): 4.

Indyk, Ivor. "Literary Theory and Architectural Practice, A Note on Agrest & Gandelsonas on Practice." *International Architect* 1 no. 1 (1979): 52–53.

Stern, Robert A.M., editor. "40 Under 40." *Architecture and Urbanism* 73 (1977): 1.

Grossman, J. "Project for the Renewal of La Villette in Paris." *La Nacion* (Buenos Aires), 15 June 1977.

Tafuri, Manfredo. "Les Cendres de Jefferson." *Architecture d'Aujourd'hui* 186 (August–September 1976).

Goldberger, Paul. "How Architects Develop Ideas." *New York Times*, 27 December 1976.

Fillion, Odile. "La Villette: Le Concours Impossible." *Cree* 43 (September–October, 1976): 80–86.

Morton, David, and Suzanne Stephens. "Singular Houses." *Progressive Architecture* (August 1976).

D'Amato, Claudio. "Roosevelt Island Housing Competition." *Controspazio* 7 no. 4 (December 1975): 24–29.

"Midtown Architecture Institute Flowering as a Student Mecca." *New York Times*, 30 October 1975.

Restany, Pierre. "La Crise de la Conscience Sud-Americaine." *Domus* 486 (May 1970): 49–54.

WORK AND RELATED WRITINGS BY DIANA AGREST AND MARIO GANDELSONAS

"The AD 100 Architects: An Exclusive Guide to the World's Foremost Architects." *Architectural Digest* (special issue) (August 1991): 20–21.

"A Symbolic Dissent, A Project for China Basin, San Francisco" (Diana Agrest). *Modulus* 21 (1991): 56–63.

"Theory and Practice." *Oculus* 53 (November 1990): 56.

"Diana Agrest Architect Para Ti." *Editorial Atlantica* (Buenos Aires), May 1989.

"The American City and the Architectural Continuum: An interview with Mario Gandelsonas." *Iowa Architect* (December 1989): 30–33.

"Project for the Renewal of the Area of Port Vittoria." *Le Citta Imaginate*. Milan: Electa, 1987, pp. 76–79.

The Chicago Tapes, Transcript of Conference at University of Illinois at Chicago (7–8 November 1986). New York: Rizzoli, 1987, p. 58–69.

"Deep Ellum: Dallas, Texas, Master Plan and Buildings." *Lotus International* 50 (November 1986): 47–57.

"Monumentality Within and Without the City, La Defense, Paris: Composite Drawings." *Summario* (1986).

"West Street Office Building." *Summario* (1986).

"Bill Robinson Showroom by Agrest and Gandelsonas." *Architectural Record* (September 1986): 134–141.

"Past and Present, Manhattan Additions I, 1980–81." *Art Press* 2 (summer 1985).

"The Gramercy Park Condominium Building, Renovation and Four Office Interiors." *Architectural Record* (April 1985): 124–129.

"Forms of a Legend: Four Follies." *Architecture and Urbanism* 172 (January 1985): 59–62.

"Shingle—Schinkle: Design for a Holiday House." *Lotus International* 44 (1984).

"Two-Pavillion House, Parents and Children." *Lotus International* 44 (1984).

"Three Buildings in Buenos Aires, Autonomous Architecture." *Harvard Architectural Review* 3 (winter 1984): 122–136.

"Agrest and Gandelsonas." *Architecture and Urbanism* (special issue) 167 (August 1984): 25–64. Includes "Urban Fragments-Building 1," "Park Square (Diana Agrest)," "Les Halles (Mario Gandelsonas)," and "La Defence."

"The Forms of a Legend: Four Follies." *Gran Bazaar* (March 1984).

"Beautification of the Town: Architecture Between Memory and Amnesia, A Project in the Minneapolis Grid." *Lotus International* 39 (1983): 55–58.

"Architecture Between Memory and Amnesia." *Lotus International* 39 (1983): 55–58.

"Una Casa a Misura Di: Three Projects and Texts by Diana Agrest and Mario Gandelsonas." *Casa Vogue* 140 (April 1983): 188–172. (Includes "Casa per una copia di Psicanalisti: Figure di contradizione," "Casa per una Copia di Avocati: Il concetto di porta," and "Casa per un Musicisata: Le scale.")

"L'architittura Bifronte." *Gran Bazar* (March 1983): 110–115.

Las Formas de una Leyenda in Follies: Arquitectura para el paisaje de finales del siglo XX, edited by B.J. Archer, pp. 38–41. New York: Rizzoli, 1983.

"The Forms of a Legend." In *Follies,* edited by B.J. Archer, pp. 38–41. New York: Rizzoli, 1983.

"Retreat-Hotel: The Agrest and Gandelsonas Studio, Fall 1983." *Student Work.* New Haven: Yale School of Architecture, 1983.

"Georgica and Le Brun Houses." *Ritual (Princeton Journal 1).* Princeton: Princeton Architectural Press, 1983, pp. 87–92.

"Manhattan Additions I." *Architectural Design* 52 (1982): 42–48.

"Architettura Urbana: Manhattan Additions II." *Domus* 627 (April 1982).

"Architectural Drawings." In *Drawings by Architects.* London: Institute of Contemporary Art, 1982.

"New York, Historical District, Design and Preservation." *Lotus International* 33 (1981): 79–83.

"The Park of La Villette, Architecture as Mise en Sequence." *Lotus International* 33 (1981): 82–84.

"Projects by Diana Agrest and Mario Gandelsonas." *Controspazio* 12 no. 2 (April–June 1981).

"Diana Agrest—Mario Gandelsonas: Ten Projects." In *Exhibition Catalogue.* New Haven: Yale School of Architecture, 1981.

"Manhattan Additions 2, Architecture Between Memory and Amnesia." In *Architettura/Idea XVI,* edited by A. Rossi, D. Vitale, and L. Meda. Milan: Electa, 1981.

"Les Echelles, Architecture Between Memory and Amnesia, House for a Couple of Psychoanalysts Idea As Model." *IAUS Catalogue* 3. New York: Rizzoli, 1981.

"On Practice." *Architecture and Urbanism* (special issue) 114 (March 1980). Includes eleven Agrest and Gandelsonas projects from 1970–78.

"Architecture Between Memory and Amnesia, La Villette City Segments." *Design Quarterly* 113–114 (January 1980): 22–25.

"Architecture Drawings 'Doors' House Dessins d'Architects Gallerie Nina Dausset, editions." *L'Equerre* (1980): 8–14.

"Urban Fragments: Three Buildings in Buenos Aires." *International Architect* 1 no. 1 (1979): 41–49.

"Arquitectura Critica/Critica Arquitectonica: Several Projects and Cover." *Summarios* 13 (November 1979).

"Arquitectura, Entre la Memoria, y la Amnesia, Centro en Minneapolis a Orillas del Mississippi." *Architectura* 218 (May–June 1979).

"Gandelsonas, En Madrid." *Arquitectura* 218 (May–June 1979): 10.

"A Suburban Center for Minneapolis." *Architecture d'Aujourd'hui* 202 (April 1979).

"Les Grandes Demeures, Summer House." *Architecture d'Aujourd'hui* 200 (December 1978).

"Paris Architecture as a Cultural Practice: Six Projects by Diana Agrest and Mario Gandelsonas." In *Assenza/Pressenza,* edited by Fulvio Irace, pp. 22–26. Bologna: D'Auria Editrice, 1978.

"The Roosevelt Island Project, New York." *Space Design* 10 (October 1977): 39–40.

"Project for La Villette, Paris." *Space Design* 10 (October 1977): 72–73.

"The Future of Architecture" (cover illustration). *Progressive Architecture* (May 1977).

"Doors: A Summer House, Suburban Center for Minneapolis." *Architecture and Urbanism* 73 (40 Under 40) (January 1977).

"Arqitectura Critica, Critica Arquitectonica: Several Projects." *Summarios* 13 (1977).

"Paris: La Villette Public Spaces." *Lotus International* 13 (December 1976): 115–117.

"La Villette Competition Project." *Architecture d'Aujourd'hui* 187 (October–November 1976).

"Roosevelt Island Competition Project, Les Echelles, Un Edifice Comme Clasificateur du Corps Humain." *Architecture d'Aujourd'hui* 186 (August–September 1976): 34–35, 75–78.

"La Villette Competition Project." *Paris Project* 15–16 (1976).

"Roosevelt Island Housing Competition Project." *Controspazio* 4 (December 1975): 24–29.

PROJECT CREDITS

LES ECHELLES
Diana Agrest
Assistants: Pat Sapinsley, Chris Barron (model)
Color Photographs: Dick Frank

BUILDING AS CLASSIFIER
Mario Gandelsonas
Assistant: Livio Dimitriu
Color Photographs: Dick Frank

DESIGN AS READING
Diana Agrest, Mario Gandelsonas, Rodolfo Machado,
Jorge Silvetti, Jack Hartley, John Nambu (model)
Project developed at IAUS, New York City
Color Photographs: Dick Frank

HOUSING IN PARIS
Diana Agrest, Mario Gandelsonas, Roldolfo Machado,
Jorge Silvetti
Assistants: Peggy Deamer, Richard Dean, Pat Sapinsley
Project developed at IAUS, New York City

ARCHITECTURE AS MISE-EN-SEQUENCE
Diana Agrest, Mario Gandelsonas, Jorge Silvetti
Assistants: Jack Hartley, Christian Hubert, David Robbins,
Pat Sapinsley, Gregory Gall, Anthony Pergola, Carter Norvak
Project developed at IAUS, New York City

DOORS
Diana Agrest, Mario Gandelsonas
Jorge Feferbaum, Marcelo Naszewsky, architects,
Associate Architects in Buenos Aires, Argentina
Assistants: Stan Allen, Greg Gall, Miguel Oks
B&W Photographs: Agrest and Gandelsonas
Color Photographs: Dick Frank

ARCHITECTURE BETWEEN MEMORY AND AMNESIA
Diana Agrest, Mario Gandelsonas
Assistants: Stan Allen, Nicholas Hoppe, Terry Kleinberg,
Miguel Oks, Robert Strong
Project developed at IAUS, New York City

URBAN FRAGMENTS, BUILDING I, II, AND III
Diana Agrest, Mario Gandelsonas
Jorge Feferbaum, Marcelo Naszewsky, architects, Associate
Architects in Buenos Aires, Argentina
Assistants: Stan Allen, Miguel Oks, David Robbins
B&W Photographs and page 30: Roberto Shezen
Color Photographs (Building 3): Dick Frank

TYPOLOGICAL MORPHING
Diana Agrest
Assistants: Elizabeth Counihan, Chris Crigenski,
Joe Langfield, Stan Allen, Turan Duda

URBAN FRAGMENTS, BUILDING V
Diana Agrest, Mario Gandelsonas
Jorge Feferbaum, Marcelo Naszewsky, architects,
Associate Architects in Buenos Aires, Argentina
Assistants: Stan Allen, Miguel Oks, David Robbins
Photographs: Roberto Shezen
Photograph page 113: Agrest and Gandelsonas

HOUSE FOR TWO PSYCHOANALYSTS
Diana Agrest, Mario Gandelsonas
Assistants: John Nambu, Leonardo Zylberberg
Photographs: Dick Frank

MANHATTAN ADDITIONS, 1 AND 2
Residential Buildings in the Upper East Side
Manhattan Addition 1, 71st Street
Diana Agrest, Mario Gandelsonas
Associate: Roberto Aisenson
Assistants: Stan Allen, Leonardo Zylberberg,
Karen Ludlow (model)
Manhattan Addition 2, 110 East 64th Street
Diana Agrest, Mario Gandelsonas
Assistants: Stan Allen, Leonardo Zylberberg,
Karen Ludlow (model)

A CRITICAL READING OF THE URBAN TEXT
Mario Gandelsonas
Assistants: Stan Allen, Gregory Gall

VARIATIONS ON A THEME
Lobby, A and G Offices, Corporate Headquarters
Diana Agrest, Mario Gandelsonas
Associate: Leonardo Zylberberg
Photographs (A and G Offices): Peter Aaron, ESTO
Photographs (CF Corporation): Roberto Shezen

THE FORM OF THE PICTURESQUE
Diana Agrest, Mario Gandelsonas
Associate: Leonardo Zylberberg
Assistants: Kathy Kling, Kevin Kennon,
Karen Ludlow (model), Jon Stark
Photographs: Agrest and Gandelsonas

MONUMENTALITY WITHIN AND WITHOUT THE CITY
Diana Agrest, Mario Gandelsonas
Assistants: Kathy Kling, Leonardo Zylberberg

DUPLICATION
Diana Agrest, Mario Gandelsonas
Assistants: Kathy Kling, Karen Ludlow (model), Michael
Stanton, Jon Stark, Leonardo Zylberberg
Photographs: Agrest and Gandelsonas

UPPER EAST SIDE TOWNHOUSE
Diana Agrest, Mario Gandelsonas
Associate: Leonardo Zylberberg
Photographs: Agrest and Gandelsonas

THE FORMS OF A LEGEND
Diana Agrest, Mario Gandelsonas
Assistants: Michael Stanton, Karen Ludlow (model)
Photographs: Roberto Shezen

FRAMINGS
Diana Agrest, Mario Gandelsonas
Assistants: Kevin Kennon, Peter Matthews, Christian
Zapatka, Leonardo Zylberberg
Photographs: Paul Warchol, pages 170-171, 172 (top, left; top,
right), 173 (bottom); Roberto Shezen, page 172 (bottom),
173 (top)

THE RETURN OF THE REPRESSED
Diana Agrest, Mario Gandelsonas
Assistants: Nancy Clayton, U. Desert, Pablo Diaz, Kevin
Kennon, J. Lehrecke
Christian Zapatka, Leonardo Zylberberg (associate)

INTERIOR ON PARK AVENUE
Diana Agrest, Mario Gandelsonas
Assistants: Kevin Kennon, Nancy Clayton, Christian Zapatka
Photographs: Durston Saylor, pages 182, 184; Jon Jensen,
pages 183, 185 (top left, bottom right); Agrest and
Gandelsonas, page 185 (top right)

OBJECT AS FABRIC
Diana Agrest, Mario Gandelsonas
Assistants: Leonardo Zylberberg, Jeff Inaba, Adriana Solazzi,
Diego Wainer, Christian Zapatka
Photographs: Agrest and Gandelsonas

INTERIOR ON CENTRAL PARK WEST
Diana Agrest, Mario Gandelsonas
Associate: Kevin Kennon
Assistants: Jeff Inaba, Tom Van Der Bout
Photographs: Paul Warchol
Photograph, page 199 (top left): Agrest and Gandelsonas

OFFICE BUILDING, NEW YORK CITY
Diana Agrest, Mario Gandelsonas
Associate: Leonardo Zylberberg

WEST STREET
Diana Agrest, Mario Gandelsonas
Associate: Leonardo Zylberberg

150 WOOSTER STREET
Diana Agrest, Mario Gandelsonas
Assistant: Tom Van der Bout
Photographs: Peter Aaron, ESTO, page 204;
Paul Warchol, page 205

URBAN READY MADES 1 AND 2
Diana Agrest, Mario Gandelsonas
Assistants: Maurice Harwell, Laing Pew, Ursula Kyle

HOUSE ON SAG POND
Diana Agrest, Mario Gandelsonas
Associate: Claire Weisz
Assistants: Tom Bader, Peter Frank, Maurice Harwell,
Thomas Kalin
Photographs: Agrest and Gandelsonas, page 25, 210
(top two, bottom), 212, 213, 223 (bottom right); Paul Warchol,
page 210 (second from bottom), 211, 214–221, 223
(top, bottom left)

VISION PLAN
Diana Agrest, Mario Gandelsonas
Des Moines Plan and Zoning, Jim Grant, Director, Patricia
Zingsheim, Bob Mickle, planner
Associate: Claire Weisz
Assistants: Maurice Harwell, Nick Arn

PRINCETON CAMPUS CENTER
Diana Agrest, Mario Gandelsonas
Associate: Claire Weisz
Assistants: Maurice Harwell, Mark Yoes (model)
Photographs: Agrest and Gandelsonas

GATE
Diana Agrest, Mario Gandelsonas
Associate: Claire Weisz
Assistant: Peter Pelsinsky
Photographs of model: Marilyn Weisz

HILLSIDE
Diana Agrest, Mario Gandelsonas, joint venture with
Environmental Design Group, Des Moines, Iowa
Associate: Claire Weisz
Assistants: Nick Arn, Karen Frome, Maurice Harwell,
David Ruff, Mark Yoes

DES MOINES INTERNATIONAL AIRPORT
Diana Agrest, Mario Gandelsonas, joint venture with Crose
Gardner Associates, Landscape Architects, Des Moines, Iowa
Associate: Claire Weisz
Assistant: Mark Yoes

THE MACHINE IN THE GARDEN
Diana Agrest
Assistants: Christian Cooper, Karen Fromme, Ursula Kyle,
David Ruff, Claire Weisz, Mark Yoes

FURNITURE AND OBJECTS
Furniture for Interior on Central Park West, New York City
Photographs: Paul Warchol
Stoppage Bar, New York City
Photographs: Paul Warchol
Canal Bar maître d' station, New York City
Photographs: Agrest and Gandelsonas
Screen, Interior on 57th Street, New York City
Photographs: Agrest and Gandelsonas
Beach Street Lobby
Photograph: Jen Fong

BIOGRAPHIES

These biographies highlight selected events in the lives of Diana Agrest and Mario Gandelsonas. They do not present a complete history of their lives, work, or writings.

DIANA AGREST

	Born in Buenos Aires, Argentina. Studied ballet and later piano.
1960	Admitted to the School of Architecture at the University of Buenos Aires, Buenos Aires, Argentina at age 16. Simultaneously studied painting and piano and taught painting to children in shanty towns.
1961	Became secretary of the New Music Association.
1965–66	Attended courses on communication and neurosis, cybernetics and information theory at the Institute for Advanced Studies, University of Buenos Aires.
1967	Graduated and received her diploma from the School of Architecture, University of Buenos Aires. Won fellowship from French government to study in Paris.
1968	Pursued urban studies at the Center for Urban Research in Paris, France and social studies at the École Pratique des Hautes Études, Section Six, Paris, France; took seminar with Roland Barthes, which became his book *S/Z*. Wrote thesis on the street as a system of signification.
1969	First built project, Blue Gold, a temporary exhibition pavilion, Buenos Aires. Designed Production of Place with Mario Gandelsonas (MG), an exhibition at the Instituto Di Tella, Buenos Aires. Co-wrote with MG and Juan C. Indart "On Semiology, Perverse Objects, and Ideological Texts" published in *Summa*.
1970	Designed and built Pierre Cardin stores in Buenos Aires. Wrote architecture Architecture manifesto with MG.
1971	Received fellowship from the University of Buenos Aires for research on the epistemology of urban planning models. Arrived in April 1971 in New York City, where that work was developed.
1972	In the spring term, taught a tutorial on film at the Department of Visual Arts, Princeton University, Princeton, New Jersey. Appointed as a full time lecturer at the School of Architecture, Princeton University in the fall. Became a Graham Foundation Visiting Fellow at the Institute for Architecture and Urban Studies (IAUS), New York City. Developed "On the Notion of Place" with a grant from the National Institute for Mental Health as part of the Generative Design Research Project at the IAUS. Lectured on "Design versus Non-Design: A Problem in the Redefinition of Architecture" at the University of California, Berkeley, California.
1972–73	Became an IAUS Fellow.
1973	Published "Semiotics and Architecture: Ideological Consumption or Theoretical Work," written with MG, in *Oppositions 1*.
1973–75	Filmed IAUS.
1974	Organized lecture series and panel discussions "Practice, Theory, and Politics" at the School of Architecture, Princeton University. Invited Manfredo Tafuri as keynote speaker and introduced him to the IAUS. Presented "Design versus Non-Design" at the First Congress of the International Association of Semiology, Milan, Italy.
1975	Designed Les Echelles, House for a Musician, Majorca, Spain and the Roosevelt Island Housing Competition, New York City. Published "The Sky's the Limit" in *Architecture d'Aujourd'hui*.
1976	Designed with MG project for La Villette, Paris, France; Architecture Between Memory and Amnesia, a project for a suburban center in Minneapolis, Minnesota; and Urban Suburban Intersections for the exhibition Images of the Mississippi, at the Walker Art Center, Minneapolis, Minnesota. "Design versus Non-Design" published in *Oppositions 6*. After leaving Princeton University, started teaching at IAUS and became

coordinator of the Design Tutorial in the Undergraduate Program in Architectural Education at IAUS until 1979. Started teaching as a visiting critic at the Irwin S. Chanin School of Architecture, The Cooper Union, New York City, where DA is currently professor of architecture, adjunct.

1977   Designed the project Doors Summer House for Two Lawyers with MG.

1977–83 Designed and built Urban Fragments, Buildings 1, 2, 3, 4, and 5, with MG in Buenos Aires.

1978   Designed the project House for Two Psychoanalysts. Published "Towards a Theory of Production of Sense in the Built Environment" based on Paris thesis in *On Streets*, Stanford Anderson, ed., MIT Press.

1979–81 Designed Manhattan Additions 1 and 2, two residential buildings in the Upper East Side Historic district, New York City.
         Exhibition of the work of Agrest and Gandelsonas shown at School of Architecture, Princeton University.
         Published "On Practice," written with MG, in *International Architect 1*.

1979   Became director of the Advanced Design Workshop in Architecture and Urban Form, IAUS, continued until 1984.

1980   Cofounded Agrest and Gandelsonas, New York City.
         Urban projects by Agrest and Gandelsonas are included in the exhibition City Segments at the Walker Art Center, Minneapolis.

1981   Work presented in exhibition Architecture, Idea at the XVI Triennale di Milano and Autonomous Architecture at the Fogg Museum, Boston.
         Published "Notes on Film and Architecture" in *Skyline*, IAUS, Rizzoli.
         Published Manhattan Additions 1 with landmarks debate in *Architectural Design*.

1982   Published *A Romance with the City: The Work of Irwin Chanin*, The Cooper Union.

1983   The Forms of a Legend, Four Follies project exhibited in Follies, Architecture for the Late Twentieth-Century Landscape at Leo Castelli, New York City.

1985   A-G summer house in Easthampton: moved an old house, barn, and toolshed and landscaped site.

1986   Exhibited master plan for Porta Vittoria, Milan, Italy, reconstruction of the city, in "Le Citta imaginate," Triennale di Milano with MG. Interior renovation of duplex apartment on Central Park West, New York City, with MG.
         Participated in the "P4 Meeting" at the University of Illinois, Chicago, Illinois.

1987   Published "Architecture from Without: Body, Logic and Sex" in *Assemblage 7*.

1988   Wrote introduction and did editorial work on *Memories and Places: The Architectural Photographic Work of Roberto Shezen*, Rizzoli.
         "The City of the 1990s: Women Architects discuss Urban Issues," Keynote Speaker at the School of Architecture and Urban Planning, University of Wisconsin-Milwaukee, Milwaukee, Wisconsin.

1989   Became professor of architecture, adjunct at Columbia
         Work displayed in exhibition New York Architecture, German Architecture Museum, Frankfurt, Germany.

1990   Schematic design for a feasibility study for the Princeton Campus Center, Princeton University.
         Design director of the Des Moines Vision Plan, Des Moines, Iowa.
         Designed and built, with MG, House on Sag Pond, Southampton, New York.
         Displayed the China Basin project, Machine in the Garden, in the exhibition Visionary San Francisco at the San Francisco Museum of Modern Art, San Francisco, California.

1991   Published *Architecture from Without: Theoretical Framings for a Critical Practice*, MIT Press. "Architecture from Without," a panel discussion on the book, with Beatriz Colomina, Mark Wigley, and Anthony Vidler, Lynne Breslin moderator.

1991–92 Designed, with MG, Hillside Residential Neighborhood, downtown Des Moines, Iowa. Designed The Machine in the Garden, phase 2, a project for China Basin, San Francisco.

1992–93 Directed "Film, Video and Urban Architecture" an urban forum program funded by the Rockefeller Foundation.
         Organized conference on "Film, Video and Urban Architecture" at the Whitney Museum of American Art, New York City.

MARIO GANDELSONAS

1938	Born in Buenos Aires, Argentina of Lithuanian parents.
1943	Started studying piano.
1954	Admitted to the School of Architecture, University of Buenos Aires, Buenos Aires, Argentina.
1955–60	Studied musical composition with Francisco Kropfl.
1958	Became a member of the board of the New Music Association.
1959–61	Internship at Organization of Modern Architecture.
1964–66	Attended courses on linguistics, semiotics, and structural anthropology at the Institute for Advanced Studies, University of Buenos Aires.
1965	Designed and built a temporary pavilion for the Ministry of Public Works next to the obelisk in downtown Buenos Aires.
1967–68	Won a French government fellowship to study at the Center for Urban Research, Paris, France.
1968	Took Roland Barthes's seminar at the École Pratique des Hautes Études, Paris, France and wrote thesis on tourism.
1969–70	Taught a course on semiology and architecture as adjunct professor at the School of Architecture, University of Buenos Aires.
	Opened an office with Diana Agrest (DA) and designed an exhibition pavilion, and two stores for Pierre Cardin in Buenos Aires.
	Designed "Production of Place" with DA for an exhibition at the Instituto di Tella.
1970	Traveled to New York City where Peter Eisenman proposed that MG spend a year at the Institute for Architecture and Urban Studies (IAUS), New York City as a Visiting Fellow.
	Published the articles "Semiology and Architecture" and "Interview with Umberto Eco" in *Summa*.
	Wrote architecture Architecture manifesto with DA.
1971	Moved to New York City and joined the IAUS with a Graham Foundation Fellowship.
1972	Became a Fellow at the IAUS.
	Published "On Reading Architecture" in *Progressive Architecture*, considered by the magazine readers to be the most polemical article of the 1970s.
1973	Codirected with Peter Eisenman the Generative Design Program funded by the National Institute of Mental Health and worked on "The Architectural Discourse," a research project, portions of which were later published in several magazines.
	Proposed to Peter Eisenman the creation of a critical magazine and suggested the name *Oppositions*. The first issue, published in the fall of 1973 with Peter Eisenman and Kenneth Frampton, included the article "Semiotics and Architecture: Ideological Conception or Theoretical Work," written with DA.
1974	Started teaching the theory seminar for the Undergraduate Program in Architectural Education at the IAUS.
1975–76	Completed the design of Building as Classifier, which was originally conceived with Marta Minujin in 1967. Designed with DA the Roosevelt Island Competition, New York City; the La Villette Competition, Paris, France; and Architecture Between Memory and Amnesia, Minneapolis, Minnesota.
1977	Designed and built Urban Fragments, Buildings 1, 2, 3, 4, and 5, with DA in Buenos Aires.
1978	Proposed the name *Skyline* for a new IAUS magazine.
1979	Published "On Practice" with DA in *International Architect1*.
1980	Designed Manhattan Additions 1 and 2, New York City.
	Designed project for the Les Halles Competition, Paris, France.
	Cofounded Agrest and Gandelsonas, New York City.
	Exhibition of the work of Agrest and Gandelsonas at PS1, New York City and at Nina Dausset, Paris, France.
	Published "The Architectural Subject" in *A+U*, later published in *Oppositions*.
1981	Became coordinator of the Undergraduate Program at the IAUS.
	Exhibition of the work of Agrest and Gandelsonas at the School of Architecture, Yale University, New Haven, Connecticut.

1982–84   Became director of the Educational Programs at the IAUS.

1983   Started to develop research work on the American city at the School of Architecture, University of Illinois at Chicago, Chicago, Illinois and at the IAUS with the "New York Studio."
Developed the New York urban drawings.
Designed The Forms of a Legend, Four Follies with DA.
Exhibited work by Agrest and Gandelsonas at AAM-COOP, Rome, Italy and in the exhibition "Idea, Progress, Results," IBA, Berlin, Germany.

1984   Taught the "Los Angeles Studio" at the School of Architecture, University of Southern California, Los Angeles, California.

1985   Agrest and Gandelsonas summer house in Easthampton.
Supported the creation of a new theoretical magazine, *Assemblage*, and became a member of the advisory board and later of the editorial board.

1986   Participated in the "P4 Meeting" at the University of Illinois, Chicago, Illinois.

1987   Taught the "Boston Studio" at the Graduate School of Design, Harvard University, Cambridge, Massachusetts, published in *Assemblage 3*.

1988   Taught the "Chicago Studio" at the School of Architecture, University of Illinois at Chicago in the fall and became a Fellow at the Chicago Institute of Urbanism, SOM Foundation in the spring for the development of the Chicago computer drawings.

1988–89   Taught the "Des Moines Studio" at Yale University.
Received the Chicago Institute of Urbanism Fellowship for the development of the Des Moines computer drawings.

1988–91   Visiting professor at the School of Architecture, Yale University, New Haven, Connecticut.

1990   Designed project with DA for House on Sag Pond, Southampton, New York.

1991   Received tenure at Yale University. MG is offered a tenured position as Professor of Architecture at Princeton University, Princeton, New Jersey, which MG accepts.
Published *The Urban Text*, The Chicago Institute of Urbanism and MIT Press.
Developed the Des Moines Vision Plan for the city of Des Moines, Iowa as project director.

1992   Designed with DA Hillside, a downtown residential neighborhood, Des Moines, Iowa.
Taught the "Red Bank Studio" at Princeton University.

Jesse Frohman